# THE LIFE AND TIMES OF

# LITTLE RICHARD

# THE LIFE AND

# LITTLE

# TIMES OF
# RICHARD
## *The Quasar of Rock*
# CHARLES WHITE

**Harmony Books • New York**

Published by Harmony Books, a division of Crown Publishers, Inc., One Park Avenue, New York, New York 10016, and simultaneously in Canada by General Publishing Company Limited

HARMONY and colophon are trademarks of Crown Publishers, Inc.

Manufactured in the United States of America

Library of Congress Cataloging in Publication Data

White, Charles, 1942-
   The life and times of Little Richard.

   Includes index.
   1. Little Richard. 2. Singers—United States—Biography. 3. Rock musicians—United States—Biography.
   I. Title.
   ML420.L773W5   1984      784.5'4'00924 [B]       84–6580
   ISBN 0-517-55498-4

10  9  8  7  6  5  4  3  2  1

First Edition

Designed by Wendy Volin Cohen

This book is dedicated to Leva Mae Penniman, Little
Richard's mother, and one of the most beautiful and spiritually dignified people I have ever met. Left a widow with
twelve children, she overcame all difficulties and reared
them successfully through her tremendous strength of
character and firm belief in the power and goodness of
God. Until her death in January 1984 at the age of seventy-
one, she remained the fulcrum of the Penniman family's
life. The secure home and never-failing love that she always
provided for Richard during his Rock 'n' Roll career in the
1950s, 1960s, and 1970s were the key factors that enabled
him to survive the excesses of life as a superstar, unlike so
many of his rock contemporaries.

May the Lord bless and keep you, Leva Mae.

# CONTENTS

# FOREWORD

At last! A book on Little Richard.

I have these fantastic memories from a very early age, singing "Tutti Frutti" at school—it was a big rave at the time. The first song I ever sang in public was "Long Tall Sally," in a Butlins holiday camp talent competition!

When the Beatles were first starting we performed with Richard in Liverpool and Hamburg, and we became close friends. Richard is one of the greatest kings of Rock 'n' Roll. He's a great guy and he's my friend today.

—Paul McCartney

# PREFACE

This is the story of Little Richard. Born Richard Wayne Penniman, he exploded onto the American music scene in 1955 with Awop-Bop-a-Loo-Mop Alop-Bam-Boom demolishing established musical structure and giving a whole generation a clarion-call to shake off the chains of repression.

With songs like "Tutti Frutti," "Long Tall Sally," "Ready Teddy," "Lucille," "Good Golly Miss Molly," and many many others, he single-handedly laid the foundations of a new music form, Rock 'n' Roll. His powerhouse voice and outlandish appearance gave the twentieth century a freer spirit, allowing later rock legends like Paul McCartney, Tom Jones, Elvis Presley, Mick Jagger, David Bowie, and Michael Jackson to do their own thing. Yet he has always been treated as a way-out demento, beyond ordinary comprehension or serious analysis. Until now...

Little Richard brought the races together in a common admiration for his music. Born in Macon, Georgia, the heart of America's gospel belt, he twice discarded superstardom for the church, typifying the conflict between sacred and secular music which is built into the black culture and which especially affects its greatest singers. The only reason that he is not a superstar today is that *he* decided not to be.

What he did was particularly amazing because he didn't have the experience of others to draw on. He had to go through it all for the first time, establish the rules, and live all the mistakes that later rock stars were able to avoid. And he is still alive and vital, unlike many of them.

Racism is woven so deeply into the fabric of America that even decent people don't realize that their attitudes are racist and that they are contributing to the outrageous holding-down of people based on their color. The creators and innovators of Afro-American music forms, the only significant musical revolution since the Strauss waltzes, should be venerated and honored. But Paul Whiteman was crowned King of Jazz, Benny Goodman the King of Swing, and Elvis Presley the King of Rock 'n' Roll, while the black geniuses like Duke Ellington, Count Basie, Billie Holiday, Joe Turner, and Little Richard, who created America's only classical music form, have always been denied true recognition in their own country.

Little Richard earned a lot of money as a Rock 'n' Roll singer. But it was only a fraction of what he would have made if attitudes toward him had not been so deeply affected by the color of his skin. Richard has always had a special magnetism, bringing his audiences together into one entity. Shining like a quasar, the most intensely radiant object in the cosmos, he seems to tap a mystical source of mental power that is only accessible to great preachers and shamans. Richard embodies everything that is America... not just Black America. Little Richard *is* America.

This is the story of a unique and dualistic psyche, an uncontrollable genius whose influence on Western culture is incalculable, but whose personal life has been tormented by outrageous and freakish sexuality and a hunger for public adulation. As a totally new phenomenon in the 1950s, he caught every stigma and label that the press could lay on a man. Yet at the same time, Richard's desire to be a minister of God and a prophet of peace among the races epitomizes man's crucial struggle—the battle between the good and the evil that exists in all of us.

# THE QUASAR

Shafts of light exploded from the podium as the spotlights hit the majestic figure. In front of sixty thousand people, clad in a suit of flashing mirrors, he stood atop the grand piano with arms upraised in the peace sign. Little Richard was on stage to close the Atlantic City pop festival.

Janis Joplin had just taken them all the way. Hair whipping across her face, she had stamped, growled, and screamed her way through her set. Between slugs of Southern Comfort, she had worked the stage like a tigress, baiting and taunting the crowd, inciting them to yell, whistle, and stomp their love message at her. They had given her three ecstatic standing ovations.

In the flush of the aftermath, as the Joplin rush subsided, few noticed the activity on stage, where the Little Richard band, formally attired as if for a nightclub date, was lining up to start the next set. Suddenly, like a mighty locomotive pounding at full speed, the sledgehammer riff to "Lucille" blasted the crowd's consciousness.

The rhythm seized their hearts and minds, its intensity obliterating all thoughts of the rain and darkening sky. The stage lights went out. For a second there was oblivion. Then the spotlights hit Richard.

The hippie audience, dazzled by his brilliance, started to cheer. Richard shimmered toward the piano. Then his fire-blizzard voice, miked so high it almost eclipsed the band, pierced the air like the battle cry of a billion banshees: "Lucille—you don't do your daddy's will..." and the massive crowd rose to its feet.

The song ended, and the roar of approval overflowed the arena. Richard now had the audience in his total control, and without pausing burst into "Awop-Bop-a-Loo-Mop Alop-Bam-Boom...Tutti Frutti!" The kids surged forward like a tidal wave, indifferent to the police line surrounding the stage. Glittering like an exotic jewel in the blackness of the night, the dispenser of joyous mayhem declared: "I am the only thing left...the King of Rock 'n' Roll, the originator and creator of soul..." The crowd screamed as one voice. A teasing tickle of the piano keys and he was into "Long Tall Sally" as the audience pushed even closer to this spellbinding shaman who had freed their spirit. Back on top of the piano, he tore off his mirrored suit, ripped it into pieces, and threw it to the crowd. His boots followed one after the other; then he swung a cape around his head, teasing the crowd into a frenzy like a stripper before letting it go.

Richard, like a panther breaking loose from captivity, left the stage. Just leaped down and left. The effect was like getting your throat cut at the very finest moment of orgasmic delight. That was how Richard had learned to treat an audience. They didn't know whether they were coming or going. They were left high. Stunned. Baying like hungry wolves for more.

# PART I
# THE SOUTHLAND

# *The Georgia Peach*

**L**ittle Richard's mother, Leva Mae Penniman, was a small, slightly built woman with a soft voice. There was an air of dignity about her, an inner calm inherent in many black people of her generation who lived in the deep South in the early part of this century.

LEVA MAE: I first met my husband, Bud Penniman, at a holy meeting in Macon, Georgia, when I was just thirteen years old. He was a fine-looking man, the son of a preacher. My sister was going out with his cousin and she introduced us. We courted for a year before we got married. I was fourteen.

Our first daughter, Peggie, was born just before I was sixteen. We lived on Pleasant Hill, in Macon, at 1540 Fifth Avenue, a nice section of the city. Bud had lived with his people on the other side of town before we were married. Bud was a man who provided. He was a brickmason, a hard worker in the construction industry. Later he started to handle a little moonshine. He didn't make the booze, now—a lot of people made it, but he didn't—he just handled it.

We called our first son Charles. That was Bud's real given name, and he was so *glad* to have a boy.

When Charles was two and my first daughter, Peggie, was one, Richard was born. It was Monday afternoon December 5, 1932. He was the biggest baby I ever had, ten pounds at birth. A big boy. A fine boy. We named him Ricardo Wayne, but it was never put on his certificate like that. They wrote down Richard Wayne, and I guess I never had sus enough to check it out and make 'em straighten it up right. So I don't worry about it. His name is Richard after my daddy.

Bud would always pick the boys' names and I always picked the girls. And we always got pretty names. Charles was the plainest name of the lot. Peggie was called Elnora. I didn't like that name so well, but my mother-in-law, she liked it, so I went along with it. I always called her Peggie, but I didn't let Bud's mother know that!

After Richard there was Marquette de Lafayette. I thought that was pretty. Then Walter Maurice, he's named after Bud's daddy. Then Horace Dearcy, who we called Tony, and then Robert Realdo. Then came Silvia, my second girl. I had six boys before she was born. She's named Leva La Leda. Then there's Elaine, Artis Elaine, then Gail June. And my last girl, Peaches, who's really named Freka Diedra. I made that up. I wanted a name I had never heard before. And last of all there was Peyton. Peyton Larry. He was born on his dad's birthday, the fifth of April. That was a good thing to happen, because Bud was dead by then.

Richard was the most trouble of any of 'em. He was very mischievous, always getting up to tricks. He got a lot of whippings. He didn't get whipped for everything he did, mind, or he wouldn't be here now, cos he did something nearly all the time!

He liked to do little mischievous things. If he did anything and he could get out of it he would. He'd just say he didn't do it. Well, you have to think for yourself. You're always supposed to understand your children—you'd know just about what they would do or what they wouldn't do.

I remember one time which I regretted so bad. I was pregnant...I think it was with Tony (I was pregnant so *many* times) I had arthritis and this knee had blew up and I was walking badly. I asked him, "Richard, put a fresh glass of water on the table for Silvia." He said, "Okay," but he didn't do it, and I could hear him outside having a good laugh. When I heard that, I was so angry, I got up and walked into the back room and picked up one of the little pop bottles that was on the shelf. I threw that bottle out back at him and I heard it hit, but I thought it had hit the fence. I turned straight around and went back into the house. I didn't know it, but I had hit him right on the head. He came in and blood was just streamin' down. I was like to have died. I was like to have had a fit. I said to Silvia, "Go get Daddy. Go get Daddy to come." He came and he said, "Honey, I've told you. You must try not to hurt these kids!" I hated to think I had done it. Richard was so bad at times that I *felt* like it, but I never meant to do nothing like that.

● My mother has always had a lot of inner strength. She was never one to talk very strong, but she would show it. Looking back, she had what it took to keep the family together and to improvise, but she was never overbearing. She was not really strict, but you had to obey. She was a good and loving woman.

Both Mother and Daddy come from big families. Daddy had five brothers and four sisters and Mother was the youngest daughter of a family of eight children. Daddy was strict. He believed in taking the belt to you if you misbehaved, but he was man enough to recognize what your qualities were and push you in that direction. Even when he wasn't around his presence was always felt. As kids we looked up to him. We were told that as long as we were

5

obedient and got our education we had a place at home. And we didn't have to work...he took care of everything. My daddy was a very independent man. We weren't a poor family and we weren't a rich family. Daddy provided for us and we had the things that normal children should have, such as a bicycle and things of that nature. We didn't beg. We went to school dressed neat. Our house was clean and at Christmas we had everything.

My daddy was one of those progressive types of people. Everyone else had gas lamps...we had electric light. My daddy's family wasn't educated like my momma's, though. My momma came from a family that was wealthy and educated. A very fair-skinned set of people, I think there was Indian blood in them. My nanny had long silver hair down to here and high cheekbones. My mother's daddy was real light and had white silver hair too. When you look at Mother you can see it.

When I was a little bitty boy, Grandaddy had a big old electric range, where everybody else had woodburning stoves, and two living rooms with glass doors. That's the house my momma was raised in. I remember the first time I went there. I couldn't believe it. I used to love to go there and just *look*. Everything was so cool. He had a bathtub the water ran into. At *our* home, we was still bathing in two little tin tubs.

My mother had all these kids, and I was the only one born deformed. My right leg is shorter than the left. I didn't realize that my leg was small. I never knew about it. Yet looking back, I can see why my mother and them was always so careful about me...cos they knew something I didn't. My mother used to let me get away with so much. I lived through a lot, and a lot of it was the way I walked. The kids didn't realize I was crippled. They thought I was trying to twist and walk feminine. But I had to take short steps cos I had a little leg. I used to walk with odd strides, like long-short, long-short. The kids would call me faggot, sissy, freak, punk. They called me everything.

One time my brother Peyton said to me, "Oh, Richard, where'd you get this body? Boy, you got a curious body," and I said to Mother, "Why is it that one of my legs is shorter than the other?" She answered, "Shut up, boy. You go and get the dishes washed and don't worry about it." But I *wanted* to hear someone talk about it. I wanted some explanation. I had this great big head and little body, and I had one big eye and one little eye.

But God gave me a strong mind, and a strong will. I've always had a fierce determination to excel. If we were cleaning the yard I would try to make my part better. It was like I had to, cos I was in competition with my brothers, and they were all good-looking.

I was the one at home that everybody thought was a nut. I would do some *silly* things. Like when Mother was cooking and I would slip a piece of chicken in my pants pocket and burn my thigh. Or, she'd send me out to do the washing, and I'd just throw the clothes in the water and wring them out. I had everybody dirty for a week! Momma didn't trust my washing *or* my cooking. She'd say, "Bro (all my family called me that. They didn't say Brother, they'd say Bro), you're a nasty cook."

I used to give people rocks and things as presents, but I once did something worse than that. I had a bowel movement in a box, in a shoebox or something like that, and I packed it up like a present and gave it to an old lady next to Mathis Groceries, on Monroe Street, in Pleasant Hill. I went to her on her birthday and I said, "Miz Ola, how you bin?" And she said, "Oh, Richard, I feel so fine. Richard, you're such a nice child." I said, "Miz Ola, I've just come to wish you a happy birthday, and I've brought you a present. Look." She said, "Ohhh, thank you so much." So she took this big old shoebox with the stuff in it. I went off and

7

waited around the corner of the house to listen for her reactions. I was hoping that she would open it while the other ladies were there, and she did. She wanted to show them what I had brought her. She said, "Let us see what Richard has brought for me." Then I just heard somebody say, "Aaaaaaa, aaaaaaahhh—I'm gonna kill him. I'll kill him!" She was crippled, but she leaped off that porch and she was walking without her stick! I laughed like a cuckoo! God bless Miz Ola, she's dead now.

Me and my cousin, Bertha May, we used to run together. We were a little team. A little evil, devilish team. I used to call her Boodlum. She had a big old black scar on her face, cos she had fallen and cut her face. And the old people back then, they didn't take her to the doctor. They just took some soot out of the stove and packed it on her face and it got well. It turned black though. That's what they used to do in those days. Well, me and Boodlum were going past Mathis Groceries and there was this big padlock hanging open on the door. I said, "Well, we might just as well lock him up in there," so we locked him up in his own store.

One day we went up the hill, and we saw my daddy's car parked, the old Model T Ford, and we said, "Well, we might as well push it on down the hill." So we pushed it, and we jumped in and were going to drive it, but it was going so fast that we had to jump out and just let it roll down the hill.

We were always looking for things to do. I did my no-manners [defecated] in a jar. I don't know why. I used to like to do things in jars and boxes and stuff. I did some in a jelly jar, and I did it very neatly, and I closed up the jar and put it up in the cabinet with Mother's preserves. As soon as she found it she hollered "RICHARD!" She didn't call out for anyone else. She knew it was me.

I was crazy, you know. Crazy. I don't know why I did all these awful things. Momma used to complain to the ladies who came round to the house, "I don't know why he does such evil dirty things like that. It must be the Devil." One lady put the bad-mouth on me—like putting on a curse— that I would die at twenty-one. I always thought that I would never live past twenty-one because she had told me I would die. I always believed that, but it just made me wilder.

I was glad to go to school though. It meant a lot to me. I had so many friends at school. Didn't trust none of 'em, though. All the kids would call me Big Head. The boys would want to fight me because I didn't like to be with them. I wanted to play with the girls. See, I *felt* like a girl. I used to play house with my cousins and I'd say, "I'm the momma," and they'd say, "Hey, Richard, you was the momma yesterday." But I wanted to be the momma, you know? So the boys wouldn't play with me cos I'd been saying stuff like that.

I had always loved Mother more than Daddy. I think it was because my mother was so close to me. I just wanted to be like her. I loved her so much. I idolized her. Every movement. I used to just love it when she put powder on her face. I used to watch her, and later I'd sneak up into her bedroom and just sit there, putting rosewater and stuff on myself. I'd imitate the things she said and the way she said them. She'd say, "Ooh, it's *so* hot." Then I would go outside and sit with my friends and say, "Ooh, it's *so* hot." I would practice it. I just felt that I wanted to be a girl more than a boy.

I knew I was different from the other boys as I got older. My cousin had a boyfriend by the name of Junior. I loved that guy. Many of the boys had crushes on other boys as friends, but mine was the whole thing. I loved that guy all the way. I loved him just like a girl would love her boy-friend and the same as a man would love a woman. My affection was not natural. It was very unnatural, but I didn't realize it then.

The older women still liked me, though. One of the ladies

I would sit around with—I'll call her Miz C, cos she's still alive—would ask me to have sex with her. She would say, "Boy, how big are you down there now?" and I'd say, "I don't know." And she'd look and she'd say, "Ohhh, you're big enough." She'd say, "C'mon over here." And then she would put it in herself and go screamin' and hollerin', "Boy, you brought me, you brought me, you brought me," meaning she had gotten a thrill. *She'd* push *me* up. I had done nothin'. She had done it all. She pushed me up. She just wanted me.

There was a lady we used to have sex with called R.M.S. She used to be there in the school grounds at night and the guys would run trains on her—six, seven, ten boys in a row.

My first homosexual experience was with a friend of my family's who the local gay people called Madame Oop.

Madame Oop lived in our neighborhood. He worked on the railroad. He used to come to our house along with another gay guy called Sis Henry. My people had known them both for years. Well, when everybody was getting off work, Madame Oop would catch them and he would use his mouth on them and he would pay them. I didn't like it. I just stared at him. But I needed him cos I would get money from him. Sis Henry too. They would give me a little money. Sis Henry would follow the seasons. He'd go to Florida when it got too cold to work in Macon. He'd be on the street and he'd talk to people in this high voice. He'd say, "How you doin', Miz Georgia? I'm doin' so fine."

My ma and dad didn't know I was associating with people like that. They never knew that we were doing these things. They would not have approved.

Madame Oop would french you. He'd suck you and tell you that he had a vagina and if you'd be nice he'd let you get some of it. You know, an older man telling you that—and you're a young guy...

You see, he'd been with so many men that his rectum had been torn out and was no use anymore, so they'd put a

10

colostomy in his side and he used his rectum as a vagina.

I went through a lot when I was a boy. They called me sissy, punk, freak, and faggot. If I ever went out to friends' houses on my own, the guys would try to catch me, about eight or twenty of them together. They would run me. I never knew I could run so fast, but I was *scared*. They would jump on me, you know, cos they didn't like my *action*. See, the girls loved you, but the boys hated you. It got so bad that I was afraid to be around guys. I remember one guy tore off my coat.

Sometimes white men would pick me up in their car and take me to the woods and try to get me to suck them. A whole lot of black people have had to do that. It happened to me and my friend, Hester. I ran off into the woods. My friend he did it. It was sickening to me. I was scared.

Homosexuality is contagious. It's not something you're born with. It's contagious.

The gay thing really came from me being with a guy called Bro Boy, who was a grocery boy. Bro Boy really laid me into that—he and Hester. It started with them and it growed.

CHARLES PENNIMAN: Richard was smaller than me, and I was more mature for my age. Richard always wanted to follow after me, but I wouldn't let him. I thought that as I was older he shouldn't be with me. But Richard would always come around. He would always be in a playful mood and trying to get something started. He would always start a commotion. I don't care where it was, he would come along and make something out of it...making people laugh. He was a showman! He wanted to be the attraction, and it didn't make any difference what he had to do to get attention. Then everybody would get mad—and that was just what he wanted. He'd run away laughing. Just hollerin' and laughing.

My friends and I, the other boys, we'd say, "Shut up, boy.

Go home, go away, stop all this hollerin' and screamin'!" I used to get mad with him and run after him, but I couldn't catch him.

When we were growing up, I used to have to fight for him. It wasn't necessarily that he was homosexual at that time, but he was getting so many problems, so much trouble. Every time somebody beat him up or something, I would have to go fight for him. He always wanted attention, and he would interfere with boys larger than him and maybe a coupla years older than *me*. My father had taught me how to box and I would fight anybody. It didn't bother me. If I found out they had messed with Richard I would go looking for them.

Peggie and I would always have to take the rap for Richard because he would get into a lot of trouble, then split from the scene and leave us there. He would do things and then say he hadn't done them. *We* would get a scolding for it and he would stand there and laugh. He was good at looking innocent!

Mother didn't get out much, and we would try to keep out of trouble for her sake, but if we did anything Richard would always tell on us. If he saw us getting into anything, he would go right home and sit right there and tell.

And another thing, he would always play tricks on older people. On their birthdays, for instance, he would take a bag of rocks to them and say, "I bought you a nice birthday present." They used to say, "He's such a nice little boy." Then they'd open up the present and find the rocks in there! But the following day he'd be right back in favor with them. He would tell Mother someone was at the door, or something was happening, or one of the kids was crying, or anything. Mother would get there and—nothing. He would just start laughing, and she would get so angry, cos she would be busy doing stuff, and she would have to stop for that...

12

Richard would holler all the time. He'd sing ever since I remember knowing him. I thought he couldn't sing, anyway, just a noise, and he would get on our nerves hollerin' and beating on tin cans and things of that nature. People around would get angry and upset with him yelling and screaming. They'd shout at him, "Shut up yo' mouth, boy," and he would run off laughing all over.

● I was always singing even as a little boy, and I'd beat on the steps in front of the house and sing to that. But the first time I got to sing before an audience was with a little gospel group that this old lady, Ma Sweetie, got together, called the Tiny Tots. There was me, my brother Marquette who sang tenor, my brother Walter who sang baritone, and a friend of ours, called Bobby Moore, who sang bass.

Ma Sweetie taught us all these church songs. She had prayer meetings just for kids every Wednesday night. We would go to her house and listen and pray and sing and learn Bible verses and stuff like that. It was really nice. We would go around different places and sing, and they would give us little things like fruit and candy and stuff like that—you know how old people like to do. She was like our manager, this old lady. They would have a prayer meeting—Ma Sweetie, Miz Stafford, Miz Hannah Jenkins, Miz Pearl Moore, Miz Dora Marshall, Miz Clarrie, Miz Edna, Miz Rula, Sis Lucy, all there—and they'd sing, and you could hear Ma Sweetie praying for five blocks! They didn't use no piano. When they sang they would stomp their feet. All these people just stomping their feet. No piano. They'd be praying, be crying to God. You could hear 'em for *blocks*.

Uncle Willard used to take us around with Ma Sweetie in my daddy's Model T Ford. His driving used to scare me sometimes, cos I remember he used to turn the corners on two wheels almost. Ma Sweetie, she used to control him,

13

though. Uncle Willard was Mother's brother, the youngest of her family, and he was just like one of the kids, almost a brother to us. We just used to call him Willard and he used to resent that a bit I think, cos all the others we used to call uncle and aunt.

Anyway, Willard would drive us around to old folks' homes and different people's houses and sit on their steps. Most of the houses had long steps and we would sing spirituals and bang on the steps as though we were playing instruments. We would go up and down the streets doing that. Sometimes we would get chased by dogs. People who didn't have fences would have dogs running loose. Sometimes they'd pay us cos they enjoyed us. Sometimes they would pay us just to leave!

Willard would take us to places like Logtown, Georgia, my father's hometown. Every fourth Sunday in August they'd have a great camp meeting there. All the churches were open, it was like a reunion. Willard would carry us to Forsyth, Perry, Cordele, small country towns around Macon, and we'd make a little money. "Precious Lord" was one of their favorites and "Peace in the Valley."

We had this old teacher, and my favorite thing was to make fun of her. She had a mole on her neck that looked like a blackberry, and her voice would quiver as she led us in songs. Well, I'd imitate her and make my voice shake. Everybody would start laughing, and when she came down on me I'd point at her and fall out of my chair and onto the floor, laughing: "Oh, the blackberry. Oh, the blackberry." After school she would stop by at home and tell Mother and Mother would get onto me, and I'd stop for a couple of days.

I was terrible to the teachers. I can remember most of them...my first grade teacher, Miz Jackson; second grade, Mrs. Graham; third grade, Miz Mason; and my fourth grade teachers, Miz Austin and Miz Phelps. I believe that all my teachers thought I was crazy. I believe they all really thought I was going nuts. I think they must have been a bit scared of me. I would sing and I would do things to make people laugh. I wouldn't *be* telling jokes, you know, but it would just come out that way. I didn't want to study. All I wanted to do was sing. I would do little bad things like tearing the teacher's stocking, and they would whup me. I never played hooky, though. I had the kind of father that would kill you if you did that. He would have knocked my head off with a switch.

*Music vibrated through the streets in the black areas of Macon. People sang as they went about their work. In the evenings people would sit outside their homes and make music together. Almost any meeting, religious or secular, would feature group singing, with everybody joining in the well-known traditional song.*

● You'd hear people singing all the time. The women would be outside in the back doing the washing, rubbing away on the rub-boards, and somebody else sweeping the yard, and somebody else would start singing "We-e-e-ll... Nobody knows the trouble I've seen..." And gradually other people would pick it up, until the whole of the street would be singing. Or "Sometimes I feel like a motherless child, a long way from home..." Everybody singing. I used to go up and down the street, some streets were paved, but our street was dirt, just singing at the top of my voice. There'd be guitar players playing on the street—old Slim, Willie Amos, and my cousin, Buddy Penniman. I remember Bamalama, this feller with one eye, who'd play the wash-board with a thimble. He had a bell like the school-teacher's, and he'd sing, "A-bamalam, you shall be free, and in the mornin' you shall be free." See, there was so much poverty, so much prejudice in those days. I imagine people had to sing to feel their connection with God. To sing their trials away, sing their problems away, to make their burdens easier and the load lighter. That's the beginning. That's where it started.

We used to have a group called the Penniman Singers—all of us, the whole family. We used to go around and sing in all the churches, and we used to sing in contests with other family groups, like the Brown Singers, in what they called the Battle of the Gospels. We used to have some good nights. I remember one time. I could always sing *loud* and I kept changing the key upward. Marquette said it ruined his voice trying to sing tenor behind me! The sisters didn't like me screaming and singing and threw their hats and purses at us, shouting "Hush, hush, boys—hush!" They called me War Hawk because of my hollerin' and screamin' and they stopped me singing in church.

From a boy, I wanted to be a preacher. I wanted to be like Brother Joe May, the singing evangelist, who they called the Thunderbolt of the West. My daddy's father, Walter Penniman, was a preacher, and so was my mother's brother, Reverend Louis Stuart, who's now pastor of a Baptist church in Philadelphia. And I have a cousin, Amos Penniman, who's a minister in the Pentecostal Church. I have always been basically a religious person—in fact most of the black people where I'm from was. I went to the New Hope Baptist Church, on Third Avenue, where my mother was a member. My daddy's people were members of Foundation Templar AME Church, a Methodist church on Madison Street, and my mother's father was with the Holiness Temple Baptist Church, downtown in Macon. So I was kind of mixed up in it right from the start. Of all the churches, I used to like going to the Pentecostal Church, because of the music. But we had fun, too. We used to go to the Holiness Church, where they had the holy water for the washing of feet, and we kids would go in and wash our dirty feet in the water! And we'd get up with everybody doing the holy dance and do it along with them. And when everybody was "talking in tongues" we used to imitate them talking in tongues, though we didn't know what we were saying.

Another thing I used to do, when I was only about ten, was to go around saying I was a healer. I would go to people who were sick and I'd sing gospels and touch them, and a lot of them would *swear* they felt better! They gave me money sometimes.

I got me a part-time job at Macon City Auditorium for a feller called Clint Brantley who used to promote shows there. I used to sell Coke to the crowd and I'd get a dime for every bucket of bottles that I sold. That was great, cos I heard all the best artists and bands that were on the touring circuit then, people like Cab Calloway, Hot Lips Page, Cootie Williams, Lucky Millinder, and my favorite singer, Sister Rosetta Tharpe. One day when Sister Rosetta was coming to play the auditorium I hung around the theater while they were unloading the cars and setting up the equipment. When I saw her come in I started singing one of her songs. She had a hit record out at that time on Decca called "Strange Things Happening Every Day." She used to travel with Lucky Millinder and his orchestra and play guitar while she sang. I sang another of her songs, "Two Little Fish and Five Loaves of Bread." She came over and talked to me. She asked me if I wanted to come up on stage that night and sing a song with her. During the show, in front of everybody, she invited me up to sing. Everybody applauded and cheered and it was the best thing that had ever happened to me. Sister Rosetta gave me a handful of money after the show, about thirty-five or forty dollars, and I'd never had so much money in my life before.

LEVA MAE: When Richard went to Hudson High on Monroe Street, things improved for him. He was still a below-average student, but his interest and musical talent were recognized by the school. He was taught to play E-flat alto saxophone. That sax has given me many a headache. He used to come home from school and blow it, and you could hear it three or four streets away. He *could* blow it, though. He started marching in the high school band so quick. A lot of them kids would be a long time before they got the hang of it, you know. But he picked it right up. He was in the band right away—and he was real good. I was glad, because before that he used to beat on the steps of the house and on tin cans and pots and pans, or whatever, and sing. He could really sing. But, oh my, the noise.

*There was a warmth and friendliness about life in Macon, a community spirit commonly found in the poorer parts of towns and cities in that period, but race barriers were an ever-present factor, rarely intruding on a child's life, but all too apparent to adults.*

● We children were looked upon as a community responsibility. People were different then, a lot different. They sort of watched over you for your parents, you know, and if we did anything wrong and our neighbors saw us it would be just like our parents seeing us. Most of the time when they spoke to you you were in more trouble than when your parents spoke to you!

But there's no doubt about the prejudice that was there. Black people weren't allowed to go into most public places, the same thing as in South Africa today. A black restaurant would be the one with stuff all over the stools, all over the floor. Just a terrible place. But you didn't have anything else. There were signs on the water fountains—"colored" and "white." The white fountain would be electric and would have cool water. The black one would be rusted, twelve or fifteen years old, no cooling. Just an old thing. You were raised in prejudice. There were certain things that you knew you were allowed to do and those were the things you did. You knew your place and you sorta stayed in your place. Your mother and father didn't want any problems, so they used to tell you your place and how to stay out of trouble. I think that's the way it still is for a lot of people in the South. Not that you really accepted it, no. You knew that if you stayed there you wouldn't be able to accomplish the things you wanted for yourself. So you always tried to do better so you could leave.

The area of the city where we lived was all black people, but a couple of streets over it was white. We lived near the borderline. Daddy made a play yard for us with swings and slides and boards and everything and the white kids used to come over and play with us, cos we'd be having a lot of fun, and children... they see you doing something they want to do, they're going to come over and do it. They would come over. But you couldn't go over there! That's where the line was. You couldn't go over that side and play with them, that was different. If you weren't aware of the prejudice people would *make* you aware. They would let you know.

It's amazing how I got out of there, you know. I just can't understand it. I really can't understand it, how I got famous and all the rest of it. Of all people, *me*. I didn't know nobody. But I think God has had something to do with me. He was with me all the time. He permitted me to go to the top of the ladder so I could show people the stairway. The grass may be greener on the other side but it's just as hard to cut.

19

# Get Rich Quick

y daddy used to sell moonshine liquor, and the police were always trying to catch him with the stuff in the house. I remember one night at about one o'clock in the morning, I had been to the store, singing at the top of my voice going down those muddy roads, and I had just got home when the police came. Daddy was inside with some people. He was selling whisky when the policemen knocked at our door, and I went to see who was there. Daddy had made a triple screen so that you could see out but nobody could see in. The police just slammed the door back. They knocked a big knot in my head. And they searched the place. Somehow Daddy had got the people out. They got away. The police went through the bedrooms anyway and pulled the covers off the kids to see if there was any whisky in the bed with them!

Daddy used to hide the jugs of bootleg whisky at Miz Stafford's next door. She had a big garden with collard greens in it. He used to pay her and bury the jugs there in the garden, putting the greens back over them, and watering them down so you'd never know nothin' was buried under there. The police used to poke sticks in the ground, but they never could catch him. He was smart. And the neighbors would never tell on him, because he was very generous and kind to the kids. He would help out the older ladies, you know, cos we lived in a depressed area. He would give them money and food and so forth. So consequently if they heard that anything was going to happen they would let him know. I guess that's why he never got caught.

Daddy was always criticizing me for the way I walked and talked and for the people I was running with. He would get real mad at me. He'd say, "My father had seven sons and I wanted seven sons. You've spoiled it, you're only half a son." And then he'd hit me. But I couldn't help it. That was the way I was.

*In trouble at school because of his lack of interest in his studies, in trouble at home because of his increasing involvement with disreputable local gays, Richard, at fourteen, was at the first crossroad of his life.*

● I was singing all the time and I used to hang around the traveling shows that came through the town. I'd get up and sing with them. I remember Doctor Nobilio, the Macon town prophet. He wore a turban and a red-and-yellow cape and he carried a black stick. I'd sing to attract the people and then he'd prophesy. People would come to see "the thing" he carried about with him. He called it the Devil's Child. It was the dried-up body of a baby with claw feet like a bird and horns on its head. Doctor Nobilio was a light-skinned black guy with a mustache that curled up at the ends. He was a spiritualist. People would write notes asking him questions. He would burn them up and then tell you what you wrote. He told me, "Boy, you're gonna be famous, but you're gonna have to go where the grass is greener!"

When I started getting into all this trouble at home, I left and joined up with Dr. Hudson's Medicine Show. I didn't tell anybody I was going. I just went. Doc Hudson was out of Macon, and he used to sell snake oil. He would go into towns, have all the black people come around, and tell them that the snake oil was good for everything. Well, they would believe him. But he was lying. Snake oil! I was helping him lie. Doc Hudson, he'd go in cryin', "Everybody come here. I got snake oil. If you got rheumatism, arthritis, if you got leg trouble, if you got toe trouble—this bottle's good for everything." Two dollars a bottle.

He had a stage out in the open, and a feller by the name of James would play piano. I would sing "Cal'donia, Cal'donia, what makes your big head so hard." That was by Louis Jordan and the Tympani Five. It was the only song I knew that wasn't a church song.

It was in Fitzgerald, Georgia, while I was with Doc Hudson, that I met Miz Ethel Wynnes. She had a club called Winsetta Patio, on East Pine Street. I used to sleep out in a field. She took pity on me and used to feed me some days. She'd feed me chitterlings and pigfeet and all the stuff that I won't even eat today. She had a son, Don, who I was very fond of.

Well, one night there was a band coming to play at her place, B. Brown and His Orchestra. They had a singer by the name of I. A. Harris. He got drunk, sick, or something, and didn't show up, so they needed a vocalist. Miz Ethel Wynnes told them about me and I sang with them. But the band members, B. Brown, a guy named Piggy, another guy named Buck, and Charlie and Roach, weren't willing to have me. I was very effeminate. I was very frisky, I was *loud*, and all these old men didn't want me. You see, Harris was their partner. The women that would come to hear Harris didn't like me, either. They liked him cos they could have sex with him. He was a grown man and I was a young child, almost. I could sing, though, and he couldn't sing like I could.

I started traveling with them. We went all over Georgia, playing in white clubs, and I would sing "Goodnight Irene" and "Mona Lisa," and all those different kinds of ballads. Then we'd go down to this place called Bellglades, Florida, on the Muck. That's black dirt, where they grow food. And we'd follow the seasons. It was a very popular band.

PEGGIE: It was the most exciting thing, I think, that had ever happened to the family. B. Brown's band came to town, and taped to the station wagon was this placard with the name "Little Richard" all over it. That was the first time he was called Little Richard. And that's when we first saw him with his pompadour. When Richard left he didn't have one because Daddy didn't want him to and he was very strict. But now Dad felt that it was part of the makeup of an artist, so he wasn't annoyed.

Daddy hadn't wanted him to go on the road to sing. But when he saw that he couldn't hold him back, he sort of accepted it and didn't say too much. I remember my mother being unhappy and not wanting him to leave again, cos he was so young. And I remember my father saying, "Well, he doesn't really want to go to school—he can sing, and he wants to do that. Let him go. He has a phone number. And if anything should happen, he can always call and we'll come and get him. We'll be right here. Let him go."

*The B. Brown band was having commercial success with their new young singer, but the atmosphere offstage was not very happy, due mainly to what would now be called the generation gap. Richard decided to make a break with the band and join another traveling show called Sugarfoot Sam from Alabam.*

● Sugarfoot Sam from Alabam was a minstrel show—the

old vaudeville type of show. It was quite something. That was the first time I performed in a dress. One of the girls was missing one night and they put me in a red evening gown. I was the biggest mess you ever saw. They called me Princess Lavonne. I didn't know how to walk in women's shoes, so they had to stand me at the mike and open the curtains. The people in the audience didn't know what was happening. There I was with this red dress on, one long leg and one short one, one long arm and one little arm. They were laughing and saying, "Look at this here." I looked like the freak of the year. When I finished they just closed the curtains so I didn't have to move. They wanted me to keep on doing the act—but it was really terrible. So, I left Sugarfoot Sam and joined the King Brothers Circus, but I wasn't with them long. Then I went back home to Macon.

Well, along comes a man wanting me to join a show called the Tidy Jolly Steppers. He offered me ten dollars a week, and that was exciting. Ten dollars a week, you know, that was all right. So I would just put on a dress again and sing, and it was all right.

After a time I left the Tidy Jolly Steppers and I went with the L. J. Heath Show from Birmingham, Alabama. It was a minstrel show, a little carnival. And *they* wanted me to dress as a woman, too. They had a lot of men dressed like women in their show. Guys like Jack Jackson, who they called Tangerine, and another man called Merle. They had on all this makeup and eyelashes. I'll never forget it.

*Richard's stage act was bringing him more and more into contact with gays. He was gaining a real reputation on the intense and varied network of whistle stop towns of the South in the early 1950s. And as he became better known, he started to get better offers. One which proved very important came from the Georgia-based show called the Broadway Follies. It took him regularly to Atlanta, the most*

24

*influential music center of the postwar gospel and R 'n' B scene. The musical life of Atlanta influenced Richard profoundly. The city was experiencing a golden era in which the interplay between performers and audiences was undisturbed by the economic pressures and image-creating agents that rule the music business today.*

*The street where black people of all ages went to meet their friends and see their favorite performers was Auburn Avenue. It bristled with clubs like the Poinciana, the Congo, the Zanzibar, the VFW, and the prestigious Royal Peacock— all of which had shows and dancing. There were many theaters in town, too, that put on live shows between films. The 81 was the only one with a proper stage. It offered four shows a day and featured local talent.*

● The man that ran the Broadway Follies was called Snake. He was a comedian, and boy, he was really something. He had another comic with him called Lightnin', and I tell you, it was some kind of a show. They had a gay guy called Madame Kilroy. Chuck Willis was part of the show, Tommy Brown, Austell Adams Orchestra, Zella Mayes, and Helen Thompson. We would play Birmingham every Thursday, and be back in Atlanta every Friday, at Bailey's 81 Theater, on Decatur Street. People would come and see these girls roll their bellies and stuff. I would go out there with my makeup on and sing a few songs. Everybody would holler at the whole thing. I thought that I was famous then. There was nobody screamin' over me but me. I really thought that I was famous.

I used to sing at the theater with all of the entertainers who'd come into town—B. B. King, Jimmy Witherspoon, and many others. And that's when I first met Billy Wright. Billy used to record at the Royal Peacock Club. Miz Carrie Cunningham owned the whole block on Auburn Avenue, including the Royal Peacock Club, at No. 187½, and the

Royal Hotel, where I used to stay. Miz Cunningham had diamonds in her teeth. I'd never seen that before, and it was really amazing to me. Her son, Red McAllister, had a cab company. They had money.

Billy Wright was an entertainer that wore very loud-colored clothin', and shoethin' to match his clothin', and he wore his hair curled. He influenced me a lot. He really enthused my whole life. I thought he was the most fantastic entertainer I had ever seen. His gospel-style-blues shouting and crying made a tremendous mark on performers in and around Atlanta like Tommy "Weepin' and Cryin' " Brown and Clyde "Blow Top" Lyn. Both of them influenced Johnnie Ray. Billy had four Top Ten R 'n' B hits in 1949–51, which made him one of the twenty best-selling artists in those years. But outside a small circle, his importance has never been recognized and his name is unknown. They used to call him Prince of the Blues. He was a great blues singer. He was recording for Savoy Records, out of New Jersey, and he had a song called "Keep Your Hand on Your Heart and Your Mind on Me," and another song he had written called "Stacked Deck," about a deck of cards. His first big hit was called "Blues for My Baby." He was a fantastic entertainer. A fantastic entertainer. His makeup was really something. I found out what it was and started using it myself. It was called Pancake 31.

*In 1951 Richard got his first recording break. Billy Wright put him in touch with a young white disk jockey called Zenas Sears, whose black-oriented radio programs had made him a pillar of the R 'n' B scene. Sears, who was working for the state-owned Radio WGST, used his influence with the RCA label to get Richard a contract. At that time there was nothing unusual in a well-known record company using the facilities of a local radio station for recording popular music. Techniques were very basic, and a*

26

reasonably good studio was all that was required. *National stars as well as local artists were recorded at WGST. The results were rough R 'n' B but at least they were authentic. The companies who sent their own producers to Atlanta, like RCA, Savoy, Okeh, Dot, and Atlantic, knew that Sears would play the records on the air to encourage local talent.*

*Richard's first recording session took place at Radio WGST on October 16. He was eighteen years old. The backing band consisted of Billy Wright's session men. Richard sounds as though he is trying hard to imitate his idol, without much success. He seems to lack Wright's vocal power. Perhaps he was overawed by his first experience in a studio, performing without feedback from an audience.*

*Whatever the shortcomings of the session, it did produce a local hit. A song called "Every Hour" was plugged by Sears and sold well in Atlanta and in Macon. Other tracks recorded at the session were "Goin' to Get Rich Quick," "Taxi Blues," and "Why Did You Leave Me."*

*The success of "Every Hour," though limited, produced one of those situations that were later to become commonplace in Richard's career. Billy Wright's producer for Savoy Records, Lee Magid, heard the song and flew to Atlanta to record a "cover" version, entitled "Ev'ry Evenin'." Using the same arrangement and possibly even the same musicians, it eclipsed Richard's version.*

*Just before he recorded "Every Hour" Richard had left Snake's variety show. A few days after the recording session, he returned to Macon.*

● I got home and I was sitting down telling Peggie, Marquette, and Bobby about making the record. They were all excited. I was telling them about being on the road, the singing and everything, and showing them my fancy clothes, which were also exciting to them, cos I didn't have none of that when I left. I could tell they half believed me and half didn't. When a couple of weeks went by and my record still hadn't been aired, they really started wondering. Then one night we were sitting there, just talking, and it came on the radio. I think it was a program called *Randy's Record Shop*, out of Nashville. We used to listen to *Randy's*. When it came on, I jumped up and started screaming and running through the house and shouting, "That's my record, my record, my record. That's my record!" Everybody who was asleep woke up, cos it was late at night. And everybody gathered round the radio to listen to my record, "Every Hour."

The record began to get a good amount of local airplay, and people came to know me. My daddy was proud of me for the first time in his life. He made sure that "Every Hour" was played on the jukebox in his club, the Tip In Inn, on Woodliff Street, as often as possible. He often put the nickels in himself! He told me he intended to buy me a car to make me more mobile in my career as an entertainer. After that first record became popular in my hometown, my daddy would have liked to have made it my fame. He thought I was famous then, but I wasn't.

Things started moving for me when a New York manager named Horace Edwards arrived at our house. He wanted me to join one of his bands, Percy Welch and His Orchestra, and Daddy gladly gave his permission.

Horace Edwards was the first man that ever booked me—really my first manager. He put me with this band, which was called Melvin Welch and His Orchestra, but he had changed it to Percy Welch because there was another band called Percy Mayfield and His Orchestra which had a hit record out at that time.

Percy played bass. He wasn't a great bass player—he was a clown more than a musician. He would play the G-string on the bass. If you play the G-string on the old stand-up bass it fits with every key. And so that's what Percy would

28

do. But he was a nice person. He was a nice man.

We'd go all around the area and play at all these clubs and things. There were so many places to play around Macon seeing that the town was originally a military area. In the war, there were four military bases in the district, Robbins Air Force Base, Cottonfield, Camp Wheeler, and Morris Air Force Base.

I used to sing at the Young Men's Club, with Gladys Williams, Marian Henderson, Baby Rose, with Luke Gonder on the piano, Earl Swanson on saxophone, Hamp Swain, Percy Welch, and all of these people. We would go to different towns. We'd go to Atlanta, and to Hopkinsville, Kentucky, where a friend of mine named Edward Babbage had a club called the Skylark Club. He'd bring me there and pay us a hundred dollars a week, which was a lot of money at the time. He would bring me to the army base at Fort Campbell, Kentucky, too. Then we would go to Nashville, Tennessee, to the Club Ravelot, for Hal Bridges, and to the New Era Club, for Sue Bridgeford and Mr. Binks. They would pay us a hundred dollars a week, too. I would sing a song called "Baby Don't You Want a Man Like Me." Everybody just loved that song. I was getting popular around these clubs. I just wanted to sing from one place to another, and everybody thought I was famous....

It was around this time that I learned to play piano. I used to mess about with Luke Gonder at home on a piano that my mamma's daddy had given us, but I couldn't really play. Then I met this gay guy, a piano player called Esquerita. I've never heard of anybody with that name before. I don't know where it comes from, but he really was SQ, too! SQ Rita. He used to joke about his name (you know, excreta!). But they said his real name was S. Q. Reeder.

I used to sit around the all-night restaurant at the Greyhound bus station in Macon, watching people come in and

29

trying to catch something—you know, have sex. I'd sit around there till three or four in the morning. Wasn't nothing else to do, cos everything was closed. One night I was sitting there and Esquerita came in. He was with a lady preacher by the name of Sister Rosa, whose line was selling blessed bread. She said it was blessed, but it was nothing but regular old bread that you buy at the store. Esquerita played piano for her and they had a little guy singing with them by the name of Shorty. So Esquerita and me went up to my house and he got on the piano and he played "One Mint Julep," way up in the treble. It sounded so pretty. The bass was fantastic. He had the biggest hands of anybody I'd ever seen. His hands was about the size of two of my hands put together. It sounded great. I said, "Hey, how do you do that?" And he says, "I'll teach you." And that's when I really started playing. I thought Esquerita was really crazy about me, you know. He was—still is—one of the greatest pianists and that's including Jerry Lee Lewis, Stevie Wonder, or anybody I've ever heard. I learned a whole lot about phrasing from him. He really taught me a lot.

They gay thing was becoming a big thing in my home-town. I was with gay people a lot because I'd fallen into their bag, you know. I used to tell my mother about the gay scene and she used to tell me to hush. I'd tell her about the words they would use and how they'd call everybody "Miss Thing." Anybody meeting you—meeting another guy—wouldn't say, "Hi, Johnny." They would say, "child," "How you doin', child." And you'd go, "How you doin', honey,... Oh child, oh, my dear, oh, my God." And they'd call up and instead of saying, "Bobby, how you doin'?" They'd say, "How you doin', Miss Thing?" I'd say, "What happened last night, Miss Thing?" They'd say, "Oh, Miss Thing, you shoulda been there..." I'd call Billy Wright's and say, "How's Billy goin', Miss Thing?" and he'd say, "She's fine ...oh honey, you should see her now."

On the scene at this time was a real good-looking gay guy named Bobby. We met in Clarksville, Tennessee, at a club called the Queens City Rainbow. He was a female imper-sonator, and he looked just like a lady. There was a soldier base not far from there called Fort Campbell, Kentucky. I used to go and play and Bobby would put on these dresses and the hair and go on stage. The soldiers would scream and go mad. You see at that time he had a shape. Bobby was very bold. He would walk by the dressing rooms leading his boyfriend by the penis, which was just like a rope.

Bobby liked to be at Fort Campbell and accost the sol-diers, to sell his body to them. Those soldiers would shoot anything down—bird or bee, tadpole or frog. Some of those soldiers would do it with a guy and they'd come back and never know they'd been with a man. It must have been good, because they came back smilin'! No, *some* of them would be mad. Bobby would come back sometimes, with the heels broken off his shoes cos those guys would have run him down the street when they found out they'd been with a man. They'd be playing with you and they'd reach-down and they'd be just smilin'—and then all of a sudden ... But some guys were pleased, you know?

*RCA got Richard back into the studio at Radio WGST on January 12, 1952. He cut four tracks, "I Brought It All on Myself," "Thinkin' 'bout My Mother," "Please Have Mercy on Me," and "Ain't Nothin' Happening," which was the only one that gave a hint of the excitement to come. None of the songs made any profound impression on the record-buying public, so Richard returned home to Macon and continued his one-night stands with the Percy Welch Orchestra.*

*Just four weeks later tragedy struck the Penniman family. During the night, Bud Penniman was shot dead outside the Tip In Inn.*

31

● Daddy knew the man who shot him. His name was Frank Tanner, and he came from a family with a bad reputation in Macon. Frank was shooting firecrackers into the coal stove that heated the room. Daddy told him to stop it but he did it again. So Daddy told him to get out. Tanner and his friends were making a commotion outside the club. Daddy took his pistol and went on outside and that's when it happened. Frank Tanner shot him. He was dead before they got him to the hospital.

I was away with the band on the night of the shooting, and it was very late when I got home. A guy met me and told me, "Your daddy's got hurt or something," but when I got home my daddy's raincoat was lying on the porch with blood on it. It was raining that night. I walked into the house and my momma was sitting there crying. She said, "Richard, your daddy's dead. No more Daddy." I thought, Oh, no... My whole body just fell out. You know, it's just awful to see your momma crying like that.

First thing I wanted to know was who killed him. My mother wouldn't tell me. She was afraid I'd go out and.... My sister Peggie wanted to go after the guy with a shotgun. She was that mad. She was the one that would fight for us. She was a great fighter back in those times.

We believe that someone had my daddy killed. They didn't keep Frank in jail, and we were too poor. We couldn't get no lawyer and fight it. We believe that the police didn't like him because... that's all I can say. I just believe that somebody had him killed, that's all.

My daddy had never been behind me in my career until then, and he was just starting to come behind me. He was going to buy me a car that Monday to help me in my traveling.

My mother took it very hard because she was pregnant at the time. It was hard, but as a mother does, she tried to hold the family together. And she did. I remember going back to Macon in 1962 or 1963, and Frank Tanner coming to us and asking us to forgive him, and we did.

The Tip In Inn was just a little place, one room, like a café. It sold food and beer and things like that. It had a jukebox and the kids would go and dance and have a lot of fun. A nice clean place for the kids to go. Peggie happened to be there that night, laughing and talking with my dad and dancing and everything. My record was on the jukebox. My father would play it all the time. He loved it and he was very proud of it.

PEGGIE: I left the club quite late and went on home, and just after I got home someone came to the house and told us that my dad was shot. They didn't know if he was dead or anything. Oh, gee, my mom and I were all upset. I ran out of the house and ran up back near the club. They said they had taken him to the hospital. So I went to a friend's house which was just up the street and sat down for a while. Then I used their phone and called the hospital and they said, "Are you his daughter?" and I said yes, and she said, "Sit down," so I sat down, and she told me he was dead on arrival.

LEVA MAE: I didn't know the man who did it, Frank Tanner. I never did understand it too much. I never did. You see I didn't have any witnesses. That's why I didn't fight it. Some of them thought I should, but I said Daddy wouldn't appreciate me spending the money on it. I had a bit of money to pay the bills and things. I only owed five hundred dollars on the house, and I paid it off. That was the first thing I did...

*Frank Tanner was indicted by a grand jury for the shooting on June 5, 1952. Bibb County, Macon, records show a district attorney dismissal of the case on October 28, 1952.*

# *Thinkin' About My Mother*

**B**ud Penniman's death vastly changed the circumstances of his family. When he died his business died, too. At the age of nineteen, Richard became the family's principal breadwinner, since his older brother Charles was fighting with the marines in Korea. He was compelled to get a regular job for the first time in his life. His second recording session for RCA had been a commercial failure. The company had lost interest, and he was getting very little work as a singer. The job was washing dishes at one of his old haunts, the Greyhound bus station in Macon.

● I didn't *have* to wash dishes, you know. I could have eaten. People then would feed each other—greens and bread and beans and rice. We helped each other. But we were really poor then. You know you're poor when you have to make a fire and you ain't got no wood. I've seen people pull wood off their houses to make a fire in the house. That's poor. And I was one of the people pulling wood off the house.

*Then along came a Macon promoter called Clint Brantley. He owned a Fifth Street supper club called the Two Spot. Booking most of the traveling stars, both for his club and for bigger concerts, at Macon City Auditorium, he would use local talent as openers for the billed acts. A former bass player with a local band in the early forties, he had become a substantial property owner in Macon, with a reputation as an expert in maneuvering local politicians and city officials. Brantley recognized Richard's talent and began to take an interest in him. Now that Richard was without a manager, he found him work in Macon and the surrounding area. Brantley told Richard, "Get yourself a band and there's plenty of work available."*

●I was playing at the New Era Club, in Nashville, on Fourth Avenue, next to the Bijou Theater. The stage was up in the bar. I was up there singing, and this friend of mine called Billy Brooks came in with Raymond and Mildred Taylor, Barry Lee Gilmore, Jimmy Swann, and a feller named Shorty. Raymond Taylor blowed trumpet and trombone and played piano and organ all at the same time. His wife, Mildred, played the drums. They had a two-man band. They saw me up there singing and they liked me. So we all got together. We formed a group which we called the Tempo Toppers.

Well, we went to New Orleans, to play at the Dew Drop Inn, on Le Sage, and at the Club Tijuana, on Saratoga. The audiences really liked us. Barry Lee Gilmore had an act where he'd take a table or a chair in his mouth and leap up and down. He'd lift a chair with somebody sat on it! I really admired that, and I practiced doing it myself.

We were down in New Orleans for a long time, and that's where I met Earl King. He was a really great singer and guitar player and he influenced my style. And then there was Patsy, a female impersonator who was working at the

35

Dew Drop Inn, too. He used to sing a song called "Hip Shakin' Mama" and he called himself the Toast of New Orleans. He had a big old vaccination on his arm the size of half a dollar, and I thought he wasn't good-looking at all. He didn't even shave off his mustache! He used to put on these dresses and sing "Oh well, oh well, I feel so fine today!" He didn't look feminine. Didn't look like a pretty woman. He looked like a woman who had been hit with a board and didn't get well. I never had relationships with him. I didn't know anybody who wanted Patsy.

*Little Richard and the Tempo Toppers did a lot of work for Clint Brantley, doing dates throughout the Southland, often as part of a blues package show. Early in 1953 the Tempo Toppers left their residency at the club Tijuana in New Orleans and moved to the Club Matinee, on Lyons Avenue in Houston, Texas. Johnny Otis, one of America's most outstanding musician/arrangers, recalls his first sight of Richard there.*

JOHNNY OTIS: I had Little Esther Philips [an Otis discovery] at the time. She had a lot of hits and was very popular. I was having lunch in the coffee shop at the Club Matinee when somebody came out and said, "Johnny, you just gotta come and see this dude in here." They were having a little entertainment. So I went through and I see this outrageous person, good-looking and very effeminate, with a big pompadour. He started singing and he was so *good.* I loved it. He reminded me of Dinah Washington. He did a few things, then he got on the floor. I think he even did a split, though I could be wrong about that. I remember it as being just beautiful, bizarre, and exotic, and when he got through he remarked, "This is Little Richard, King of the Blues," and then he added, "And the Queen, too!" I knew I liked him then. He's just great. He was new to a lot of people around then, and they were just saying, "Boy, that's something else."

*The buzz about Richard and the Tempo Toppers attracted the interest of the president of Houston-based Peacock Records, Don Robey. He went along to listen to the band and signed them up to record for his label. On February 25, 1953, they recorded four songs, "Always," "Ain't That Good News," "Fool at the Wheel," and "Rice, Red Beans and Turnip Greens." They all failed to make any significant impression on the record-buying public.*

*Robey had a reputation for being tough and aggressive— probably a necessity for a black man in the recording industry at that time. Known as "The Black Caesar," he acted like a Damon Runyon character, never moving without pistol-packing bodyguards, "like a czar of the negro underworld."*

*Nearly twenty-one, Richard had matured into a self-confident, swaggering young showman with a bizarre lifestyle, who was not afraid to say exactly what he thought and say it at the top of his voice. The very antithesis of the compliant black singers who were grateful for anything doled out to them. Richard and Robey clashed like a prairie chicken and a rattlesnake. Called to the Peacock Records office for a dressing-down about his attitude, Richard so angered Robey with his backtalk that the record boss lost his temper completely.*

● He jumped on me, knocked me down, and kicked me in the stomach. It gave me a hernia that was painful for years. I had to have an operation. Right there in the office he beat me up. Knocked me out in one round. Wasn't any second or third round—he just come around that desk and I was *down!* He was known for beating people up, though. He would beat everybody up but Big Mama Thornton. He was scared of her. She was built like a big bull.

Don Robey was a disciplinary person, almost like a dictator. He was a black guy that looked like a white guy and he was very stern. He wore great big diamonds on his hand and he was always chewing this big cigar, cussin' at me round the end of it. I never knew how he smoked it, cos he was chewing it all the time. He was so possessive. He would control the very breath that you breathed. I resented him being so mean. He didn't want to give me any freedom. He had artists like Clarence "Gatemouth" Brown, Bobby Bland, and Johnny Ace. He controlled all of them. He had his own booking agency, called Buffalo, run by a lady named Evelyn Johnson. I refused to let him control me. If I can't have freedom, I can't be happy. Contracts don't mean nothing to me if I can't be relaxed. A contract is only your word. Paper don't mean nothing to me.

Well, I was telling people how rude he was, how nasty he was, how he didn't pay me, and that he was a crook and was just using all these people—using them up. I spoke out against him loudly—louder than I could today cos I had more breath to do it with then. He was very angry with me about all this.

On October 5, 1953, in one last attempt to make something out of Richard, whom he now regarded as a very bad bargain indeed, Robey teamed Richard up with Johnny Otis and his band to record four more songs, "Directly from My Heart to You," "I Love My Baby," "Maybe I'm Right," and an up-tempo jam called "Little Richard's Boogie." The tracks were not released at the time.

The crisis with Peacock spelled the end for the Tempo Toppers and they parted company. Richard continued playing dates for Clint Brantley, with a backup guitarist named

*Thomas Hartwell, who hailed from Memphis, Tennessee. But after a year of working with a competent band behind him, Richard found solo work unsatisfactory and he began looking for a new kind of band. He wanted more emphasis on hard-driving R'n'B rather than the gospel-oriented sound of the Tempo Toppers.*

*He struck lucky very soon, happening across ace drummer Charles (Chuck) Connors, who came from New Orleans, and a pianist-sax-player named Wilbert "Lee Diamond" Smith. They had been working at Nashville's Club Ravelot with a male-female duo called Shirley and Lee.*

● Clint Brantley set up a tour around Georgia and Tennessee—Nashville, Knoxville, Milledgeville, Sparta, Fitzgerald, and Tallahassee, places like that. We used to draw the crowds all the time. The places were always packed. I was popular around those states before Chuck and Lee Diamond joined the band. I got two sax players and named the band the Upsetters. It made me outstanding in Macon at that time, to have this fantastic band in a little town like this. The other bands couldn't compete. So when it said "Little Richard and the Upsetters" everybody wanted to come. We had a station wagon with the name written on it, and I thought it was fantastic.

We were each making fifteen dollars a night, and there was a lot you could do with fifteen dollars. We would play three, four nights a week—that's fifty dollars. And sometimes we would play at a place on the outskirts of Macon at a midnight dance. That would pay ten dollars and all the fried chicken you could eat. We were playing some of Roy Brown's tunes, a lot of Fats Domino tunes, some B. B. King tunes, and I believe a couple of Little Walter's and a few things by Billy Wright. I really looked up to Billy Wright. That's where I got the hairstyle from and everything. "Keep Your Hand on Your Heart," that was one of them.

We'd play all around Georgia, Tennessee, and Kentucky, cos we had a big name around those places. We would draw packed houses every place and we'd get a guarantee and a percentage of the take over the guarantee. We were making a darned good living. One song which would really tear the house down was "Tutti Frutti." The lyrics were kind of vulgar, "Tutti Frutti good booty—if it don't fit don't force it..." It would crack the crowd up. We were playing without a bass and Chuck would have to bang real hard on his bass drum in order to get a bass-fiddle effect.

Macon was a good place to live if you were in the entertainment business. The years of the early 1940s, when the military bases were in the area, had left the city with lots of nightclubs, big and small, like the Manhattan, the Elks Club, Club Fifteen, Anne's Tick-Tock Club, Mann's Drive-In, Sawyer's Lake, and many others. All of them had live entertainment. Within a couple of hours' drive from Macon was Atlanta and the border towns of Columbus, Georgia, and Phoenix City, Alabama, which they used to call "Little Las Vegas" cos gambling was legal there.

Little Richard and the Upsetters got this tremendous name. Fats Domino would come to the Manhattan Club, in Macon, and I would go out to see him. He was a star then, but he was singing blues. Chuck Berry was a star too, but they were blues singers. They were all afraid of me, cos they had heard people talking about me, saying, "Have you been to Macon? Have you seen this guy Little Richard? Y'know, he's terrible. Have you heard him play the piano?" My name was getting all over the place. I was really out there with the people.

Lloyd Price came to Macon to play the Auditorium and I met him. He was a big star—he'd had a big big hit with "Lawdy Miss Clawdy"—and he had a black-and-gold Cadillac. I wanted one just like that. There weren't that many Cadillacs about. The only place that had one was the funeral home, and you had to *die* to ride! So I talked to Lloyd Price and he told me to send a tape to a guy called Art Rupe at Specialty Records in Los Angeles. I went to the radio station in Macon by the call-letters WBML, and I recorded some blues. That was in February 1955. One of the songs was "Wonderin'," which I had stole from a friend of mine. He wrote it and I had got it. I used to hear him singing it, so it just stayed in my mind. So I took the song. The other one on the tape was "He's My Star." I sent it off to the address Lloyd had given me, and just carried on playing with my band. Weeks and weeks went by and I never heard from Specialty. Even when I called I couldn't find out what was happening. Then I got into trouble with the law and had to stop appearing in Macon clubs.

There was this lady by the name of Fanny. I used to drive her around so I could watch people having sex with her. She'd be in the back of the car, the lights on, her legs open, and no panties on. I'd take her around so that the fellers could have sex with her. She didn't do it for money. She did it because I wanted her to do it. She wasn't very old. I used to enjoy seeing that.

Well, I got put in jail for it. I went into the gas station and the gas station man reported me to the police. They put me in jail. Lewd conduct, they called it. I wasn't in jail for more than a few days. I wasn't treated badly. Then my mother got a laywer by the name of Lawyer Jacob. He told the court, "This nigger's going to get out of town. He ain't gonna be here no more." So they let me go, and I left Macon. I couldn't go back and play there no more because of that. We just stayed on the road.

Then, ten months after I'd sent them my tape, Specialty sent for me. We had been playing in Fayetteville, Tennessee. I got the call early in the morning, "Meet us in New Orleans." I slipped away and left my band in the motel, except for Henry Nash, Lee Diamond, and Chuck Connors.

We loaded up the car and drove right down into New Orleans. As we were crossing Lake Pontchartrain Bridge it was raining so hard that we couldn't see to drive. The wipers on my Chrysler were not working, so we took coat hangers and tied them to the blades and worked them by hand so that the driver could see the road. We didn't want to stop cos we were afraid we would miss the session next morning.

And so I recorded "Wonderin'," "He's My Star," "Directly from My Heart to You," and "I'm Just a Lonely Guy," because at that time Specialty wanted me to be a blues singer, like B. B. King and Ray Charles. And then I did "Tutti Frutti."

# Awop-Bop-a-Loo-Mop Alop-Bam-Boom

O n February 17, 1955, Little Richard's audition tape arrived at Specialty's head office, 8508 Sunset Boulevard, Hollywood, California. It was just one of many such shots in the dark that landed on the front desk every week from young hopefuls.

The man whose job it was to bend an ear to these offerings was a conservatory-educated black musician named Robert "Bumps" Blackwell. He had joined Specialty following a distinguished musical career in his home city, Seattle, Washington, where he had nurtured and taught such budding geniuses as Ray Charles and Quincy Jones.

Specialty Records, founded in 1944 by Arthur N. Rupe, had enjoyed ten years of moderate success recording black gospel and R'n'B. The war-related industries attracted an estimated two million working people, a large majority of them black, to California from the southern states. They found plenty of work and a new level of prosperity, which created a big demand for musical entertainment, both live and on record. But black people, still unwelcome in white theaters and clubs, wanted black music, not the white artists and records produced by the major record compan-

*ies. This led to the formation of a number of small indepen-
dent labels. One of the earliest was Art Rupe's Specialty
Records.*

*After listening to hundreds of top selling records and
using a stopwatch to determine what made a record a hit,
Rupe decided that he wanted "a big-band sound expressed
in a churchy way." He toured L.A.'s after-hours clubs looking for artists to record and found a rich vein of talent
among the many gifted black singers and musicians.*

*Over the next decade, Specialty had a number of R'n'B
hits with artists like the Sepia Tones, Roy Milton and His
Solid Senders, Camille Howard, and Jimmy Liggins. Rupe
realized that there was a huge demand for sanctified black
music. The company signed and recorded gospel groups
like the Pilgrim Travelers, the Swan Silvertones, the Chosen
Gospel Singers, and the famous Soul Stirrers, whose lead
singer was a charismatic young man called Sam Cooke.*

*Then, in 1952, Rupe struck gold for the first time. Im-
pressed by the records coming out of New Orleans, he made
a talent-spotting trip and stumbled across a singer called
Lloyd Price, who wrote and sang Specialty's first really-big
seller, "Lawdy Miss Clawdy." It hit number one on the
R'n'B chart and sold a million records in six months.*

*But in 1955, Rupe, faced with a rapidly changing music
and social scene, had little idea of where he and his label
should be going. Having no musical training himself, apart
from an instinct picked up from listening to records, he
placed control of Specialty's musical policy in the hands of
Bumps Blackwell. It was an inspired move which was to
make the company millions of dollars over the next two or
three years.*

BUMPS BLACKWELL: I arrived in Hollywood in 1949 to
study advanced classical composition at UCLA and took a

job with Specialty Records under Art Rupe. Within the first year I had a string of hit records which now seems incredible. I started out by recording religious music, and under my direction Specialty got the greatest stable of gospel stars in history. Then I began to record rhythm-and-blues and had a succession of hits.

In those days the Negro market was the exclusive domain of a few independent record companies. The major companies, like RCA Victor, Columbia, Okeh, and Decca-Brunswick, did not maintain distributors in the mainly black South and hardly competed in that area. The companies that dominated the southern market were Modern, Crown, Aladdin, Imperial, Federal, Chess, King, and Specialty. Specialty had the best Negro artists in both the gospel and R'n'B fields, and under my direction had a virtual monopoly on these sounds.

There was a definite trend toward a more basic and simple music in which the feeling was the most important thing. A singer could make a hit recording if he sang with a lot of feeling, regardless of how imperfect everything else might be. Lloyd Price was one of those kind of singers, and his success prompted Little Richard and others to follow. You couldn't get a learned piano player to give you that simplicity and put that much energy and excitement into it. And that was the rhythm that the people loved and danced to and were buying. People were buying feel, and if you check every one of my hit records that's what they have.

I was recording Lloyd Price, and I was also recording a fellow by the name of Eddie Jones, known as Guitar Slim. His piano player was R. C. Robinson, a youngster who had played in my band in Seattle and had come to L.A. shortly after me. Guitar Slim had a string of good hits, including "The Things That I Used to Do," but he was quite a drinking

45

man. He later died from overindulgence. R. C. Robinson changed his name to Ray Charles, joined Atlantic, and became a superstar in his own right.

Okay, so Ray Charles stopped trying to sound like Nat "King" Cole and started copying Clarence Fountain, of the Alabama Blind Boys. That's how he made it with Atlantic Records, by taking gospel songs and developing them in a blues setting with a beat. He became a sensation. Atlantic also had some other hot artists, and started to become serious competition to Specialty, grabbing a larger share of the market every day. Art Rupe instructed me in the late winter of 1954 or early spring of 1955 to find someone to compete with Ray Charles. I began to search and was auditioning artists. One day a reel of tape, wrapped in a piece of paper looking as though someone had eaten off it, came across my desk.

The tape was from Little Richard. It contained two gospel-inclined songs, "He's My Star," and "Wonderin'." The voice was unmistakably star material. I can't tell you how I knew, but I knew. In spite of the poor quality of the tape, I could tell that the singer had something to say and could say it better than anyone I could think of. The songs were not out-and-out gospel, but I could tell by the tone of his voice and all those churchy turns that he was a gospel singer who could sing the blues. And that's what Art Rupe had told me to find.

I played it for Rupe with the strong recommendation that the artist be signed immediately. But Rupe didn't seem to have any conviction. My theory was he never made a decision because he couldn't bear the thought of being wrong.

I felt the reason some companies dealt with black artists was because black guys wouldn't sue. I will say for Rupe, though, that he would give you what he said he would. When you accepted his terms he'd pay you what he

46

offered—which was not very much—but at least he wasn't a liar.

ART RUPE: We received the tape about seven or eight months before we recorded. Richard kept bugging us on the phone, "Are you going to record me?" "When are you going to record me?" Every fourth or fifth day we'd get a phone call from him. One time from Fort Lauderdale, Florida, another time from Atlanta, then from Jacksonville. I'd never seen Richard, and neither had Bumps Blackwell—this was all by mail and phone. When we were ready to record, we found out that he was still under contract to Peacock. So he made a deal to buy his contract back for six hundred dollars, and we loaned him the money and then signed him.

Richard had told me he liked Fats Domino's sound, and I thought maybe lightning would strike twice if we recorded Richard at J and M Studios in New Orleans, like we did Lloyd Price. We even planned to do eight sides instead of four.

BUMPS BLACKWELL: When I got to New Orleans, Cosimo Matassa, the studio owner, called and said, "Hey, man, this boy's down here waiting for you." When I walked in, there's this cat in this loud shirt, with hair waved up six inches above his head. He was talking wild, thinking up stuff just to be different, you know? I could tell he was a megapersonality. So we got to the studio, on Rampart and Dumaine. I had the Studio Band in—Lee Allen on tenor sax, Alvin "Red" Tyler on baritone sax, Earl Palmer on drums, Edgar Blanchard and Justin Adams on guitar, Huey "Piano" Smith and James Booker on piano, Frank Fields, bass, all of them the best in New Orleans. They were Fats Domino's session men.

Let me tell you about the recording methods we used in those days. Recording technicians of today, surrounded by

47

huge banks of computer-controlled sound technology, would find the engineering techniques available in the 1950s as primitive as the *Kitty Hawk* is to the space shuttle. When I started there was no tape. It was disk to disk. There was no such thing as overdubbing. Those things we did at Cosimo's were on tape, but they were all done straight ahead. The tracks you heard were the tracks as they were recorded from beginning to end. We would take sixty or seventy takes. We were recording two tracks. Maybe we might go to surgery and intercut a track or cut a track at the end or something, but we didn't know what overdubbing was. The studio was just a back room in a furniture store, like an ordinary motel room. For the whole orchestra. There'd be a grand piano just as you came in the door. I'd have the grand's lid up with a mike in the keys and Alvin Tyler and Lee Allen would be blowing into that. Earl Palmer's drums were out of the door, where I had one mike as well. The bassman would be way over the other side of the studio. You see, the bass would cut and bleed in, so I could get the bass.

The recording equipment was a little old quarter-inch single-channel Ampex Model 300 in the next room. I would go in there and listen with earphones. If it didn't sound right I'd just keep moving the mikes around. I would have to set up all those things. But, you see, once I had got my sound, my room sound, well then I would just start running my numbers straight down. It might take me forty-five minutes, an hour, to get that balance within the room, but once those guys hit a groove you could go on all night. When we got it, we got it. I would like to see some of these great producers today produce on monaural or binaural equipment with the same atmosphere. Cos the problem is, if you're going to get a room sound with the timbre of the instruments, you can't put them together as a band and just start playing. All of a sudden one horn's going to stick

48

out. So I had to place the mikes very carefully and put the drummer outside the door.

Well, the first session was to run six hours, and we planned to cut eight sides. Richard ran through the songs on his audition tape. "He's My Star" was very disappointing. I did not even record it. But "Wonderin' " we got in two takes. Then we got "I'm Just a Lonely Guy," which was written by a local girl called Dorothy La Bostrie who was always pestering me to record her stuff. Then "The Most I Can Offer," and then "Baby." So far so good. But it wasn't really what I was looking for. I had heard that Richard's stage act was really wild, but in the studio that day he was very inhibited. Possibly his ego was pushing him to show his spiritual feeling or something, but it certainly wasn't coming together like I had expected and hoped.

The problem was that what he looked like, and what he sounded like didn't come together. If you look like Tarzan and sound like Mickey Mouse it just doesn't work out. So I'm thinking, Oh, Jesus...You know what it's like when you don't know what to do? It's "Let's take a break. Let's go to lunch." I had to think. I didn't know what to do. I couldn't go back to Rupe with the material I had because there was nothing there that I could put out. Nothing that I could ask anyone to put a promotion on. Nothing to merchandise. And I was paying out serious money.

So here we go over to the Dew Drop Inn, and, of course, Richard's like any other ham. We walk into the place and, you know, the girls are there and the boys are there and he's got an audience. There's a piano, and that's his crutch. He's on stage reckoning to show Lee Allen his piano style. So WOW! He gets to going. He hits that piano, didididididididididi...and starts to sing "Awop-bop-a-Loo-Mop a-good Goddam—Tutti Frutti, good booty..." I said, "Wow! That's what I want from you, Richard. That's a hit!" I knew that the lyrics were too lewd and suggestive to record. It would never have got played on the air. So I got hold of Dorothy La

Bostrie, who had come over to see how the recording of her song was going. I brought her to the Dew Drop.

Dorothy was a little colored girl so thin she looked like six o'clock. She just had to close one eye and she looked like a needle. Dorothy had songs stacked this high and was always asking me to record them. She'd been singing these songs to me, but the trouble was they all sounded like Dinah Washington's "Blowtop Blues." They were all composed to the same melody. But looking through her words, I could see that she was a prolific writer. She just didn't understand melody. So I said to her, "Look. You come and write some lyrics to this, cos I can't use the lyrics Richard's got." He had some terrible words in there. Well, Richard was embarrassed to sing the song and she was not certain that she wanted to hear it. Time was running out, and I *knew* it could be a hit. I talked, using every argument I could think of. I asked him if he had a grudge against making money. I told her that she was over twenty-one, had a houseful of kids and no husband and needed the money. And finally, I convinced them. Richard turned to face the wall and sang the song two or three times and Dorothy listened.

Break time was over, and we went back to the studio to finish the session, leaving Dorothy to write the words. I think the first thing we did was "Directly from My Heart to You." Now that, and "I'm Just a Lonely Guy," could have made it. Those two I could have gotten by with—just by the skin of my teeth. Fifteen minutes before the session was to end, the chick comes in and puts these little trite lyrics in front of me. I put them in front of Richard. Richard says he ain't got no voice left. I said, "Richard, you've *got* to sing it."

There had been no chance to write an arrangement, so I had to take the chance on Richard playing the piano himself. That wild piano was essential to the success of the

50

song. It was impossible for the other piano players to learn it in the short time we had. I put a microphone between Richard and the piano and another inside the piano, and we started to record. It took three takes, and in fifteen minutes we had it. "Tutti Frutti."

### TUTTI FRUTTI
(Penniman/La Bostrie/Lubin)

First Specialty Record

*Womp-Bomp-a-Loo-Momp Alop-Bomp-Bomp*

*Tutti Frutti, Aw-Rootie (5 times)*
*Awop-Bop-a-Loo-Mop Alop-Bomp-Bomp*

*I Got A Girl, Named Sue*
*She Knows Just What To Do*
*I Got A Girl, Named Sue*
*She Knows Just What To Do*
*She Rock To The East, She Rock To The West*
*But She's The Girl That I Love Best*

*Tutti Frutti, Aw-Rootie (5 times)*
*Awop-Bop-a-Loo-Mop Alop-Bam-Boom*

*I've Got A Gal, Named Daisy*
*She Almost Drives Me Crazy*
*I've Got A Gal, Named Daisy*
*She Almost Drives Me Crazy*
*She Knows How To Love Me, Yes Indeed*
*Boy You Don't Know What She's Doin' To Me*

*Tutti Frutti, Aw-Rootie (5 times)*
*Awop-Bop-a-Loo-Mop Alop-Bam-Boom*

# PART II
# TUTTI FRUTTI

# *Tutti Frutti*

'd been singing "Tutti Frutti" for years, but it never struck me as a song you'd *record*. I didn't go to New Orleans to record no "Tutti Frutti." Sure, it used to crack the crowds up when I sang it in the clubs, with those risqué lyrics: Tutti Frutti, good booty/If it don't fit, don't force it/You can grease it, make it easy...

But I never thought it would be a hit, even with the lyrics cleaned up.

Well, I was at home in Macon when I heard them play it on *Randy's Record Mart*, Radio WLAC out of Nashville, Tennessee. The disk jockey Gene Nobles said, "This is the hottest record in the country. This guy Little Richard is taking the record market by storm." I couldn't believe it. My old song a hit! Then I got a call from Specialty to come to Hollywood—the record was breaking wide open. I left the band and went to make personal appearances there.

HENRY NASH: I first met Richard when he was blowing saxophone in the Hudson High School band in 1947. I was aware of him and friendly with him at that time. Then I began singing with a group I formed called the Dominions. We idolized the Dominoes so much that we wanted to be as close to them as possible. We hoped people would see the

55

signs and think it *was* the Dominoes! My group and Little Richard's were managed by Clint Brantley. We would travel together doing dates throughout the Southland—all over the states of Tennessee, Mississippi, Florida, Alabama, Kentucky, South Carolina, and in the southern parts of Illinois. Our last package together was called the Blues Express.

When Richard left us, Clint Brantley was very angry. He had to find a singer to replace Richard for the dates which had already been booked. We remembered a young black singer who had gate-crashed Richard's show in a South Carolina club. During the intermission he and his band had put on a great performance and brought the house down. Clint traced the singer, but discovered he had recently served time in a correctional institution at Toccoa, Georgia, for theft and general delinquency and was still on parole. Clint used his influence with the state's political chiefs, managing to clear things with his parole officer. He got the young man together with the Upsetters for the remaining dates of the tour. The singer's name was James Brown.

James Brown was a tremendous singer and dancer, with a lot of voice. He wore his hair in a process, very high at the front. Apart from that, he by no means *looked* like Richard, although he could sing and perform like him. Each night Luke, who did the M.C. work, would bring him on and say, "Ladies and gentlemen—the hardest-working man in show-business today—Little Richard!"

Another young singer that we took on the road with us later was a guy named Otis Redding. He idolized Richard. Otis won a talent show at the Douglass Theater in downtown Macon run by D.J. Hamp Swain. His impressions of Richard were word perfect and he had all of his moves down pat. He quit high school to come on the road with the Upsetters.

56

BUMPS BLACKWELL: When Richard first arrived in Hollywood, he was so far out! His hair was processed a foot high over his head. His shirt was so loud it looked as though he had drunk raspberry juice, cherryade, malt, and greens and then thrown up all over himself. Man, he was a freak. Well, I had to go around with him. I fixed him up with clothes and things to prepare him for personal appearances. My folks got a look at him and held a family meeting to ask me if I'd changed my ways!

Richard had been a pro for years. But he lacked polish. When he buttoned his shirt his suitcase was packed. He had that magic, that perception, which made him able to handle any audience. But there were a few things he still had to learn.

*Specialty's deal with Richard was typical of the company's dealings with their artists. In the fifties the standard royalty received from record companies was 5 percent of 90 percent of the retail price of the record. At that time a 45 sold for eighty-nine cents. The performer could expect to receive about four cents for each record sold, plus a broadcast fee, calculated on the number of airplays it received, which could be one or two cents. The song's publisher retained the "mechanical right" to the song, which meant that the record company paid out one cent for each of the songs on the record. If the songwriter nominated himself as the publisher of the songs, he received, in addition to any royalty and broadcast fees, two-cent mechanical fees on every copy sold. Specialty boss Art Rupe owned the publishing company that bought Richard's songs. He leased them to his own recording company at one-half rate, which cut Richard's share of the mechanicals to half a cent.*

● I had signed a very bad deal with Specialty. If you wanted to record you signed on their terms or you didn't record. I got a half cent for every record sold. Whoever heard of cutting a penny in half!

It didn't matter how many records you sold if you were black. The publishing rights were sold to the record label before the record was released. "Tutti Frutti" was sold to Specialty for fifty dollars.

The tragedy about show business in the early days was that, like me, most performers were young, inexperienced, and uneducated. We just wanted to be away from home and travel around the country. So we were exploited, abused, misused, and just plain ripped off by record labels and managements as they quickly became aware of the money to be made in the early era of Rock 'n' Roll.

So the people who got recorded were the ones who didn't know or care too much about the money angle of it. And when one came along who showed signs of knowledge of the business, he was called a smart nigger who knew too much for his own good. That is why many of the old acts were never heard from after their first one or two recordings. They were shuffled around and their records just sat on a shelf and were forgotten.

So we knew that to make money we had to go on the road, and it had to be with the best show in the U.S. We got some of the old Upsetters, Chuck Connors on drums and Lee Diamond, who played sax and piano, plus Grady Gaines and Clifford Burks on tenor saxes, Sammy Parker on baritone, Olsie Robinson on bass, and Nathaniel Douglas on guitar, with Henry Nash as road manager. We rehearsed until I had the best show band in the United States. Then we went on the road. I called my brother, Marquette, who was in Chicago, and got him to come with me, as my valet and companion.

JOHN MARASCALCO: I was a novice in this field in the

fifties, and whatever royalty checks came in I was glad to get them. I wrote or cowrote six of Richard's hits on Specialty. I did not, until I became my own publisher and own record company, realize what had been going on. I only found this out about ten years ago, but a lot of the early rhythm-and-blues companies had their own publishing companies, which owned the record companies. So they licensed their songs to their own record companies at whatever rate they wanted to. When I went back into my files on my BMI performances I started to look at those old royalty statements, and I saw that Art Rupe had licensed the songs to himself for one-half rate. Instead of a two-cent rate he had licensed it to a one-cent rate. So the publishers would get half a cent and the writers would get half a cent rather than a whole cent!"

CHUCK CONNORS: We surely did a lot of rehearsing. For instance, Richard said to us, "I want 'Tutti Frutti' to have a little more energy to it. I don't want just that single back-beat like when Earl Palmer played it in the studio." He made me change so it was more heavy on the bass drum. When I think of it now, it sounded almost like what's known as the disco beat.

A whole lot of other bands had started to play "Tutti Frutti." They cottoned on to Richard's record, but they never played it like we did. They always used the single back-beat, never the beat we used. That's too much trouble for the drummer. Playing it like that with the hand and arm up there you get tired. But I'm from the old school. I was taught relaxing. I can play "Tutti Frutti" for five hours like that and never get tired.

We had a good band. It was so tight and well organized that everybody was almost thinking alike. We were the only Rock 'n' Roll band out there on the road that could read music and play behind other acts. A whole lot of other bands could play behind their own artists, but if they had to play behind anyone else they blew it, cos they couldn't read. But we did all that. We could play anything. Jazz or anything.

*As "Tutti Frutti" climbed the R'n'B charts it was covered by two white artists—Pat Boone and Elvis Presley. Boone, a young churchgoing schoolteacher from Nashville, already had two hits that were cover versions—Otis Williams's "Two Hearts, Two Kisses" and Fats Domino's "Ain't That a Shame." Boone's version of "Tutti Frutti" only had a fraction of the vitality and humor of Richard's. His crooner's voice made the song slightly ridiculous. In spite of that, Pat Boone's record went gold.*

*This actually helped sales of Richard's original version, as people who had never heard Rock 'n' Roll before became turned on to the new sound. But in general, the policy of the "white" record companies covering the songs of black artists was a cruel larceny of original talent.*

BUMPS BLACKWELL: The white radio stations wouldn't play Richard's version of "Tutti Frutti" and made Boone's cover number one. So we decided to up the tempo on the follow-up and get the lyrics going so fast that Boone wouldn't be able to get his mouth together to do it! The follow-up was "Long Tall Sally." It was written by a girl named Enortis Johnson and the story of how she came to us seems unbelievable today.

I got a call from a big disk jockey called Honey Chile. She *had* to see me. Very urgent. I went, because we relied on the jocks to push the records, and the last thing you said to them was no. I went along to this awful downtown hotel, and there was Honey Chile with this young girl, about sixteen, seventeen, with plaits, who reminded you of one of these little sisters at a Baptist meeting, all white starched collars and everything. She looked like someone who's just been scrubbed—so out of place in this joint filled with pimps and unsavory characters just waiting to scoop her up when she's left alone, you know?

So Honey Chile said to me, "Bumps, you got to do something about this girl. She's walked all the way from Appaloosa, Mississippi, to sell this song to Richard, cos her auntie's sick and she needs money to put her in the hospital." I said okay, let's hear the song, and this little clean-cut kid, all bows and things, says, "Well, I don't have a melody yet. I thought maybe you or Richard could do that." So I said okay, what *have* you got, and she pulls out this piece of paper. It looked like toilet paper with a few words written on it:

*Saw Uncle John with Long Tall Sally*
*They saw Aunt Mary comin'*
*So they ducked back in the alley*

And she said, "Aunt Mary is sick. And I'm going to tell her about Uncle John. Cos he was out there with Long Tall Sally, and I saw 'em. They saw Aunt Mary comin' and they ducked back in the alley.

I said, "They did, huh? And this is a song? You walked all the way from Appaloosa, Mississippi, with this piece of paper?" (I'd give my right arm if I could find it now. I kept it for years. It was a classic. Just a few words on a used doily!)

Honey Chile said, "Bumps, you gotta do something for this child." So I went back to the studio. I told Richard. He didn't want to do it. I said, "Richard, Honey Chile will get mad at us...." I kept hearing "Duck back in the alley, duck back in the alley." We kept adding words and music to it, to put it right. Richard started to sing it—and all of a sudden there was "Have some fun tonight." That was the hook. Richard loved it cos the hottest thing then was the shuffle.

Richard was reciting that thing. He got on the piano and got the music going and it just started growing and growing. We kept trying, trying it, and I pulled the musicians in and we pulled stuff from everybody. That's where Richard's "Ooooooh" first came in. That's what he taught to Paul McCartney. Well, we kept rerecording because I wanted it faster. I drilled Richard with "Duck back in the alley" faster and faster until it burned, it was so fast. When it was finished I turned to Richard and said, "Let's see Pat Boone get his mouth together to do *this* song."* That's how it was done, and if you look at the copyright you'll see it's Johnson, Penniman, and Blackwell.

*Released in February of that year, "Long Tall Sally," backed with "Slippin' and Slidin'," zoomed almost instantly to number one on the R'n'B charts. The record eventually became a double-sided hit on the national top-twenty charts. It sold half a million copies by March, despite numerous cover versions and the refusal of many white stations to give it airplay. The record also boosted the sales of "Tutti Frutti," which was on the national pop charts for twelve weeks and on the R'n'B charts for twenty weeks, pushing the sales to a million. Up-and-coming rock star Elvis Presley had recorded his own version of "Tutti Frutti" and had sung it on the Dorsey Brothers' TV show.*

---

*Boone did cover "Long Tall Sally." An anemic version in which he reverses the Midas touch and turns gold into dross, managing to sound as though he is not quite sure what he is singing about. It sold a million.

## LONG TALL SALLY
### (E. Johnson/Blackwell/Penniman)

*Gonna tell Aunt Mary 'bout Uncle John,*
*He claims he has the mis'ry but he has a lotta fun*
*Oh, baby, yes baby, woo baby*
*Havin' me some fun tonight.*

*Well, Long Tall Sally she's built for speed, she got*
*Everythin' that Uncle John needs*
*Oh, baby, yes baby, woo baby*
*Havin' me some fun tonight.*

*Well, I saw Uncle John, with bald-head Sally*
*He saw Aunt Mary comin' and he ducked back in the*
*  alley,*
*Oh, baby, yes baby, woo baby*
*Havin' me some fun tonight.*

*Yeah! We're gonna have some fun tonight*
*Gonna have some fun tonight—woo!*
*We're gonna have some fun tonight,*
*Everythin's all right.*
*We're gonna have some fun, gonna have me some fun*
*  tonight.*

● When people started admiring me and my songs went gold I decided to buy a home in Hollywood and bring my family there to live. Art Rupe gave me ten thousand dollars to put down on a house at 1710 Virginia Road, in West L.A., the Sugar Hill district. The house cost twenty-five thousand dollars. It was next door to the world champion, Joe Louis, who was raised in Macon, like me. Rupe wasn't giving me nothing that wasn't mine, you understand. He deducted it from my royalty checks. That's how it was. You made the hits, you sold the records, then when the royalty statements arrived you'd find you owed *them*.

But that was the happiest moment of my life, when I bought my mother that lovely home and moved her out of that little three-room house in Macon. Macon was country then, red mud everywhere, and my mother was a country woman. She didn't want to come at first and leave all her friends and neighbors. I had always wanted to do this for my mother and I also felt obligated to my sisters and brothers—through love. It was a great period in my life.

When Mother saw the house she couldn't believe it. She had never seen black people living in this type of house. It was the kind of house that white film stars lived in—big staircase, chandeliers, marble floors, plants, bedrooms upstairs and downstairs, and statues. Really lavish.

I tell you, until they saw the house and my 1956 gold Fleetwood Cadillac in the garage they never realized what a big hit record really meant. And I didn't either. None of us will ever forget that.

*With the success of "Long Tall Sally" immortality in the world of Rock 'n' Roll would have been Richard's even if he had never recorded again. But he continued to produce classic singles at an amazing rate. His third release, in June 1956, was "Rip It Up," coupled with "Ready Teddy." Both songs were written by Johnny Marascalco and Bumps Blackwell. It became a double-sided number-one hit on the R'n'B charts. And the songs were quickly covered by Elvis Presley, Bill Haley, and Buddy Holly. The top-side lyrics sublimely sum up the good-time feelings of Rock 'n' Roll:*

### RIP IT UP
### (M a r a s c a l c o / B l a c k w e l l)

*Well, it's Saturday night and I just got paid,*
*Fool about my money, don't try to save.*
*My heart says, go go,*

*Have a time*
*'Cause it's Saturday night, and I feel fine.*

*I'm gonna RIP IT UP!*
*I'm gonna rock it up!*
*I'm gonna shake it up      I'm gonna ball it up!*
*I'm gonna RIP IT UP and ball tonight.*

*Got me a date and I won't be late,*
*Picked her up in my eighty eight.*
*Shag on down by the union hall*
*When the joint starts jumpin' I have a ball.*

*I'm gonna RIP IT UP! etc.*

*Along about ten,*
*I'll be flyin' high,*
*Walk on out into the sky.*
*But I don't care if I spend my dough,*
*'Cause tonight I'm gonna be one happy soul.*

*I'm gonna RIP IT UP! etc.*


*Richard was taking America by storm. The demand for personal appearances, even in the southern states, was eroding the taboos against black artists appearing in white clubs and dance halls. Everyone wanted to see the creator of this joyous new sound. America, however, was still a country where terrible things could happen to a black man who was seen as sexually attractive to white women, so Richard established a wild and bizarre image which was to stick throughout his career.*

● We were breaking through the racial barrier. The white kids had to hide my records cos they daren't let their parents know they had them in the house. We decided that my image should be crazy and way-out so that the adults

65

would think I was harmless. I'd appear in one show dressed as the Queen of England and in the next as the pope.

*His act was a whole new experience to audiences used to seeing groups like the Penguins or the Cadillacs, who were super-cool and concentrated on their singing, doing little rehearsed dance steps and hand gestures. He freed people from their inhibitions, unleashing their spirit, enabling them to do exactly what they felt like doing—to scream, shout, dance, jump up and down—or even more unusual things. . . .*

*It was at a Little Richard show in the Royal Theater, Baltimore, Maryland, that U.S. concert history was changed forever. The beat was charging the packed and fervid crowd with super-excitement as the Upsetters pumped out the music. People had to be restrained from jumping off the balcony. The show had been stopped twice while police drafted for the concert removed a dozen hysterical girls who were climbing on stage, trying to rip souvenirs from a wild-eyed and sweat-soaked Richard. Suddenly something flew through the air and landed on Chuck Connors's high-hat—a pair of panties. One of the frenzied girls in front had peeled off her briefs and thrown them at the band. Within seconds the air was filled with flying undergarments as the other girls followed suit.*

CHUCK CONNORS: We didn't know what was happening. Grady and the rest of 'em were ducking and shouting "Hey!" bumping heads trying to avoid all these flying panties. We cracked up. Stopped playing. We were laughing so much. I picked a pair up on my stick and waved them in the air. After that it happened lots of places we played. The girls would actually take their panties off and throw them at the bandstand. A shower of panties!

To watch the guys in the band playing on the stage was

amazing. You couldn't miss a beat because those bodies were always moving in time. It was very exciting. Those guys were the first band to come out with dance steps. They would look like a well-drilled chorus line. And then Richard, out there in front of them sweating, all that water and everything, and his hair falling all over his face—you'd get a natural high just by looking at him.

Some of the wildest theater dates we did were at the Howard Theater, Washington, D.C. Wow! They used to have two or three shows a day. The kids wanted to see Richard so bad they would play hooky to come and see the show. For the kids just to *look* at Richard was really something. They had never seen a man like that, with long hair and all that makeup, and shaking his head and all that. And the band there, playing behind him, really exciting 'em.

In the intermission, you went to the bar to get a drink, people'd mob you. They'd recognize you—"That's one of 'em right there..." You know. And the band was so close and warm. We used to walk down the street with our arms around Richard, and that made people love us, to see that the band was warm, good friends. We used to get respect out of black and white, like we were heroes. We never had a serious argument or anything like that, cos everything was going so well. Everyone was happy. It was a good experience to work in an environment like that, and I would like to live it again.

In those days, you didn't see many people with long hair. Well, they arrested Richard for that in Texas. We were playing El Paso, Texas, and the police came in and stopped the show, stopped the band and everything and put Richard in jail. He had this long hair, and he was shakin' about up on the stage, you know? Elvis Presley was due to be coming into that town a couple of weeks later, and the police told Richard, "If you see that guy Elvis Presley tell him we're gonna lock *him* up, too, cos he has long hair." Real rednecks.

Richard used to go to the beauty shop to get his hair done, and the band had to go too. I was wearing my hair curled in a process. We would go and get our hair curled, then the next week we had to go get a touchup. But what made us feel so great was that we had a whole lot of good-looking guys in the band, good builds and everything. We had different sets of colored suits and shirts and black and white and gray tuxedos, uniform shirts, and things. Everybody dressed alike.

Those times were all wild. It was always a new experience. Really something. We had a beautiful time—wild parties, pretty girls, wild girls. A beautiful time.

H. B. BARNUM: When I first saw Richard, he was headlining a big package show—Etta James and the Peaches, the Five Chords, the Five Keys, the Robins, and Bill Doggett. I was fourteen years old, playing saxophone with Chuck Liggins and Big Jay McNeely, making about ninety dollars a week. I'd come on with the show band and play the opening number. Then I'd run off stage and change clothes and come back on with the next group and then the next. I guess Richard took a fancy to me because he would let me play with his band, too.

You knew not, night to night, where he was going to come from. He'd just burst onto the stage from anywhere, and you wouldn't be able to hear anything but the roar of the audience. He might come out and walk on the piano. He might go out in the audience. His charisma was just a whole new thing to the business. Richard was totally out of this world, wild, and it gave people who wanted to scream a chance to go ahead and scream instead of trying to be cool.

We would go into the first number and we might vamp that first number for four to five minutes before he even got to the piano. He'd be on the stage, he'd be off the stage, he'd be jumping and yelling, screaming, whipping the audience on, whipping them on. Then when he finally hit the piano and just went into di-di-di-di-di-di-di-di, you know, well nobody can do that as fast as Richard. It just took everybody by surprise.

I'd been playing with Fats for a couple of years and I'd seen some pretty wild suits as far as colors go, but Richard with the diamonds, the different-colored stones and sequins, the capes, the blouse shirts, the way he used makeup, the way he did his eyes (Richard has eyes that would just look through you, but when he accentuated them with makeup—wow!), it was really very way out for the times. That's the first time I ever saw spotlights and flicker lights used at a concert show. It had all been used in show business, but he brought it into *our* world.

He pulled out all the stops. The audiences, they'd rush to touch him. Each night he could go to new heights. He could just come out and sing the same song and another dimension would happen. I've worked with some top artists, Presley, all those, and nobody's ever had that kind of magic. When Richard opened his mouth, man, everybody in the world could enjoy it. He's got a voice that would make 'em jump up and down.

Richard opened the door. He brought the races together. When I first went on the road there were many segregated audiences. With Richard, although they still had the audiences segregated in the building, they were *there* together. And most times, before the end of the night, they would all be mixed together. Up until then, the audiences were either all black or all white, and no one else could come in. His records weren't boy-meets-girl-girl-meets-boy things, they were *fun* records, all fun. And they had a lot to say sociologically in our country and the world. The shot was fired here and heard round the world.

● They were exciting times. The fans would go really wild. Nearly every place we went, the people got unruly. They'd want to get to me and tear my clothes off. It would be standing-room-only crowds and 90 percent of the audience would be white. I've always thought that Rock 'n' Roll brought the races together. Although I was black, the fans didn't care. I used to feel good about that. Especially being from the South, where you see the barriers, having all these people who we thought hated us, showing all this *love*.

We were doing one-nighters and we were doing one *every* night! We were working seven nights a week, two and sometimes three shows a night. The schedule was indescribable. You would get there and not even have time to unpack your bags. Whatever you were wearing that day, the valets would press with those little steam irons or send down to the hotel to be pressed. We'd barely have time to get ready and get to the show.

There we'd be, the band in all these pink-and-white suits, looking fine and feeling great. I was there with my hair long and beautiful. We used potato and lye and hot combing and curlers, because we had to have that new image. We knew we had it. We knew we could draw ten thousand people every night, and we were making more money than we had ever made before. We all had to change our clothes two or three times because of all the sweating. So, there I was doing this dancing. Chuck would call it my freaky-deaky dance. I used to have women coming up and throwing naked pictures of themselves on stage, with their phone numbers on 'em.

When we booked the hotel we might rent four or five different rooms. Probably the whole top floor. There would always be a lot of people come around. It was quite a show. Barnum and Bailey, you name it! There was never any problem getting girls. At the end of the show, they'd either come around to the dressing room or the hotel, and we'd sort them out—which ones we wanted. We had some parties!

There was one time we were in this hotel in Bloomsfield, West Virginia. They had a rule like you couldn't bring in any girl unless she's your wife. Well, this girl came over and she was really wild. She would take anything. All the band guys at once. We didn't know she was married. Her husband was downstairs trying to find out if his wife was up there with us. He was banging on the door, and we were trying to get her out. But she didn't want to go! She said, "I don't wanna leave now, I'm enjoying myself." The guys didn't care and I had to plead with them to let her go. Eventually we sneaked her down the fire escape, but it was close. The hotel was a wooden building and this guy was downstairs threatening to put a match to it and burn it down! That's the fun part, you see, when you're sneakin'. Makes it very much more exciting.

But it got difficult to have sex parties after a time, because we were so popular. People couldn't get to you. I wasn't used to that. It made me feel so important. So big. I felt unusual, you know, like I was a special person.

ETTA JAMES: I was so naïve in those days. Richard and the band were always having those parties and I'd knock on the door and try to get in. They'd say, "Don't open the door, she's a minor!" Then one day, I climbed up and looked through the transom—and the things I *saw!*

● I used to like to watch these people having sex with my band men. I would pay a guy who had a big penis to come and have sex with these ladies so I could watch them. It was a big thrill to me. If the girls didn't think they could take it, I would watch him make them take it. As I was watching, I would masturbate while someone was eating my titties. They should have called me "Richard the Watcher."

My whole gay activities were really into masturbation. I used to do it six or seven times a day. In fact everybody used to tell me that I should get a trophy for it, I did it so much. I got to be a professional jack-offer. I would do it just to be doing something, seven, eight times a day. Feel bad after I did it though. I'd always be mad after I finished. Be mad at myself, don't want to talk about it, don't wanna answer no questions. I'd think, Why did you do it? You crazy? You could've... Most gay people fall in love with themselves.

Then I met Angel. We were in Savannah, Georgia. I was sitting in the hotel room with some of the band looking out of the window. I saw this beautiful young girl with this fantastic body, fifty-inch bust and eighteen-inch waist. It's true that nothing grows in the shade! She was with another girl walking toward the theater. I asked one of my band men to go across the street and ask her to come over to the hotel. She told me she was about to graduate from high school.

A few weeks later she turned up at a concert in Wilmington, Delaware. She had decided to come with me. When we left for Washington, D.C. that night Angel traveled with us in my car. We checked into the Hotel Dunbar, in Washington, and we shared a room. She was a wonderful lover. She changed her name to Lee Angel and worked as a nude model, a dancer, and a stripper. From the beginning she seemed to know exactly what I wanted in sex. She would do anything to excite me, including having sex with other guys while I watched. I loved Angel and Angel loved me, but in different ways. Marriage was a dream of hers, but I never wanted to marry her.

I loved Angel because she was pretty and the fellers enjoyed having sex with her. She could draw a lot of handsome guys for me. She was like a magnet. She drew everything to me. You ain't never seen a woman made like Angel. That fifty-inch bust. Natural, too. She was never a fat woman. She looked like a white girl, but she's black.

Angel would take in four guys at one time, and she wouldn't let 'em out. Most of 'em didn't want to get out, I noticed. I'd see some big guy and I'd say, "Hey, c'mon by," and Angel would say, "Yeah, c'mon. I'd like to see what you got there." She was some girl.

LEE ANGEL: Richard and I became very close friends to the point where we almost got married. He sent me to Tennessee to work with a piano player called Ray Charles. I was there about three weeks before Richard got there. He had planned to have his new record, "Send Me Some Lovin'," released on that particular day all over the country. That night, at the show, Richard told me and about seven thousand other people that I was his fiancée and that we were getting married. That's how I found out. He dedicated "Send Me Some Lovin' " specially to me.

We were so close that we could read each other's mind. I would be in a room with him and I'd start cursing him out because I'd know what he was thinking. Everybody in the room used to wonder what was going on between us. If he was away on the road and I wanted to talk to him, I would really concentrate on him and he'd call me within a few minutes.

I traveled with him when he was doing one-nighters. It was always fun. One time we were at the Civic Opera House, in Chicago. Richard introduced me to the audience. The place was packed with thousands of people. As we were leaving the auditorium his fans came up and ripped my dress off!

*After his third hit record, "Rip It Up," backed with "Ready Teddy," smashed the charts, Richard felt confident enough to directly challenge Art Rupe's decision to record in New Orleans.*

● I told Art Rupe that my band was the greatest in the world, better than those studio musicians from New Orleans. I didn't see why the Upsetters couldn't back me on my records the same way as they did on the stage. The Upsetters were good, and I wanted them on my records, too.

The New Orleans guys, Earl Palmer, Lee Allen, and the others, had a fellowship. They were on my recordings, on Fats Domino's recordings, on Shirley and Lee's, and Guitar Slim's. When people got around to recognizing that it was the same musicians on all those records, they broke up the syndicate. But that was much later.

Rupe told me I had to make the record in New Orleans. He said that he knew what was best for me. I told him I would break my contract if he insisted. He was really mad, but there was nothing he could do. He set up the session at Masters Recording Studio, down on Fairfax. We cut "She's Got It," "Heeby-Jeebies," "Send Me Some Lovin'," and "Lucille." I think those recordings are as good as the others.

JOHN MARASCALCO: Richard had recorded a song called "I Got It." Mr. Rupe had asked me to change it to "She's Got It" for the film *The Girl Can't Help It*. So I wrote new lyrics. Richard was out on the road at the time.

Richard had really started getting on an ego trip. He was refusing to go to New Orleans to record. He thought that he was God at the time, and I guess he was! It was like a blackmail session. If they didn't let him record with his band, they were going to have problems.

I had never seen Richard work in the studio, though he'd already recorded several of my songs. I asked Bumps if I could go along to the session, and he said okay. They were doing "She's Got It" and a couple of other songs. Bumps had been in complete control of the Studio Band. But at this particular session Richard was the whole show. I wasn't there the whole time. When I arrived they had already started recording. Mr. Rupe and Bumps were there, but I don't remember Bumps conducting or suggesting, apart from saying, "You said '*I* got it' again, Richard. Stop." Art Rupe just kinda sat back and said, "Yeah, that's good" or, "Get a little more of that in or a little more of that." Richard had *demanded*, and it was his session.

BUMPS BLACKWELL: There was nobody else ever got a hit record out of Richard but me. Other people recorded him, but they didn't make it. And the reason they couldn't make it? I dunno. Whatever you want to work it out to be, they just didn't do what I did, that's all.

Richard screamed so hard. His dynamic range was so terrific. Richard would be singing like this [whispers] and then all of a sudden BOW!! The needles would just go off the dial. I never overdubbed Richard's voice. Richard was on, full on, all the way. Richard's style of playing really brought the piano to the forefront in this music. He was such a powerful player, he'd beat the piano out of tune and break the strings. He was the only guy I knew who would beat the piano so hard he'd break an eighty-gauge piano string. He did it several times.

● A lot of songs I sang to crowds first to watch their reaction, that's how I knew they'd hit, but we recorded them over and over again. "Lucille" was after a female impersonator in my hometown. We used to call him Queen Sonya. I just took the rhythm of an old song of mine called

"Directly from My Heart to You" slowed down and I used to do that riff and go "Sonya!" and I made it into "Lucille." My cousin used to live in a place called Barn Hop Bottom in Macon, right by the railway line, and when the trains came past they'd shake the houses—*chocka-chocka-chocka*—and that's how I got the rhythm for "Directly from My Heart" and "Lucille." I was playing it way before I met Bumps. I was playing "Lucille" and "Slippin' and Slidin' " in my room in Macon way before I started recording for Specialty. I'd make up the music while I was making the words fit.

"Good Golly Miss Molly" I first heard a D.J. using that name. His name was Jimmy Pennick, but you know it was Jackie Brenston that gave me the musical inspiration. Jackie Brenston was a sax player with Ike Turner's Kings of Rhythm when he did "Rocket 88" and "Juiced," and Ike Turner's band backed him, but they didn't take any credits because of their contracts. I always liked that record, and I used to use the riff in my act, so when we were looking for a lead-in to "Good Golly Miss Molly" I did that and it fitted."

*Little Richard sang songs in which the words were vague and often nonsensical. He made them classics with the intensity and power of his unique voice, which was so frantic and exhilarating that the listener was compelled to follow its incredible pace to the end. Even in the slower-paced ballads, Richard's voice embellished the lyrics like a volcano bursting through an arctic wasteland. His extraordinary range embracing both the wildest Rock 'n' Roll falsetto and the precision and control of a virtuoso opera singer, ripped through the words with a pulsating power, never less than that of a* Saturn 5 *rocket at full thrust. His voice left the listener intensely high as though he had sniffed a gram of toot, drunk a bottle of Jack Daniel's, and reached a sexual orgasm all at once. Instant ecstasy.*

*Elvis Presley had sexuality, Chuck Berry his masterly lyrics, and Fats Domino his rich New Orleans R'n'B beat, but it was Richard's voice, with its sheer naked and joyous energy, which broke through established musical structures and changed the way of life for a whole generation.*

● I tried to take voice lessons, but I found I couldn't because the way I sing, a voice teacher can't deal with it. I'm out of control. True singers, people who know something about music, not Rock 'n' Roll, have told me there is something special there. I thank the Lord for it.

You know I was havin' so much fun in 1956, I didn't realize how much impact my music had. Sure, I knew that Elvis cut four of my songs that year. Pat Boone had two gold disks with my "Tutti Frutti" and "Long Tall Sally." Bill Haley had a big big hit with "Rip It Up." Gene Vincent, Carl Perkins, Jerry Lee Lewis, the Everly Brothers, and Eddie Cochran, they all recorded my songs. When I met them on tour they were always asking me, "When's your new record comin' out, man?" "How did you get that full sound on 'She's Got It'? " "Please play 'Ready Teddy' tonight."

I was selling so many records that Specialty brought in an old buddy of mine called Larry Williams, who used to work around New Orleans with Lloyd Price and Fats Domino, to cut some records imitating my sound and style. They were "Short Fat Fanny," "Dizzy Miss Lizzy," and "Bony Moronie" and they, too, became million sellers. At this time there were dozens of singers trying to imitate me, not always my songs but my style. Joe Tex did "You Little Baby Faced Thing," Long Tall Marvin had a number called "Have Mercy Miss Percy" and many more crazy things like that. It flattered me—but it also annoyed me because it went on and on.

Most of my hits were cut in New Orleans. Earl Palmer

was my session drummer—he is probably the greatest session drummer of all time—and Lee Allen was my tenor sax player—he, too, is the greatest and they both have influenced so many musicians.

But you know if Specialty had recorded me live with the Upsetters that would have been the most exciting Rock 'n' Roll of all.

*The relationship between Little Richard and Robert Blackwell was an intricate one. Bumps molded Richard's career from 1955, not only masterminding the million-selling records of his Specialty days, but also managing his career on the road from early 1956 until he was forced by Art Rupe in 1957 to relinquish this job to Henry Nash and Cherie Landry.*

*A deeply perceptive and philosophical man, he knew better than anybody else what made Richard tick and how to motivate him. He succeeded by blunt speaking and the power of his personality, which is very forceful. He treated Richard like a wayward but loved son. The father-son relationship, however, had built-in conflicts.*

● Don't let anybody tell you that Bumps doesn't know what he's doing. He started Herb Alpert, Connie Stevens, Larry Williams, Sly and the Family Stone, Lloyd Price, and Sam Cooke. He should be a millionaire. He was abused and misused. He took it because if you don't belong to certain people you don't get any down. I didn't know we had a hit with "Tutti Frutti" till Bumps discovered me. But Bumps hasn't had any dealings with me for years. Bumps wasn't managing me in the hard years. My brother Robert was. All the television stuff in these late years, Andy Williams, Jack Good, Richard Nader, were all my brother, and my last tour through Europe was with my brother. Now I book myself all over the country in my ministry.

78

When I first came to Hollywood, Bumps dressed and acted like a white executive. He was the city cat and I was the southern boy up from the sticks. Then when I became a big star, I believe Bumps was a little jealous of my fame. He has a superiority complex. He gets resentful at times and becomes bossy and nasty. Then I leave him and I don't bother with him.

Me and Bumps like each other, but we conflict because of his ego. We really started conflicting with each other at the end, and that was one of the reasons for the relationship parting. But you know, deep down inside, I really love Bumps.

BUMPS BLACKWELL: Richard is a supreme star. A once-in-a-millennium talent. And like many unique talents, he gets paranoid and I understand that. He loses any sense of time or obligation. It's not deliberate, it's just him. Those were the times when I was managing him that I'd get mad at him and we'd conflict. But the people who know us know that I can cope with him and get the best from him. So they contact me. Richard, too. He suffers from what I call decidophobia. He finds it hard to make a decision. And when he can't he comes to me.

# Don't Knock the Rock

he first Rock 'n' Roll movie starred Bill Haley and
the Comets and was called Rock Around the
Clock. It was a box-office smash, and Columbia
Pictures rushed out a follow-up, cashing in on
teenagers' desperate hunger to see their heroes
perform. This was Don't Knock the Rock, which featured
Bill Haley and the Comets, the legendary D.J. Alan Freed,
and Little Richard.

Both films were produced by Sam Katzman, who had
spent many years making B movies for Columbia. The story
lines were brain damage on celluloid, as no one was prepared to gamble a lot of money on what might be a passing
craze. But neither the yawn-making dialogue nor the hectic
shooting schedules could dampen the excitement of the
music.

Richard sang "Tutti Frutti" and "Long Tall Sally." And by
all accounts, his performance wrenched the film from
Haley. After being introduced by Alan Freed, Richard, in a
baggy silver suit, stands for a second as if lifeless, then
explodes into "Awop-Bop-a-Loo-MopAlop-Bam-Boom."
Hammering the piano, staring ferociously as the camera
moves in for a closeup, throwing his head from side to side,
arms flailing like a tree in a tornado, Richard puts on a
spectacular performance. Bowing graciously, as though he
has just played a Chopin nocturne, he wallops straight into

*"Long Tall Sally,"* as sax player Grady Gaines solos on top of the grand piano. *The wild freedom of it changed the lives of hundreds of thousands of young people. It was a box-office smash hit in the U.S. and after its release in Europe two years later it instigated riots in England, Germany, and Ireland.*

*Following his success in* Don't Knock the Rock, *Richard was signed to appear in the best Rock 'n' Roll movie ever,* The Girl Can't Help It. *Featuring sex symbol Jayne Mansfield, the film had an impressive array of Rock 'n' Roll stars like Fats Domino, Gene Vincent, Eddie Cochran, the Platters, and Eddie Fontaine. Richard had the principal musical spot, singing three numbers, including the title song.*

The Girl Can't Help It *showed that Hollywood was at last taking Rock 'n' Roll seriously. The film was in color, which was extravagant for a rock film in the fifties, and the writing was put in the hands of one of the genre's best-respected figures, writer-director Frank Tashlin, who had produced some hot box-office films starring comedian Jerry Lewis. It set a standard for rock films that was not approached again until Richard Lester's* A Hard Day's Night.

*Tashlin used Little Richard to send up American attitudes toward sexuality and racism. Early rock films featured black artists only musically, never as part of the plot. Tashlin placed Richard, probably the most overtly sexual Rock 'n' Roller ever, in the central scene, in which the incredibly endowed Jayne Mansfield captures the attention of the audience in a plush nightclub by undulating across the floor. Richard, cast as the headline act at the club, manically sings "She's Got It," as the camera cuts between Mansfield's inflated charms and Richard's jet-black, sweat-shiny, lascivious response. "She's Got It" became another million-selling single.*

*At the premiere Mansfield told the press that Richard was her favorite singer.*

81

● I had never thought that I would be in the movies. To feel that all your friends all over the world will be able to see you. It's such an opportunity. It really just shook my mind up, you know. I was so nervous. I had never done anything like that before. *The Girl Can't Help It* was a very big hit and a very big record. The movie was meant for Fats Domino but they gave it to me. Jayne Mansfield was really a wonderful person, really pretty. Her breasts were fifty inches, and she didn't wear a brassiere. They didn't hang down. They stood straight out, and the nipples were easily four and a half inches across. She was one of the prettiest people I had ever seen, and we really hit it off together.

*To kids all over the world, Little Richard became, like James Dean and Marlon Brando, a symbol of rejection of middle-class values. To adults, however, Richard was a wild and bizarre, almost demented, creature. They could not understand or appreciate his music. But they did understand that Rock 'n' Roll was changing their nice, safe, conformist (and racist) American society, into some place where young people were developing their own counterculture.*

*There were those who saw rock music as a serious threat to the existing social structure. Racists in the South began putting out blunt and inflammatory statements that sent vibrations through the American establishment. The North Alabama White Citizens Council declared on TV: "Rock 'n' Roll is part of a test to undermine the morals of the youth of our nation. It is sexualistic, unmoralistic and ... brings people of both races together."*

*One circular distributed in the South read: "Notice! Stop! Help save the youth of America. Don't buy Negro records. If you don't want to serve Negroes in your place of business, then don't have Negro records on your jukebox or listen to Negro records on the radio. The screaming idiotic words and savage music of these records are undermining the morals of our white youth in America. Call the advertisers of radio stations that play this type of music and complain to them!"*

*But Little Richard kept clicking up hit after hit—"She's Got It," "Heeby-Jeebies," "The Girl Can't Help It," "Lucille," which had twenty-one weeks on the* Billboard *"Hot 100," "Send Me Some Lovin'," "Miss Ann," and "Jenny Jenny," twenty weeks on the "Hot 100."*

*American conservatism moved into action. Radio, TV, and newspapers began to smear live rock performances as incitement to violence, Rock 'n' Roll performers as evil and corrupting, and Rock 'n' Roll promoters and sympathizers as grasping and money-mad. D.J. and rock promoter Alan Freed, the "father" of the Rock 'n' Roll cult, was subjected to media harassment that resulted in his indictment under antianarchy laws a year later and his eventual destruction over payola allegations. But despite the smears, Freed can never be said to have pushed a record that he did not like. He refused to play the bland cover versions of black artists' songs by people like Pat Boone and the Crewcuts, and he slammed the D.J.s who did so. "They're anti-Negro," he told a contemporary writer. "If it isn't that, what is it? They excuse it on the grounds that the covers are better quality, but I defy anyone to show me that the quality of the original 'Tweedlee Dee' [LaVern Baker] or 'Seven Days' [Clyde McPhatter] is poor."*

*Freed's courageous and imprudent efforts to promote the music he loved deserves to be remembered. He ran nonsegregated dances often in defiance of local custom and enraged the segregationists by his preference for black artists.*

● Alan Freed was a fantastic person. One of the greatest. Dick Clark and the rest of them don't come near him. He was a fair man to deal with, and he always paid, unlike many of the promoters I've worked for. He'd bring us to the Brooklyn Paramount and we'd tear the place down. One of his favorite songs was "Send Me Some Lovin'." He'd get in back of the curtain while I was on and whisper the title to me and I'd always do it.

*One of the regular support acts in the Alan Freed package shows was the Crickets, a young group from Texas. Their lead singer was a tall, bespectacled young man named Buddy Holly. The Crickets' first record, "That'll Be the Day" (it went to number one), clearly showed how much young Buddy Holly was influenced by Little Richard.*

● Buddy and I were real good friends. He was a nice guy and he used to idolize my music. He'd go out and do my songs before I came on. On one of our tours he invited me to his home in Lubbock, Texas, for dinner. In those days racial segregation was a big thing. Lubbock was a very conservative southern town. When his daddy saw who his son had brought home he wouldn't let me in. But Buddy told his daddy, "If you don't let Richard in, I'll never come back to this house again." So they let me in, but they weren't too happy. I'll bet they washed them dishes I ate off of about twenty times after we'd gone.

Buddy liked Angel. He was a wild boy for the women. One time we were playing at the Paramount Theater and Buddy came into my dressing room while I was jacking off with Angel sucking my titty. Angel had the fastest tongue in the West. Well, she was doing that to me and Buddy took out his thing. He was ready, so she opened up her legs and he put it in her. He was having sex with Angel, I was jacking off, and Angel was sucking me, when they introduced his name on stage! He was trying to rush so he could run on stage. He made it, too. He finished and went to the stage still fastening himself up. I'll never forget that. He came and he went!

When we were on tour, other artists would come to the side of the stage and watch my act—Jerry Lee Lewis, Chuck Berry, the Dells, the Coasters, the Clovers. And I used to watch theirs, too. See, I couldn't allow anybody to take an audience from me. If I saw the audience really clapping and going for another artist, it was as if something aroused up in me and said "I can't allow this." I would do anything that was within me, *anything* to keep the house—even if I had to go onstage and throw money into the audience!

One thing I would do was to dance with a table or a chair in my mouth while they were doing their act. I had seen Barry Lee Gilmore doing that at the Dew Drop Inn when I was young. I used it when I felt I wasn't coming across to people. I'd pick up a table and hold it with my arms straight out ahead and let kids stand on the table and dance. I'd do *anything*. And truly I did feel in my heart that nobody could take a show from me. I didn't care how great they were. I didn't care how many records they had. I would say, "This is my house."

I always demanded to go on last. I'd hassle with some of these singers who had been stars for a long time. Everyone knew that the star went on last. Well, I tell ya, if I didn't go on last, I went on next to last. And if I had to go on next to last, boy, were they sorry they had decided to be last. Because I made it a point to try to kill them!

When I recorded "Keep a-Knockin' " in Washington a young fan, who later was to become a good friend of mine, hung around me and my band, then he started to drive me places. I called him "pretty boy"—he wrote a song based on that title and I said he could use my band to record it— he did—and that was his first record—his name was Don Covay.

CHUCK CONNORS: We appeared with a lot of different artists, Jerry Lee Lewis, Buddy Holly, Jackie Wilson, the

Drifters, people like that. But usually, we would be the main act. Little Richard and the Upsetters. Richard would always stand in the wings behind the curtain. We'd be peeping out, and a lot of times when these people saw Richard their energy level would drop. They'd be thinking, "Look, man, we're not doing so good. Look who's gonna come behind us. I'm glad we don't have to follow that guy." We were a hard act to follow. Richard was aware of that, too. He's such a good-hearted guy. He'd smile and say, "Hey, okay," and otherwise give 'em confidence like that. But a lot of times the guys couldn't cut it, you know?

Chuck Berry was a powerful act when he wasn't on a bill with Richard. We met Chuck a lot of times on the road. He was down there and Richard was up here, though. Chuck would have been bigger if he'd had a regular band. See, he'd have the house band backing him. They'd be good musicians, studio musicians, but they'd actually be downing the guy they were playing for. They'd say, "Chuck Berry? It's a drag. Just play anything." And a lot of the drummers who'd do those dates were *ashamed* to play back-beat. They didn't want to play the blues or Rock 'n' Roll, they wanted to be like Max Roach or Buddy Rich. But they found they couldn't make money that way, so they *had* to play back-beat. Yet they were ashamed to do it. Ask 'em to play Fats Domino's six-eight stuff, and they'd say, "It's too simple, man."

Richard knew this, you see, which was why he had formed the Upsetters. There were a lot of good musicians in the band, and we all loved Richard. We were dedicated to him and we were out to make him look good. Although he was the star he'd make you feel good, too. He'd look at you and say, "Hey, Charles, man," and "Hey, Grady." It was encouragement. You'd do anything for him. He was a good boss. He was a good guy. Remember, at that time, Richard was not drinking anything but coffee. He wasn't smoking no cigarettes, neither. The most I saw Richard drink in the fifties was one half can of beer.

● This was my richest time, with all my hit records selling over the country and me and my band working every night. The river was running. The river of loot. And I was on the bank at that time. At the height of my career our initial guarantee had risen to about twenty-five hundred dollars a night, plus 50 percent of the take over double the guarantee amount. Most often we would walk out with maybe ten thousand or fifteen thousand dollars as our part of the total gate receipt. And understand that during that era the price of a concert ticket was at the maximum three dollars and fifty cents."

BOBBY BYRD: I was the founder of the original gospel group James Brown joined and which later became the Flames. I sang, played keyboards, and cowrote many of James's hits.

One time we were appearing on the same package as Richard in New Jersey—though much lower down the bill. The Famous Flames were stranded in New Jersey with no money to get us back to Georgia. We asked Richard for a loan. He opened the trunk of his car, reached in, and scooped out a handful of dollars without even looking. The trunk of the car was *full* of loose notes of all denominations!

PEGGIE: I had never seen so much money before. I just put it on the bed and wallowed in it. I thought about taking some of it for myself. Then I thought, No, I'm not going to steal. Whatever I want Richard will give to me. So I just rolled in it.

Could Richard look after money? No. But he didn't have to. Money was no problem. He made so much that all he had to do was spend it. When he set off on a tour he'd take a big suitcase to put the money in. We'd put some bundles of bills in the bottom to pay for the start of the tour. When he came back, weeks later, we'd find this same money that we'd counted before, still at the bottom of the case. He'd have just taken bills off the top as it was needed, then piled more in there.

He'd give money to anyone who asked for it. I've seen people around him with cash stuffed down their socks and in their shorts. I certainly never knew who was taking what and I'm sure that Richard didn't either.

● Have people stolen from me? Oh, my! I tell you something. If I had the money that's been stolen from me, I could build a church the likes of which you'd never seen. They took everything but my clothes—and they would have stolen them if I hadn't been sleeping with my socks on! But I was having so much fun I didn't really know what was going on.

When I was home between tours, Virginia Road was a sort of open house for the big names in the Rock 'n' Roll world. Nearly all of them came by at that time. Mother was always cooking big dinners for all sorts of entertainers. Chuck Berry came on his first appearance in L.A. James Brown, Jackie Wilson, Etta James, the Coasters, everybody came there. They were exciting times. My sisters were young and Mother always kept entertainers away from them, but they used to sneak downstairs and peek through the banisters.

*The incredible adulation Richard was receiving brought a "river of loot" to be sure. But the intensity of the performances he gave on every appearance took their toll of his resources. There were deep contradictions in Little Richard's character. The clash between religion, which had*

88

*been a big part of his life, the music he was producing, which was being denounced as evil, and his powerful sexuality were creating a mental conflict which made him want to turn away from show business and toward God.*

*One day early in 1957 when Richard was at home taking a break from his tight touring schedule, there came a knock on the door of 1710 Virginia Road. The echoes of that knock were to change Little Richard's life and shake the music world to its foundations.*

*The apocalypse for millions of Little Richard fans all over the world came in the unlikely shape of Brother Wilbur Gulley, a mild and soft-spoken "missionary" for the Church of God of the Ten Commandments. He went from door to door in what was then the Los Angeles "star belt" making important converts for his church and selling evangelistic literature. His call on Richard came at an important psychological moment.*

*The Bible was Richard's main reading matter. It was not unusual for participants in one of the famous after-show orgies to be waked up in the morning by an earnest Richard quoting passages from the Gospels. But that was not the whole story. He deeply resented the way in which racism dominated the music business and the way Specialty was exploiting his talent.*

● I was very impressed with Brother Gulley when he called at my house to sell me some religious books. He was a very *good* man. He would just come on by and talk to me about the Lord and his work and try to get me into the church. He put me in touch with Joe Lutcher, who had also been in the music field and had left it to come to God. I had a lot of talks with him, too. They were beautiful people.

*Joe Lutcher had been a noted saxophonist and bandleader in the 1940s, playing with Nat "King" Cole and*

89

*Sammy Davis in 1949. Hit records "Mardi Gras Mambo,"
"Rockin' Boogie," and "Society Boogie" brought him to
fame as the King of Mambo before he turned his back on
the world of show business to become an evangelistic
preacher.*

JOE LUTCHER: Brother Wilbur Gulley called and said he
wanted me to talk to someone called Little Richard. He
said Little Richard was touring around, going crazy or
something. I said I'd never heard of him. So Brother
Wilbur told me about some of his hit songs, "Good Golly
Miss Molly" and "Tutti Frutti."... But I told him no, I'd
still never heard of him. I had completely divorced myself
from that type of music.

Well, Brother Gulley said Little Richard would be calling
me, because he had been very impressed with the books
and wanted to know more. He wanted to be in a situation
where he could help more people, rather than just in the
Rock 'n' Roll field. He wanted to be able to reach people on
a higher level. Which was a good idea.

So Richard finally called me one night. He asked me
some things about my experiences with the Lord. He
wanted to know how I had come to know the Lord. I was
able to tell him from the point of view of someone who had
been out there—out in show business. Although I was
never as big as he was, I'd had a couple of hit records.

You see, you don't belong to yourself. You belong to the
people. You're at their disposal. You've got to keep smiling
regardless. They'll tear your clothes off as a souvenir and
you get tired of going through that kind of thing. You want
to be free. Totally free.

So we talked and talked. Richard was very much impressed with me and I was very much impressed with him.
He told me he wanted to leave show business. In spite of all
the money he was making, he needed and wanted a spiri-

tual regeneration. There was something missing from inside him—from his life at this time.

*Richard was ready, both spiritually and economically, to make the break with the world of show business. Misused, ripped off, and cheated by racists, promoters, and companies, he was also being hassled by the Internal Revenue Service for an accounting of his huge earnings. He was becoming very tired of the heavy traveling schedules and of the business of being a star in general. The spiritual pressures were such that he needed only a sign that he could interpret as divine to clinch the decision.*

*Richard announced his retirement in the middle of a tour of Australia. Headlining a package of artists that included Eddie Cochran, Gene Vincent and the Bluecaps, and one Alis Lesley, billed as "the female Elvis Presley," Richard found himself at the center of scenes of frenzied and riotous adulation from the Rock 'n' Roll-starved Australian teenagers.*

● I had never liked flying and I had never been so far on a plane before. It worked on my mind. When it got dark and I could see the engines on the wings glowing red hot, I thought the plane was on fire. My mother had a religious book called *The Great Controversy* by Ellen G. White, which showed angels with yellow hair flying. In my mind I pictured these angels flying up under the plane holding it up. It was like a sign to me. It came to me later that the plane wasn't on fire—it was just that I had never been that far away before. It was very strange to me.

Then, on our fifth date of the two-week tour, we had left Melbourne for Sydney, and forty thousand people came to see me at the municipal outdoor arena. That night Russia sent off that very first *Sputnik*. It looked as though the big ball of fire came directly over the stadium about two or three hundred feet above our heads. It shook my mind. It really shook my mind. I got up from the piano and said, "This is it. I am through. I am leaving show business to go back to God."

The very next day we were leaving Sydney on the ferry, and I had told the fellers in the band that I was quitting. Clifford didn't believe me. So I said, "Would you believe it if I throw this ring in the water?" Clifford tried to grab it and nearly fell into the water behind the boat.

There were ten days of the tour left to run, but I would not work any more. Our tickets home were bought on the basis of a two-week tour, but I demanded passage back to the States for the total entourage ten days early. The incredible thing is that the plane we were originally scheduled to return on crashed into the Pacific Ocean. That's when I felt that God really had inspired me to do the things I did at the time.

*So the Little Richard entourage returned to the United States, each member asking himself where his future lay. Richard had left behind half a million dollars' worth of canceled bookings in Australia, and several pending lawsuits because of that. But at least he knew where he was going. Into religious seclusion. What about the other people who for more than a year had been riding the Little Richard gravy train?*

CHUCK CONNORS: We were not really too surprised. Richard had been talking about giving up Rock 'n' Roll and devoting his life to God for a long time. Whenever he got down in the dumps. We were not too worried, either. The tours had been lasting for months and we never really got a break. We knew the band was hot, we knew we were good, and we were young and on a bit of an ego trip. We were sure that someone else would grab us. Richard told us we would all have enough money in our pockets and a place to live until we got fixed up again. So we weren't too worried.

MARQUETTE PENNIMAN: I was really shocked when it happened. I didn't really think he'd do it, although I did know that Richard was changing. We used to have these really wild parties. People would come around, expecting that there was going to be one of these incredible parties, and Richard would sit them around on the floor and pull out his Bible. And he'd do a show. That was a strong indication that he was changing, but I didn't know it was *that* strong. He had kept telling me he was going back to the church. But I didn't think he was going that quick, because he was getting so many hits. Hit after hit after hit.

PEGGIE: We felt we might lose everything. It was so upsetting not having time to prepare for it. Then we started remembering. We used to count all his money, *thousands* of dollars, and we said, "Oh, we should have put away some of that money," cos we felt our whole world was going to collapse.

LEVA MAE: There wasn't much to say when he told me. If Richard had done something that made him happy, then we were happy. He was the one that had cared for us and provided after Bud's death. That was something we could never forget. Richard's life was his own. If he had decided to change, and come to the Lord, all I could say was Amen.

JOHN MARASCALCO: Richard told me when he came back from Australia that he was going to break that contract with Specialty. He said, "The only way I can do it is if I die or by an act of God. So I'm going to join a ministerial college. I'll go in for a year or a couple of years and then that's it." We both had this bad deal, the Specialty

specialty—half a cent a record. Richard said to me, "I know I'm getting screwed and I know that you're getting screwed, and I'm going to break this damn contract." Richard told me that directly.

● My friends and fans all over the world couldn't understand a guy at the height of his career quitting with the whole world in his hands. One reason *was* Art Rupe. It seemed that he wanted to buy me body and soul—with my own money. Bought things for me, then took it out of my money and said he had bought it. Can you image that? Beginning in 1959, although I had settled my dispute with Rupe for the recording royalties on my biggest hits, he took the position that this release also covered songwriters' royalties and has refused to pay me any songwriters' royalties from that day to this one. Consequently, I was forced to institute a federal law suit against him and his companies for the millions of dollars I say he owes me.

The very thought of it is sickening to me now. He's made millions and he should owe me millions.

But this was not the only reason I left show business. I wanted to work for Jehovah and find that peace of mind. I had always wanted to be a preacher and dedicate my life to God. I knew I had a message to say to the world outside of show business. I was not sure what it was till I met Joe and Brother Gulley. When I knew I came to God.

*The story had broken all over the world by the time Richard and his band arrived back in the United States. Journalists and broadcasters let their imaginations run riot. The airliner incident and the ring-throwing episode became distorted out of all proportion. A Chicago radio station reported that Richard had committed suicide. Some newspapers announced that Richard was in a lunatic asylum. Others, that he had seen a vision and was in a monas-*

*tery. Hoping against hope that the worst had not really happened, Rupe ordered a news clampdown from Specialty, and media questions were evaded.*

*Although arenas were booked and deposits paid for nearly fifty engagements, Richard refused to work. A friend such as Alan Freed, however, could not be denied, and Richard played his farewell concert at the Apollo Theater in New York to a hysterical crowd. Then roadies drove the Cadillacs across the U.S. and into the big garage at Virginia Road. They turned the ignitions off and handed the keys to Leva Mae.*

# The Most I Can Offer

I f Little Richard's decision to leave the world of show business was a blow to his millions of fans around the world, Specialty boss Art Rupe must have felt as though the Empire State Building had fallen on top of him. Richard was the biggest jewel in the Specialty crown. Every record had produced a shower of gold for the company.

Over the past year and a half, Specialty was the envy of every major record company for having a megastar like Richard. But in 1957, there was very little in the can. Rupe had kept Richard on the road. With better treatment, he might have been in the recording studio putting down songs that could have been released later on.

Richard brought to evangelism all the personal magnetism and energy that had made him a legend in the music world. The church realized that in him they had a very hot property indeed—a man who could well have the messianic powers that would bring thousands of people to the church. So they set about grooming him for his new role in life.

● Me and Joe Lutcher got a team together called the Little Richard Evangelistic Team. We started traveling across the country, and we helped many people through the ministry. Joe had a mission in downtown L.A. with a

96

feller named Edward D'Amato. I would go down there and preach, sort of like a little school. We would call it our own seminary. We were able to help a lot of people on the skid row. We fed them and gave them a place to sleep. We didn't push them into anything, just let them know the difference between right and wrong. If a person wanted what we had, good, but we never would push a person or try to make him into religion.

I served at the tent meetings, doing all the menial tasks like ushering, tightening the ropes, showing slides, and collecting questions from the audience. I shared in the ordinance of humility by washing the feet of other members before taking communion. My life changed completely. All those steaks, pork chops, chitterlings, Cokes, and coffee had to go. I ate only vegetables cooked in vegetable oils, as the church instructs.

I was taking a Voice of Prophecy course, reading my Bible, and praying. Every time I started my Cadillac I said a prayer. On arriving to my destination, I said a prayer. I prayed in the homes of my friends; I prayed with people I met in the street. I was just living a life of prayer. I was waiting to become a sophomore student at Oakwood College, a commandment-keeping college in Huntsville, Alabama, on a three-year course aimed at my becoming ordained as an elder of the church.

Everybody was telling me I needed a wife. They said, "You gonna study religion, you gonna study in school, you need a wife." And I was afraid that if I didn't marry I would go to hell. So I decided to start looking for a wife.

*Ernestine Campbell, the girl who was to be Richard's wife, was just out of high school. One of four daughters of a Washington navy family, she was working temporarily for the Department of the Navy before going to college when Richard entered her life.*

ERNESTINE CAMPBELL: I met Richard in November 1957 when he came to speak at an evangelistic meeting being held by our church at a convention center in Washington, D.C., called Turner's Arena. I had heard of him, but I hadn't bought his records then because I wasn't into that kind of music. I was so impressed with him at the meeting. He was so clean-cut. He was suited and he looked just great. I had heard his music, of course, and heard interviews on the radio, but I had never seen him before.

There was something about him that made me feel he was more than just some crazy Rock 'n' Roll singer. I walked up to him after the meeting and introduced myself, welcoming him to the city. We invited him to dinner at our house. I don't know whether I fell in love with him then. In the summer of 1959, in July, we married. I guess that's a pretty long courtship, from November 1957 to July 1959.

We had a happy marriage for a time, but I think from the beginning we didn't have a chance because I could not adjust to the life-style. Having to share him with so many people was very hard to get used to. I hadn't appreciated the extent of his popularity worldwide. People adored him. Worshiped him. And it was like I was kind of intruding upon something the public wanted. It was as though we didn't belong to each other. We belonged to the world, the public. We honeymooned as Richard was on his way to a meeting. I wanted to make him *mine* and happy and I could not do that.

Somebody like Richard can't be made into that kind of man. You can't expect it. I later understood that, but I was not able to at first, so it made the adjustment difficult.

CHARLES PENNIMAN: I wasn't happy at all about the marriage. I felt like the Church of God was putting Ernestine on to Richard getting him to do something they wanted him to do. I felt like they were using Ernestine to promote their own denomination. I felt they were using Richard to bring other entertainers and other people to their church.

LEE ANGEL: I was only seventeen years old and I didn't want to get mixed up with the church. So I disappeared. I saw Richard about three months later. I was working as a stripper at the 81 Theater, in Atlanta. He found out and came over to see me. He had changed, both in his appearance and in himself. Richard wanted to go on seeing me. I liked the change, but I got to the point where I couldn't go around with him. He was a preacher and I was a stripper and I felt guilty about it.

*The marriage hardly stood a chance from the start. It would have been hard to find two people of more widely differing backgrounds and personalities than the ex-King of Rock 'n' Roll and the shy, well-educated young secretary from Washington, D.C.*

*The wedding took place at 1710 Virginia Road. It was scheduled for 9 P.M. on July 11, 1959, but, typically, Richard was away somewhere. No one knows where and he cannot remember. He kept the bride, the preacher, the family, and the guests waiting for six hours (just about par for a Richard appointment today).*

*That was hardly the start of a dream marriage for a romantically minded young bride, but worse was to come. The honeymoon set the pattern for what was to be a union dominated by the needs of the church.*

*The tutors at Oakwood found Richard as frustrating a pupil as the teachers had at Macon's Hudson High. He turned up late for class, usually in one of his garishly colored Cadillacs. He skipped lectures, and he was a disrupting influence in what was a quiet, well-ordered quasi-religious liberal arts college. But what the elders had in*

*Richard was too valuable to lose just because of failed grades. He was a natural preacher with a gift for absorbing passages from the Bible. He could translate them into simple rhetoric, capturing the hearts and minds of his listeners.*

● I had one or two problems at Oakwood. The elders didn't like me taking my yellow Cadillac on the campus. They didn't like the way the kids swarmed around me asking me to sing my Rock 'n' Roll hits. Then I squashed my studies. I didn't like school any better than I did when I was a boy in Macon. I was taking biblical courses, and I was taking English an' all, but English was so hard for me I had to let it go. Oh, I tell ya, I realized that I'd have to chew my words for the rest of my life.

I really went to Oakwood to be indoctrinated. I never finished high school, and you had to finish high school to enter Oakwood. But Oakwood gave me a special course in Bible. It was fantastic. It taught me how to love God better. I studied books called *Daniel and the Revelations, Steps to Christ, Daniel and the Prophets*, about Moses, about Pharaoh, about God's great plan for man, and about how black people have ruled before. King Solomon was black. I believed wholeheartedly. I studied about how you can praise God through music. A lot of people are devoted to music because music can bring something to people that nothing else can. But I thought that everyone who went to Oakwood would be an angel. Then I learned that there were some devils there, too.

They had discovered that I was a homosexual and I resented the discovery. I had worked with a young guy and I had him show himself to me. I didn't touch him, but he went back and told his father, who was a deacon of the church. The church had a board meeting to let me know that it was wrong. I was so mad, I felt I could have whupped all of them at one time. I would have. I was that mad. I cursed them out. I said some nasty words that shouldn't have been said in church.

You see, I was angry that they had found out about my unnatural affections. You know how when you find out the truth about someone they get mad. Well, I was caught point-blank and I hated it. At the time I thought they were being hypocritical. But really, to be truthful, they weren't. I was. I was supposed to have been living a different life and I wasn't. They forgave me. Oh, definitely they did forgive me, but I couldn't face it and I left the church.

*In the meantime, Specialty was issuing Little Richard tracks which had not been considered worthy of release when they were recorded in 1956 and 1957. The name Little Richard still had such commercial appeal that they sold very well. His friends were urging him to get back into the studio, record some more Rock 'n' Roll, and make some more money. But Richard could not bear the thought of making such a drastic about-face in his life.*

*While Richard was traveling and preaching in 1960 he ran into the Upsetters. They had been doing well appearing in New York, backing Little Willie John. But Richard felt that they never had the exposure they deserved. He set up a secret Rock 'n' Roll recording session in New York with an old friend, H. B. Barnum as producer. Richard sang and played on the session but did not want his name to go on the record. It was just to be the Upsetters. They recorded enough material for an album, including two Fats Domino cover songs.*

*Richard recorded twenty sacred songs for record entrepreneur George Goldner, who issued them on his label, End. That move set the stage for negotiations with one of the bigger record companies, Mercury. Bumps Blackwell was now their chief A and R man.*

101

*Richard, once again reunited with Bumps Blackwell, re-corded an album called* Little Richard, King of the Gospel Singers. *Blackwell's former pupil, Quincy Jones, was musical director. He used a forty-piece orchestra to back Richard, cushioning the solo voice with the lush tones of Howard Roberts' Chorale.*

*Out of these sessions came four singles, "Joy Joy Joy" backed with "He's Not Just a Soldier," and "He Got What He Wanted" backed with a song written by Joe Lutcher, "Why Don't You Change Your Ways." He and Richard set up a publishing company, Woodman Music Inc., for religious books and music.*

*The public, hungry for new Little Richard releases, bought the album expecting the frantic urgency of the Specialty recordings. But they were shocked, as the vocal delivery on these sacred songs had a completely different tone and range, like a rich classical tenor.*

QUINCY JONES: As a jazz musician and director I have participated in scores of recording sessions, but I can recall none that moved me more than this one. There was soul in the singing of Little Richard during this session. He was more than just an entertainer, he was a true believer ...his was the "spirit feel." During the recording of "It's Real," all of us gathered there amidst the electronic devices knew that he wasn't just singing it. He was preaching it. One take was all that was needed. The man felt it all the way as only someone who has the call feels it. Yes, this was Richard Penniman. Little Richard, the Rock 'n' Roll darling. Yet this was a different man. Gone was the six-inch-high pompadour. Gone the wild mannerisms. Forgotten were "Tutti Frutti" and "Long Tall Sally." Here was a serious young gospel singer. "Do, Lord, remember me," cried Richard. It was the cry of a triumphant man; of one who had been saved. All of us in the studio were deeply moved and impressed. He reached me. It was an experience that proved once again that deep religious feeling and fervor go hand in hand.

Little Richard was not only a giant but a pioneer of the so-called Rock 'n' Roll music industry. He had such a unique voice and style that no one has matched it, even to this day (and if you don't believe me, ask Mick Jagger). I had the pleasure to record with Little Richard "Joy Joy Joy" and "He's Not Just A Soldier" for his albums. He also sang the title song "Money, Money" for the soundtrack I produced for the film $, starring Warren Beatty and Goldie Hawn. It was truly a joy working with Little Richard in New York, though he was still very religious I noticed that he never lost his feeling for Rock 'n' Soul.

Bumps Blackwell, a one-of-a-kind producer and band leader, has been very influential in my life from the beginning. It's fantastic to see that he's going back in the studio with Little Richard. I know this unique collaboration is a long awaited one by everyone. Rock 'n' Soul is here to stay!

● That album was the thing that really put me back in business. It was just the kind of music I had always wanted to record. After it was released the offers for gospel concerts started pouring in. I gave concerts all over the country, often with my very good friend and inspiration Mahalia Jackson—the true queen of spiritual singers. I had admired her for a long time, but I didn't get to meet her until just after I had come to God. She was doing a concert in Los Angeles and I stopped her on the street and asked her to come and hear me sing in Mount Maria Baptist Church.

MAHALIA JACKSON: I didn't know what to expect in view of Richard's wild reputation as a Rock 'n' Roll performer, but I was delighted to learn that he had been saved and was returning to the music he had heard in church as a small boy—the music of the Lord. I went, and I was delighted. First of all, his stage demeanor impressed me. I could tell he had been raised right, for he was singing gospel songs the way they should be sung. He had that primitive beat and sound that came so naturally. By primitive I don't mean untamed or wild. I'm referring to the authentic way in which church music should be sung. The soul in his singing was not faked. It was *real*. I do believe that Little Richard had found himself. As a person and as a singer.

*That sort of praise does not come to many ex–Rock 'n' Roll singers and teenage idols. But during the sessions for the album Richard proved that while his spiritual conversion was for real, his volatile personality was unchanged.*

BUMPS BLACKWELL: We were recording one session on Sunday, and there were forty musicians in the studio on double time. Richard was due to arrive at 10 A.M. and he kept us all waiting around until 8 P.M., when he turned up to announce calmly, "The Lord does not want me to record today." Manny Klein, who had organized the session, broke down and wept.

● I had dropped a guy off at the Trailways bus station in Long Beach. I went down into the restroom, to look, to see who was doing what, to watch people take out and urinate, like I always did. While I was down there the police raided the place. Once you walk into a raid you don't get out of it. These young boys with jeans on came into the place and pulled out their badges and said "You're under arrest." Just boys! And while I was trying to talk to them, cos they wouldn't let me go, they hit me and knocked blood out of my face. My face was bleeding. I didn't know what was going on. I wasn't innocent. I went there and I got caught and I had to pay the price. My lawyer told me to plead guilty and let it go. He said don't say anything, cos they'll make a case out of nothing. So I paid the fine. I could have gone back and had it erased, but I never did.

*Richard's reversion to his former life-style, coming on top of two and a half years of neglect and turmoil, proved the last straw for his wife, Ernestine. She set divorce proceedings in motion, citing "extreme cruelty by the infliction of grievous mental suffering." The action was uncontested.*

● Ernestine was right. I was a neglectful husband. A terrible husband. I wouldn't have married *me* if I'd had diamond toenails and ruby eyeballs. We were not compatible the way we should have been. When I met Ernestine I liked her a whole lot, but I never loved her in the way a man should love his wife. I loved her more like a sister. Ernestine was jealous and she had reason enough to be, because I wasn't a husband. I didn't give her any attention. I was gay and I wasn't concerned. I was like a lot of men today who have got wives. I had to think of someone else to be with her, to be complete. I was thinking about Johnny. About Jimmy. I had to think about someone I wanted and couldn't get. Ernestine was too much woman for me. She was a whole lotta lady and I was just like a little mouse. I couldn't do nothing.

ERNESTINE: We had normal husband-and-wife relations, definitely. That's why it was so easy for me to discount anything that anyone said to me at that time about him. If he was gay he was *very* good about hiding it from me! And if he was he never wanted it to affect me. I don't recollect any incident that indicated that. It was only things that people said. There were times when I felt that I wanted to ask him about it because people, being unkind, or perhaps not realizing they were being unkind, asked *me* about it. Why he dressed like that. Why he acted like that. But it never affected my relationship with him because it had nothing to do with me. I accepted his act. I even explained it later to people who asked me about it. I said, "Well, you know, people have various gimmicks that they use, and if this is what it takes to draw and make money, okay. If you're going to pay to go and see him and wonder whether he's gay or not, go and see him. He's making money out of it." But that had nothing to do with our separation or break-up. It was just that I was not able to make the adjustment to Richard's way of life.

I don't regret that we didn't have children because we always had each other. We're still very close. It doesn't matter who comes or goes, I'm usually in touch with him and he stays in touch with me. I'm in real estate now, and I consider myself a good businesswoman.

*At this severe psychological moment in Richard's life, British promoter Don Arden came on the scene. Arden had already promoted successful tours in England and Europe for Jerry Lee Lewis and Brenda Lee. Despite Richard's retirement his records were still selling well in England, even though Rock 'n' Roll was in a slump back in the United States.*

*Whether Arden intentionally misled Richard over the nature of the tour he was planning is not clear. What is clear is that Arden began the publicity and advertising for a Rock 'n' Roll package show featuring Richard and Sam Cooke. Sam was very hot at the time with his hits "You Send Me" and "Only Sixteen." Richard engaged as his organist a prodigy of the keyboards named Billy Preston.*

*Although only sixteen years old, Preston was already a veteran musician. He had performed with an L.A. symphony orchestra at the age of ten, conducted his local church choir, and appeared with such greats as Mahalia Jackson and Bessie Griffin. The two began to rehearse and prepare for a gospel tour.*

● I wanted to go to England. Don Arden made it sound as though everyone was buying my records, and I was wanting to get right back into show business because I had been an entertainer all my life. But I accepted Arden's offer believing it was for a gospel tour.

*The tour was scheduled to open in the northern England coal-mining town of Doncaster on October 8, 1962. Richard was advertised as the headline artist, Sam Cooke got second billing, British bass-guitar star Jet Harris was support, with Sounds Incorporated, a four-sax band modeled on America's Piltdown Men, as support band and all-purpose backing group. Gene Vincent was also billed, but he could only present the show as he had no English work permit and was forbidden to sing on the stage.*

● I had toured with Gene and Eddie Cochran in Australia in 1957. Gene was a good friend of mine, but he was an annoying fella sometimes. I remember Gene would get drunk and want to put you out of the car while you were traveling along the highway. I thought he was totally mad when he'd had some drink.

*When Richard had retired in 1957 the British public had been exposed to a barrage of misinformation about him. So when rumors began to circulate that Richard would sing only gospel music, Arden became worried that attendances might be hit. He took space in Britain's leading music papers in September to tell the public, "Little Richard has been booked purely as a rock artist, and his repertoire WILL consist of old favorites like 'Rip It Up' and 'Long Tall Sally.' Little Richard is back in business and has chosen Britain as the base from which he will launch his comeback bid."*

# PART III
# SECOND COMING

# J'm Back

ichard arrived in England with Billy Preston convinced that he was booked as a gospel singer. He had refused to fly and had sailed from New York in the aging liner SS Rotterdam ("it was dam' rotten all the way," he quipped on arrival), treating fellow passengers to gospel singing and preaching sessions en route. One bewildered passenger told the press: "I thought at first that it was all part of the shipboard entertainment."

Richard's gospel recordings had never had much exposure in England, and the audience at the opening concert had never heard him sing anything other than Rock 'n' Roll. Richard strode onto the stage of the Gaumont Theatre, Doncaster, in a long religious-type robe to the sobbing organ of Billy Preston, and began to sing religious songs "Peace in the Valley" and "I Believe." The scene was chaotic. No one could figure it out. Arden saw that if the show was repeated it would mean the end of his heavily promoted tour. He was frantic. He pleaded with Richard to sing his rock hits and called in top British disk jockey Jimmy Savile to reinforce his arguments.

Due to plane delays, Sam Cooke had failed to turn up for the first show. When he did arrive and was preparing for the second house, Arden sought out Cooke's manager, J. W.

111

*Alexander, an old colleague of Richard's from their Specialty recording days, and tried to enlist his help.*

J. W. ALEXANDER: We were late because of fog and had to be driven to the show and we missed the first one. When we got there Don Arden was like having a fit. Richard had gone on the first show and done the religious thing and Arden wanted to know if we would talk to Richard and try to persuade him to do his Rock 'n' Roll. You know, if we would talk to him. I said, "Look, if I know this guy right he's a competitor. Don't need anyone else to say anything to him. Sam'll just go out there and he'll kill that audience. Richard'll come out and take care of himself."

*Alexander certainly knew his man. Sam Cooke turned in a power-packed performance, giving polished versions of his hits and ending with a wildly received "Twistin' the Night Away." The applause lasted well into the intermission. Richard carefully watched all this. While the second-half opening acts were doing their stuff, including Gene Vincent beating the union-imposed ban by singing "Be-Bop-a-Lula" offstage, Richard talked with the band and prepared his presentation. When the time came, Richard went onstage and spent about a minute in absolute darkness warming up with Billy Preston, creating an almost unbearable tension with the audience. Then, suddenly, a spotlight illuminated Richard standing at a grand piano in the center of the stage in an all-white suit and pounding out the opening bars of "Long Tall Sally."*

*The effect was shattering, and the house erupted. With high-jumping, hip-shaking, spine-tingling renditions of his everlasting hits, "Lucille," "Good Golly Miss Molly," "Tutti Frutti," put over with incredible verve, Richard kept his entire audience spellbound. With the audience on their feet and near-hysterical girls in the aisles, he walked off to a*

**Richard at age thirteen.**

Richard's father, Charles (Bud) Penniman, was the proprietor of The Tip In Inn.

Little Richard's family. *Top row:* Peggie, Richard, Sylvia. *Second row:* Gail, Peaches. *Third row:* Elaine, Leva Mae, Charles. *Fourth row:* Walter, Marquette. *Bottom row:* Peyton, Uncle Willard, Robert.

**Little Richard sporting the Penniman pompadour complete with marcel waves.**

Richard's trademark, his pompadour, was
inspired by the notorious Esquerita, a.k.a.
The Magnificent Malucci.

*Above:* Don Robey and Johnny Otis holding a copy of "Little Richard Boogie" (Peacock).

*Left:* Henry Nash, Richard's close friend and road manager in the 1950s.

6

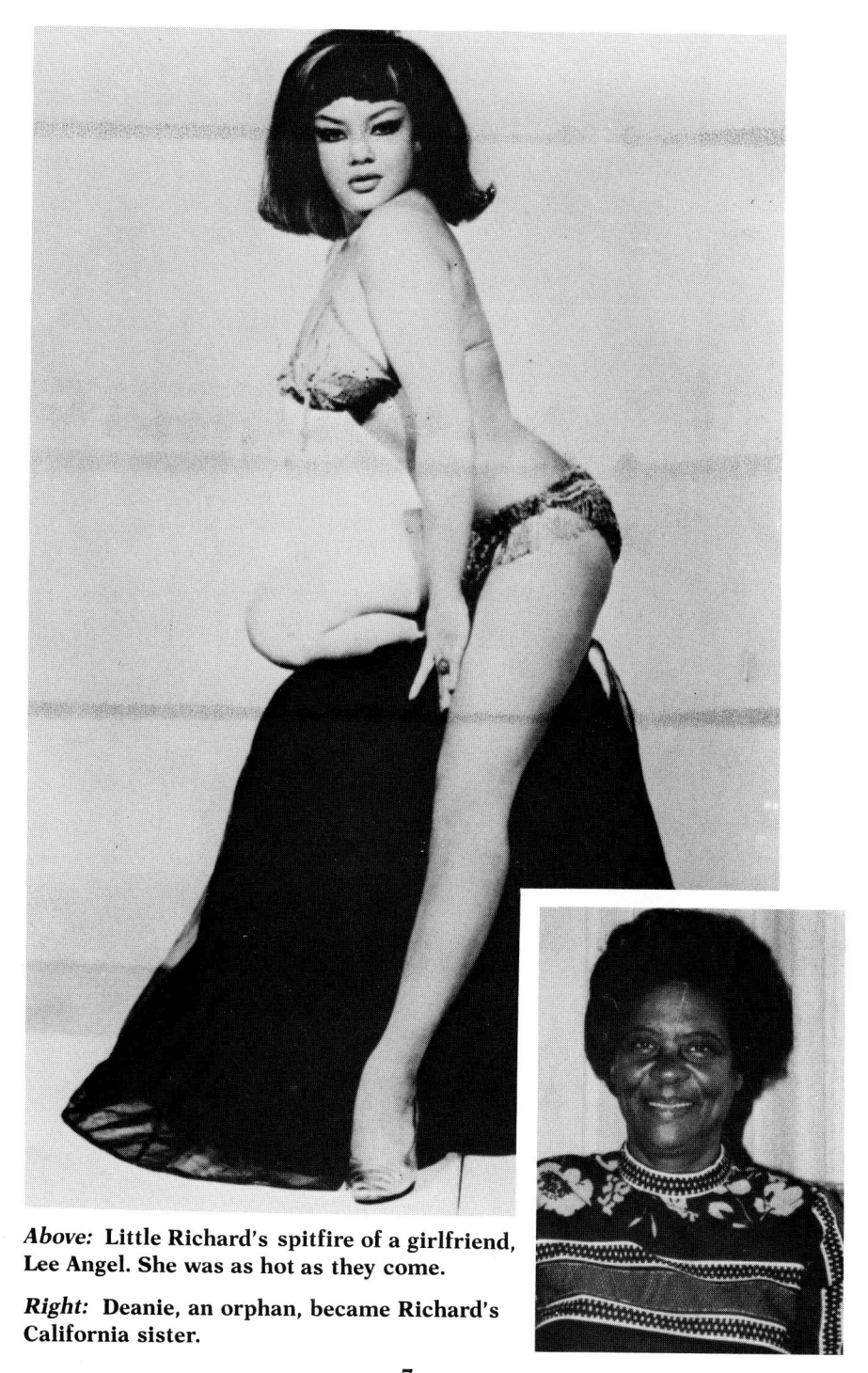

*Above:* Little Richard's spitfire of a girlfriend, Lee Angel. She was as hot as they come.

*Right:* Deanie, an orphan, became Richard's California sister.

7

Robert (Bumps) Blackwell. Richard's best friend, manager, and the creative genius behind Specialty Records.

**Little Richard in Hollywood after "Tutti Frutti" hit the charts.**

Little Richard and the Upsetters on their first tour for Specialty Records. *From left to right:* Nathaniel (Buster) Douglass, guitar; Chuck Conners, drums; Olsi

(Baysee) Robinson, bass: Wilbert Smith (Lee Diamond), sax, piano; Clifford (Gene) Burks, tenor sax; Little Richard; and Grady Gaines, tenor sax.

11

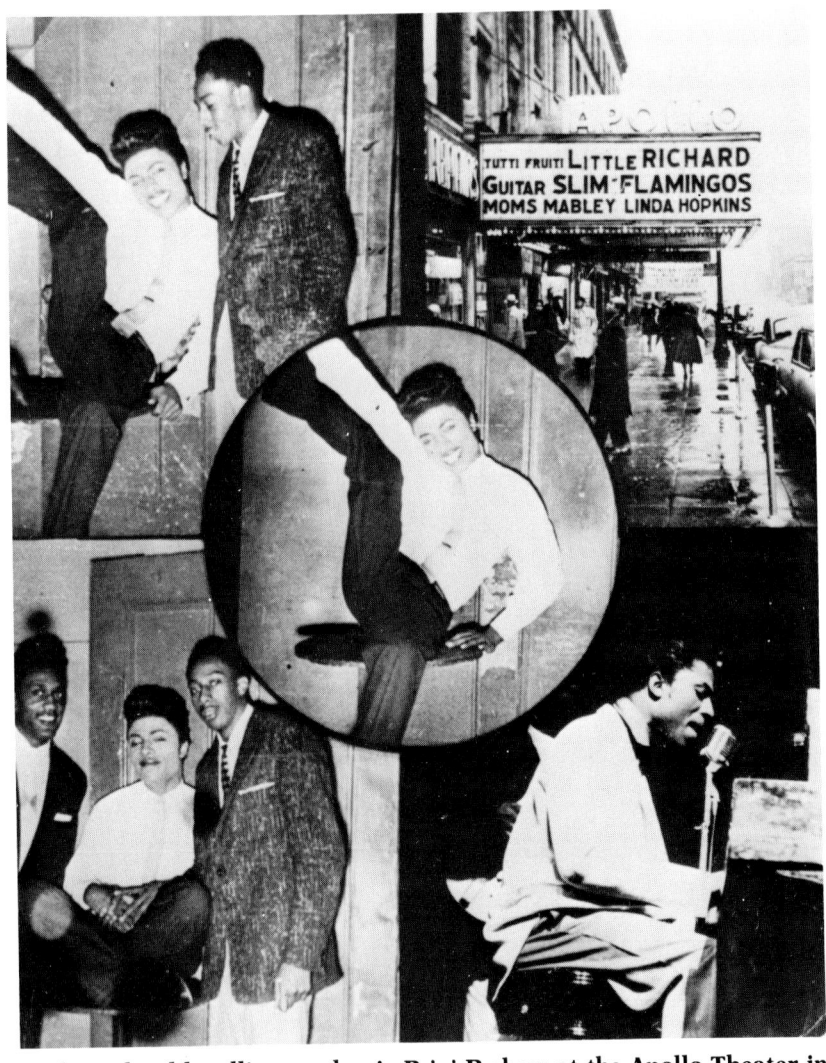

Little Richard headlines a classic R 'n' B show at the Apollo Theater in Harlem, 1956. Note spelling of "Tutti Fruiti."

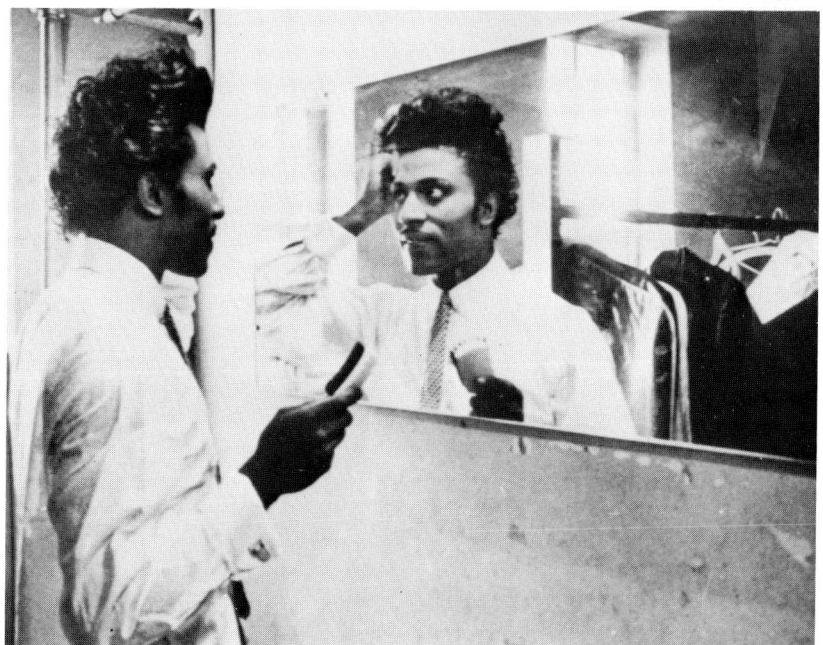

*Top:* Richard lays down the sounds for his first album.
*Bottom:* Pumping that pomp.

**Pure Rock 'n' Roll. Little Richard and The Upsetters.**
*Right:* **Little Richard and Bill Haley, 1956.**

Bumps, Maybelle Jackson, and Richard celebrating the success of their collaboration, "Heeby-Jeebies," 1956.

Richard headed an all-star line-up featuring Alys Leslie (the female Elvis) and Eddie Cochran, Australian tour, 1957.

*thunderous ovation. It was a night to remember—the night a king returned to his throne.*

*That scene was to be repeated everywhere he appeared. In the seaside resort of Brighton, the Hippodrome crowd erupted and there was hysteria the likes of which had never been seen in an English venue. Little Richard whipped the audience into such a frenzy that the hall management warned that the show would be stopped. Ignoring them, Richard jumped on and off the piano, threw his jacket, tie, and shirt to the audience, leaped into the orchestra pit— causing a rush of girls to the front of the auditorium to try to touch him, and finished his act on his knees soaked with sweat and wrapped in a bathrobe.*

**J. W. ALEXANDER:** Richard just wrecked the place. The kids got so wild. We went out and we got in the bus and they all gathered around the bus. I guess we sat there an hour before they could clear them and we could get away.

*At Mansfield's Granada Theatre, Richard had polished his act and introduced new features. A huge grand piano stood in the middle of the stage, but no Richard. The tension mounted as all the theater lights went out, leaving only a spotlight on the piano. The music stopped. The audience held its breath. Then, from the back of the auditorium came Richard's incredible and unmistakable voice shouting out the titles of his hits: " 'Long Tall Sally'! 'Tutti Frutti'! 'Good Golly Miss Molly'!" He ran down the aisle toward the stage, dressed in a white silk suit, not quite avoiding the clutching hands of the delirious crowd. One of them ripped off his white bow tie.*

*A giant leap took him onto the edge of the orchestra pit and from there onto the stage, where he immediately grabbed the microphone and began singing "Good Golly Miss Molly" and pounding the piano. Within seconds every-*

113

*body was standing on their seats. Halfway through a mind-blowing version of "Lucille" he leaped onto the piano top, mike in hand, and boogied around. Then, without warning, he fell rigid from the piano as if struck by a high-velocity bullet. The band stuttered to a halt, the good-time atmosphere shattered.*

*Richard lay like a corpse in the center of the stage, as compere Bob Bain rushed frantically onstage and asked "Is there a doctor in the house?" A member of Sounds Incorporated ran offstage shouting for help. The audience was stunned into silence. Shocked, strained, and anxious faces were everywhere as a buzz of concern rose. Then from the center of the stage burst Little Richard's voice, very much alive, singing the opening of "Tutti Frutti." Inebriated with joy, the audience surged forward and the hysteria caused the stage staff to bring down the safety curtain, ending the show.*

*Richard's amazing showmanship attracted a tremendous amount of press comment. The manager of a young Liverpool group had the idea of using the publicity generated by Richard to promote his protégés.*

*The manager was Brian Epstein, and his group, the Beatles, were having a local hit in Liverpool with their single, "Love Me Do" backed with "Please Please Me." Epstein approached Richard to do two extra dates there at the end of his tour, one at the Tower, New Brighton, and the other at the Empire Theatre. The Beatles were the main support group and several other Merseyside bands filled in the rest of the bill.*

PAUL McCARTNEY: We'd been to Hamburg several times, we were really popular on Merseyside, and everybody was telling us that we were going to make it big. But I never thought I'd ever meet Little Richard. He was my idol at school. The first song I ever sang solo in public was "Long

114

Tall Sally," at a Butlins holiday camp talent contest when I was fourteen. We never thought we'd be playing on the same bill with a big star like that. So when Brian told us he'd set up this gig at the Tower at New Brighton, with Richard and about ten other groups, we were knocked out. We were going to meet Little Richard!

When we got there we told Brian we wanted to have a photograph with Richard to prove that we'd played with him, but there was so much going on that he couldn't fix it. My brother, Mike, had a new camera. He found a hole in the scenery, and was taking pictures of Richard on stage while we stood in the wings at the other side, taking it in turns to try to get in the shot with him. It didn't work. Mike said Richard moved too fast in his act for him to catch. I think one shot of Ringo and Richard's shoulder came out.

● At the show Brian said to me, "These boys worship you. You're the only famous artist they've ever met. They've never met a famous person in their life. They want their picture taken with you." So they grabbed my hand and Paul wanted to be next to me. He said, "This is my seat."

When I first saw the Beatles I didn't think they'd make it. I remember Brian Epstein had booked me to play at the Cavern with them. A couple of weeks later he had me headlining a big concert at a theater in Liverpool. They were a support band, with the Swinging Blue Jeans, Cilla Black, and Gerry and the Pacemakers. The Beatles went on and sang "Love Me Do." They couldn't do my numbers, "Lucille" and "Long Tall Sally," cos I was there. When they came off, Brian Epstein said to me, "Richard, I'll give you fifty percent of the Beatles." I couldn't accept cos I never thought they would make it. Brian Epstein said, "Take the masters [of Beatles songs] back to America with you and give them to the record company for me." I didn't do that, but I did call up some people for them. I phoned Art Rupe and I also got in touch with Vee Jay, but I didn't take a piece of them.

So then I was booked for a tour of clubs in Hamburg for Don Arden, and I took the Beatles with me. We spent two months in Hamburg. John, Paul, George, and Ringo. They would stay in my room every night. They'd come to my dressing room and eat there every night. They hadn't any money, so I paid for their food. I used to buy steaks for John.

Paul would come in, sit down, and just look at me. Like he wouldn't move his eyes. And he'd say, "Oh, Richard! You're my idol. Just let me touch you." He wanted to learn my little holler, so we sat at the piano going "Ooooh! Ooooh!" till he got it.

I threw my shirt in the audience and Paul went and got one of his best shirts. A flash shirt, a beautiful shirt, and he said, "Take it, Richard." I said, "I can't take that," but he insisted, "*Please* take it. I'll feel bad if you don't take it. Just think—Little Richard's got on my shirt. I can't believe it."

They asked me, "Richard, how does California look? Are the buildings in New York real tall? Have you ever met Elvis Presley? Is he nice-looking?"

I developed a specially close relationship with Paul McCartney, but me and John couldn't make it. John had a nasty personality. He was different from Paul and George, they were sweet. George and Paul had humbler-type personalities. You know, submissive. John and Ringo had strange personalities, both of them. John would do his no-manners [break wind] and jump over and fan it all over the room, and I didn't like it. You know, sometimes he would do two in a row and say "Oooh whee! He did two tonight." It would bother me. I didn't want to hear that stuff, y'know.

116

ART RUPE: Richard called me from England. He wanted to tell me about a group who were on his bill. Four guys who were singing. He said they can imitate anybody. That was the Beatles. He wanted to know if I would be interested, and I said, "Richard, I am not interested in anyone but you. I want you to come back and sing like you did before."

BILLY PRESTON: I was surprised when that tour turned out to be Rock 'n' Roll, but I was quite happy. I had never played that stuff before and it was all exciting to me. Richard was very unpredictable to work with. Every show was exciting because you never knew what he was going to do. He was one of the greatest performers ever. He inspired me as a performer because he put everything into the show. He really worked hard and he knew just how to get the kids going. I remember how excited the Beatles were to meet Richard. He had been their idol for years. In Hamburg they'd always be with him asking him questions about America, the cities, the stars, the movies, Elvis, and all that. And when Richard left to go back to the United States they cried.

That's when the Beatles and I became very close. You see, Richard left me in Hamburg without a ticket home. He was supposed to meet me at the train station but he never showed up. So I went back to Don Arden's office and the Beatles happened to be there as well. They were hurt because Richard had left me and I guess their hearts kinda went out to me from then.

● Billy wasn't ready to come back. He was having such a good time with the Beatles. They all went to the Star Club. I had to leave and I couldn't find them. So I left his ticket with Arden and went to catch the ship. I didn't leave him stranded. Why should I have done a thing like that?

*Back in the United States Richard spent Christmas at home with his family in a state of indecision about his future. He hung around a lot with J. W. Alexander and Sam Cooke, who now had his own recording studio. He recorded some gospel songs with a choir for Atlantic Records, but refused all offers to record rock music. Then he put a toe in the water, recording a song called "Well Alright" which Cooke had written around a well-known Richard catch phrase.*

*The success of Cooke, who was making enormous amounts of money, made Richard wonder whether he was missing his chance. In England he had gotten back into his old life-style—staying in good hotels with the best of everything and traveling around in limousines. His soul craved the star treatment he saw Cooke receiving.*

*In the middle of the summer Don Arden approached Richard to do a second tour of England. Again the offer came at just the right psychological moment, and he accepted. He kept it a secret from his family and his friends in religion. Partly because he still could not entirely submerge the thought that Rock 'n' Roll was evil and partly because he wanted to retain their respect, he wanted to leave his options open for a possible return to his role as preacher. Ernestine, who had just won her suit for divorce, knew his plans but kept silent.*

ERNESTINE: I did understand him going back into show business. I was disappointed because I liked him where he was, but I understand what makes him go. He was accustomed to a certain life-style and he thrived on that and missed it a lot. Being around people and doing things and being the center of attention is part of his makeup. If you take that away you're going to hurt him. He draws people. He thrives on that, and they thrive on him.

118

*Arden's plans and publicity for the tour were well in hand when he approached Richard. Headliners were to be the Everly Brothers, with Bo Diddley as support act and another young British group who had just released their first record—the Rolling Stones.*

● It was a last-minute thing to get me on the tour. They had my old friend Bo and the Everly Brothers as headliners. I think the bookings weren't going too well or something, so Don Arden remembered my success of the previous year and made me an offer. I know I had said I wouldn't do another rock tour but...I went because I wanted to.

I had never heard of the Rolling Stones before I went to England. Mick Jagger used to sit at the side of the stage watching my act. Every performance. They had a little record out, a cover of Chuck Berry's "Come On," but they had never done a tour before. Mick opened the show with the Rolling Stones. They were making fifty dollars a night. He couldn't even pay for his room. Mick used to talk to me all the time. He'd sit there and talk all night if I let him. He and the others used to sleep on Bo Diddley's floor in the hotel.

MICK JAGGER: I'd heard so much about the audience reaction that I thought there must be some exaggeration. But it was all true. He drove the whole house into a complete frenzy. There's no single phrase to describe his hold on the audience. It might excite some and terrify others. It's hypnotic, like an evangelistic meeting where, for want of a better phrase, Richard is the disciple and the audience the flock that follows. I couldn't believe the power of Little Richard on stage. He was amazing. Chuck Berry is my favorite, along with Bo, but nobody could beat

119

Little Richard's stage act. Little Richard is the originator and my first idol.

KEITH RICHARDS: The most exciting moment of my life was appearing on the same stage as Little Richard.

MICKEY MOST: One night Richard asked if he could borrow a shirt from me. He went out onstage and I saw it torn to pieces by the fans. When he asked me again the next night I had to say no. I was a struggling singer earning about ten pounds a week and he was making thousands.

*Richard had thrown his cufflinks away with the shirt so he asked Don Arden, who happened to be backstage, if he could lend him a pair. Not knowing what had happened to Richard's own links, Arden slipped off his solid-gold set and passed them to Richard. They, too, went to the crowd in the next performance, along with the shirt. Arden smoldered with rage when he found out.*

*The Stones got a hostile reception at some shows, as did Mickey Most, whose facile Chuck Berry imitation died a thousand deaths in front of fans who had no patience for anything that stood between them and Little Richard.*

*The last engagement of the tour was Richard's appearance in a TV spectacular produced by Britain's biggest independent TV company, Granada Network Ltd. The Little Richard Spectacular was filmed in the company's Manchester studio, with U.S. female vocal group the Shirelles ("Will You Still Love Me Tomorrow?" and "Tonight's the Night") as backing vocalists and Sounds Incorporated as the backing band. They came close to Richard's original sound and to re-creating the excitement of the Upsetters.*

*The spectacular was aptly named. After hilarious rehearsals, during which all the musicians seemed to have a bottle of spirits stashed away, filming started with Richard storming on set and straight into "Rip It Up," "Lucille," and "Long Tall Sally." With so much intensity and power, it seemed as if he* must *have a heart attack. But he went on from strength to strength, producing more and more energy the harder he worked. He crouched over the piano to play his driving boogie riffs, then leaped away to shout "Oooh my soul!" "My my my," and "Well, all right" between numbers, bringing the young invited audience ("Sweater, jeans, no ties, leathers, feet to tap, hands to clap," read the invitation cards) to their feet to dance wildly about the studio floor. His excessive energy astounded viewers. "You think I'm tired, but I'm not!" he shouted, launching full throttle into more nonstop powerhouse Rock 'n' Roll.*

*The program, thirty-eight minutes long, was first shown on British commercial television in May 1964. Billed as "Little Richard's final farewell performance," it was repeated twice by public demand after Granada received sixty thousand fan letters. Much of the footage was used for a TV special on Rock 'n' Roll called* Don't Knock the Rock, *and a shortened version was seen all over the world. To this day excerpts are used to illustrate the frenzy and excitement of a quintessential Rock 'n' Roll performance.*

*The producer of Granada's show was John Hamp, who must be given credit for putting onto the small screen some of the greatest rockers ever. He says: "I've recorded Jerry Lee Lewis, Gene Vincent, the Beatles, and many others—but by far the most exciting was Little Richard in his Granada special. When it was shown at the National Film Theatre in 1971 in an exhibition of rock movies, everybody got up and started dancing and jiving, which shows the power and impact of the music and Little Richard's personality, even on film."*

*But toward the end of the thirty-date tour there were signs that the old conflict between the sacred and secular was once more affecting Richard.*

● I wanted people to forget Little Richard as a Rock 'n' Roller. I was soon to be qualified as an evangelist like Billy Graham. I was taking my exams that spring and I wanted to be an evangelist. But when I got home after the tour and saw what was going on in America, I became restless and dissatisfied. Sam Cooke was a big, big star. The Beatles' music was sweeping the country, and I had taught them to rock! I was their idol and they were my apprentices! In England and Europe they had treated me like a real star. The kids were screaming for my music, just like it was in 1956, when I was in my fame. But back home I was forgotten. It made me want to get back into show business properly again. If they liked me so much in England, why couldn't it be the same in the U.S.?

# The King of Rock'n'Roll

T he second coming of Little Richard started where the first had, in the recording studio. With three former Specialty men, producer Don Weiss, guitarist Dewey Terry, and bass player Don "Sugarcane" Harris, Richard recorded his first "official" Rock 'n' Roll music in seven years, abandoning the big sax sound of his 50s hits for the currently popular guitar sound. Weiss persuaded him that Specialty was the only company that could bring him back to popularity. So despite the bad memories, Richard agreed to let the company hear the tapes and he signed with them again. But just for the one record, no more.

When Art Rupe heard the tapes he flipped. His label had been in the doldrums since Richard's retirement. The main title on the demos, a song called "Bama Lama Bama Loo" recaptured the excitement of Richard's old hits. This was the boost needed to put Specialty back on the map! He agreed to the terms, bought the tapes, secured Richard's release for a thousand dollars from Atlantic, and issued "Bama Lama" as a single, with "Annie's Back," on the B side.

Little Richard's climb back to U.S. popularity was just beginning.

Before setting out on a third Don Arden–promoted tour of

*England, Richard had one hard task to face. He had to tell his friends in the church and his family that he had decided to go back to show business.*

MARQUETTE: Richard asked me to go to England with him as road manager. The family didn't know he was back in show business. Richard used to keep his life separate from Mother and the family. There were so many rumors about him and so many stories that we just ignored them. Perhaps we had been a little suspicious for a year or so when he had let his hair grow back, but he had never told us what was going on and we had never asked. I thought I was going on his first tour of England, and it was his third!

*The U.K. tour was triumphant and it was followed by dates all over Europe, ending with a delirious and riot-provoking concert at the Paris Olympia. On returning to the U.S., Richard was given the disappointing news that "Bama Lama" had flopped, only reaching number eighty-two on the* Billboard *charts.*

● It was a fantastic record. I had gone into the guitar thing just like the groups were doing and Dewey's rhythm was terrific. His solo was really great. But although Specialty did their best, the whole thing had turned around by then and it was all white groups with hits on the charts. The establishment wouldn't let "Bama Lama" through because they were afraid that I might blow the whole thing open again. See, the entertainment business is run by a whole hidden system. It doesn't matter how good a record is. If it gets enough airplay it'll grow on the public. They can guarantee you a hit, or stop you from having one. In the 1950s there was nothing they could do. People just wanted my records. They couldn't do anything about that. My hits just slipped through. "Tutti Frutti" just fruitied on outa there and they couldn't stop it. The Southern Child came in and they couldn't stop him. The Southern Child from down in Macon, Georgia. But in the sixties they had gotten organized.

When "Bama Lama" flopped, it was devastating to me. It was like to've killed me. So I just got me a band together and went on the road. I went all over the country touring, one-night stands. I played in some dumps. I played some snake holes, some rat holes, and some pigpens. Oh, my God! The Domino Lounge, in Atlanta, Georgia; Soul City, in Dallas, Texas; I went everywhere. I was singing "Good Golly Miss Molly" and "Tutti Frutti" and "Long Tall Sally," and my hair was so high over my head, I was leaping all over the piano and tearing it up everywhere.

You see, I had been out of the public's eye in America for so long that they had forgotten me. It was like starting all over again like when I was just a teenage boy. I needed to break through again. Things had changed. There were all these English groups, the Beatles, the Stones, Herman's Hermits, Gerry and the Pacemakers, and they just over-shadowed my thing. But I was determined to make it.

*The phone rang in Bumps Blackwell's North Hollywood home. Bumps pushed away the manuscript on which he was roughing out an arrangement for a Sam Cooke album track and picked up the receiver. "Hi, Bumps. This is Richard. Bumps, I want you to help me. I need to change my image. I want to come on loud and gaudy. I want to come back as the Living Flame!"*

*It was going to cost a lot of money, and raising that without ending up as someone's property was a difficult job, but Richard was determined never to be owned again. If he made it, it was going to be all his this time. The bulk of the cash probably came as an advance from the Vee Jay record company. He can't remember exactly, except that it came.*

*One of his old band colleagues, Percy Welch, who was a*

125

*member of his road crew at the time, told a story about Richard going to the Mafia and borrowing fifty thousand dollars to set up his show but refusing to accept any control or interference from "the Man." But Richard denies this and it is barely believable that he could have gotten away with it. Wherever the cash came from, Richard went on the road again with a nine-piece band, Guardsmen, a throne, dancers, and an outrageously camp image.*

● The King returned to his rightful throne, to push everybody off that can't hold his own. When I retired from show business millions of my fans were stunned. They weeped and they moaned and they groaned because the King had left his subjects. I sacrificed millions of dollars, but I had no regrets. Now I was back, and I was a tornado, fast and round, faster than sound. I put sixteen thousand dollars into my new act, which was very, very glamorous and elaborate. Something no one else had. I was the star and leader of my own troupe of seventeen musicians, singers, dancers, and comedians. The Little Richard Show. My voice was the most exciting voice in the world. It was a sassy voice, and I gave a message and it was sassy. Then I would get very sweet and lovable and it fit my beautiful personality. I was not in harmony with the church at that time. I still believed what they taught, but I wasn't doing that then. My music made your liver quiver, your bladder spatter, your knees freeze. And your big toe shoot right up in your boot!

*The touring started all over again. Along the way Richard acquired a new guitar player. A young man who wanted to be known as Maurice James but later would burst onto the music scene as Jimi Hendrix.*

● I first met Jimi Hendrix in Atlanta, Georgia, where he

126

was stranded with no money. He had been working as guitarist with a feller called Gorgeous George, a black guy who sported a blond wig and wore these fabulous clothes which he made himself. My bus was parked on Auburn Avenue and Jimi was staying in this small hotel. And so he came by to see us. He had watched me work and just loved the way I wore these headbands around my hair and how wild I dressed. He wanted to come with me, so Bumps, who knew his folks back in Seattle, rang Mr. Hendrix to see if it was okay for him to join us. Al Hendrix told Bumps, "Jimi just idolizes Richard. He would eat ten yards of shit to join his band." So he came with me. He wasn't playing my kind of music, though. He was playing like B. B. King, blues. He started rocking, though, and he was a good guy. He began to dress like me and he even grew a little mustache like mine. I grew mine when I was just a boy, to cover a scar on my lip.

HENRY NASH: Gorgeous George was valeting for Hank Ballard and the Midnighters, and helping the other tour stars with their needs. In Atlanta, George asked me if I would allow Jimi Hendrix to come on the tour as his valet. I saw the manager of the package and we gave Jimi the opportunity to load the bus as Gorgeous George's helper.

I never will forget Jimi loading his belongings on the bus. His guitar was wrapped in a potato sack. It had only five strings on it. Well, we left Atlanta for Greenville, South Carolina. After the concert that night, we went to an after-hours club and began working the after-the-concert date. Gorgeous George talked me into allowing Jimi to sit in with the Upsetters. He played the entire night with only five strings to his guitar. He made a good impression on the band, though, and they welcomed having him on stage with them. So throughout the tour, whenever he would have after-hours dates to play, Jimi would ask to sit in and

I would allow him to. Jimi to me was never a precision guitarist. I know he was not a reading musician in those days, though he played well by ear. I regarded him as being innovative, creative, and something of a stylist. He would sometimes play with his teeth and then put the guitar behind his neck and play with his fingers. This brought raves from the audience. Once the tour ended I didn't see any more of Jimi, and I don't know whether he went back to Atlanta with Gorgeous George.

*Hendrix and Gorgeous George worked at intervals for Henry Wynne. It was on one of these tours that Hendrix met blues guitarist Albert King. King, like Hendrix, was a left-handed player who used a right-handed guitar upside-down. He passed on to the eager young musician his own trademark—a sound that slurred up and then dropped down, like a saxophone sound. He taught him fingerings using the thumb and the frettings on the guitar to bend the strings horizontally instead of vertically.*

*With his technique developing rapidly, Hendrix desperately needed to play regularly with musicians of a higher caliber than Gorgeous George. His Atlanta meeting with Little Richard came at just the right time for him. Touring with Richard, the most charismatic show-business figure ever, gave him an insight into the techniques of a master and saved him from stagnation on the chitterling circuit, just one among dozens of talented young black guitarists.*

*It has been alleged that Richard suppressed Hendrix's talent as a guitarist, bawling him out for wearing a ruffled shirt while playing and for doing anything onstage that might take attention away from himself.*

MARQUETTE: Richard *didn't* hide Jimi. He used to allow him to do that playing with his teeth onstage and take solos. It became part of the act, all that playing behind his back and stuff. If Richard had been trying to suppress him, he wouldn't have allowed that. The only thing he wouldn't allow his musicians to do was play at some other places when we were in town to do a show. Richard was a little strict with the band. Sometimes on off nights the guys would want to appear in places, to sit in, so that they could be heard as individuals. Richard would say, "No. No. To-morrow night you're going to be on stage with me and I want it to be a whole new thing. I don't want people to say, " 'Oh, yes, those are the same guys we saw last night over at such-and-such a club. Richard must have picked them up. They're not *his* band.' " Maybe that's what they mean by saying he suppressed his musicians. He would limit them by saying, "You work for *me*."

Richard taught Hendrix a lot of things, and Hendrix copied a lot of things from Richard. That's where he got the charisma. Richard used to say, "Look. Don't be ashamed to do whatever you feel. The people can tell if you're phony. They can *feel* it out in the audience. I don't care if you're wild. I don't care if you're quiet. They'll know if you're putting yourself into it, whatever it is."

HOSEA WILSON: Today I head up a Hollywood production agency, but I was Richard's road manager at that time. Jimi was a real strong rhythm-guitar player. He was a hell of a talent. Everybody knows that now, but you could tell even then. The thing is that when Jimi was with the band he wasn't on the hard stuff. He wasn't flamboyant or anything then. He was all quiet—to himself. Most guitar players are introverted. Jimi was like that. Richard brought Hendrix out. Helped him a lot to be what he became.

*Randy Wood, the enterprising president of Chicago-based Vee Jay Records, called Richard and his band into a Los*

Angeles studio to record some material in return for the cash advanced earlier in the year.

The sessions produced an album of rock and R 'n B standards entitled Little Richard Is Back and There's a Whole Lotta Shakin' Goin' On. His first Vee Jay single release was a new version of the old standard "Goodnight Irene" backed with the album title track. Both featured the guitar work of Hendrix. Vee Jay rerecorded many of Richard's original Specialty hits, too. But, blinded by commercial considerations, they rushed the session without concern for quality. The result was dreadful. Low-key promotion and the overwhelming "invasion" of British groups prevented the records from making it.

The Little Richard Show went back on the road. Then Vee Jay folded, just as it was releasing its last single, "I Don't Know What You Got" and putting Richard back on the Billboard "Hot 100."

After this, Richard's recording career became very erratic. His stage act was rapidly becoming a form of self-parody. The undiscriminating audiences, who seemed to love his camp fooling more than his music, encouraged his displays of narcissistic nonsense and he became even more eccentric.

Then things started to move. Richard signed with the prestigious Okeh label, a division of Columbia Broadcasting, and began recording under the direction of Larry Williams, his friend from their Specialty recording days. Bookings for live performances rocketed.

The gay act went down well in the clubs and lounges, but it was working against him in other areas. When Richard was told by his booking agency that they were unable to get him television work because the producers objected to his long hair and his general image, he gave Soul magazine the story. They splashed it their front cover with the headline "Little Richard Declares War" (on the knockers in the TV

130

*companies). The article was accompanied by photographs of Richard working, with his long hair falling over his heavily madeup face.*

● Some of the television shows were refusing me because of my hair. *Ninth Street West* told me they didn't want the image I was building with the kids on television. They really couldn't explain it. I was very hurt. This was my style and my living. Everybody was wearing long hair. I just don't understand it. Every big artist in Rock 'n' Roll today had recorded my songs. The Beatles, the Stones, Mick Jagger, Herman's Hermits, they'd all been to see me. They were complaining about me—a legend, one of the originals—wearing my hair long?

HOSEA WILSON: Richard always went on stage with this guy he, you know, liked. We had three guys, who later became Earth Wind and Fire, backing us at this time. Right in the middle of the program he would say, "Ladies and gentlemen, Liberace has George. And I have Ray." It was embarrassing to me, cos every night I'd be collecting the money and it was sorta difficult to face the guys who were paying me. I said, "Richard, why don't you take that part out of the show?" He said no. So what I decided to do was wait until he got through with that part, and *then* go and collect the money. So this night in Atlanta, Georgia, I waited and waited until I thought he must have said that part already. So I go up behind, and the guy's counting out the money, and Richard says, "Liberace has George and I have Ray." And then he said, "The reason I did that, ladies and gentlemen, is because my road manager is over there collecting the money. He don't like that part of the show."

I don't know whether he was really gay or whether it was just the act. I never saw anything. I never used to get mixed up with these things. He had wild parties, plenty of ladies,

131

plenty of fellers, but I seldom went to them. I was busy doing other things. I used to get the money and give it to Richard, but he wasn't very quick about paying the guys. I remember going to him in New York and saying, "Hey, the guys wanna be paid," and Richard saying, "I haven't had my morning jack yet! Don't tell me I gotta pay them before I have my morning jack."

*Some musicians take to life on the road as though they were born to it. Jimi Hendrix was not one of these. Little Richard's journeyings around America had an expectant buzz about them. Every performance was wild, outrageous. Sometimes working the audience into an enthusiastic frenzy, sometimes not quite reaching them, sometimes visibly offending. The tour was taking them to a lot of out-of-the-way places. In the South they were getting caught up in the atmosphere generated by the civil-rights disorders. Often Richard flew from one venue to the next while the band traveled by bus. Jimi Hendrix was not happy, though he loved to play. His unhappiness showed itself in deliberate flouting of the band rules and in bad timekeeping. He had to go. Richard's brother, Robert, who was managing the tour, wielded the ax.*

ROBERT PENNIMAN: I fired Hendrix, who was using the name Maurice James all the time I knew him. He was a damn good guitar player, but the guy was never on time. He was always late for the bus and flirting with the girls and stuff like that. It came to a head in New York, where we had been playing the Apollo, and Hendrix missed the bus for Washington, D.C. I finally got Richard to cut him loose. I believe when you're paying people they've got certain obligations. I told Richard, "Hey, man, he can't keep doing this." So when Hendrix called us in Washington, D.C., I gave him the word that his services were no longer required. We had some words. I explained why we were doing this. I was running the road for Richard and I didn't accept that kind of bullshit.

I have read that Richard canned him in England and left him stranded. It makes better reading that way, sells books and things, but it's a damn lie. I know. I canned Hendrix myself in New York. Later—years later—I was flying some place to meet Richard and the program on the headset kept listing "Jimi Hendrix." Well I had been reading about this guy making all this money, like a hundred thousand dollars for forty-five minutes, and I mentioned it to Richard. He said, "Robert, do you know who that is?" He let me hang for a couple of minutes; then he said, "That's Maurice James." I had never related Jimi Hendrix to Maurice James until then.

*The traveling went on, week after week, month after month. A welcome break was a trip to England. Brian Epstein had set up a deal for Richard, headlining a series of concerts at London's Savile Theatre, with British bands the Alan Price Set, the Quotations, and a new group, Bluesology. The piano player with Bluesology, which opened the shows to shouts of "Off, off" from Richard's fans, was a young man called Reggie Dwight. He said, "When I saw Little Richard standing on top of the piano, all lights, sequins, and energy, I decided there and then that I was going to be a Rock 'n' Roll piano player." Not long afterward he went solo and changed his name to Elton John.*

*The British rockers found Richard's shows as dynamic as ever, though some were a little confused by the homosexual overtones in his act. It was still the hottest rock show in town, however, and the concerts sold out. Richard received nonstop attention from newspapers and television, concluding his visit with a top spot on the BBC's premier TV rock program, singing his new U.S. release, "I Need Love."*

*Epstein, impressed by Richard's tour de force, set up a recording session at EMI's famous Abbey Road Studios, where such music greats as Caruso, von Karajan, Elgar— and the Beatles—had recorded. The man who produced the session was Norman Hurricane Smith, who had just finished working with the Beatles.*

HURRICANE SMITH: I wasn't happy with Richard at first. He had a bad throat and was using a throat spray, and he was drinking a lot of whisky. But he was really great. I've never seen an artist work so hard—or perspire so much— in the studio. We cut four tracks, and the best was "Get Down with It," a powerhouse rocker in which Richard's voice is so clear and strong you'd never believe he had a bad throat at the time.

*The British trip had been a tremendous ego boost, but back home Richard found things little changed.*

● I was in the second year of the Okeh contract and there was still no hit record. So I tore it up. The contract gave me no say in the material I recorded with them or in what was released. Larry Williams was the worst producer in the world. He wanted me to copy Motown and I was no Motown artist. They made me use their band, which was all trumpets. I got so I wanted to throw all the trumpets in the world into the river. They wanted me to use all that electronics stuff. I wanted the natural real thing. The real people wanted the real thing. The Okeh stuff didn't sell at all because Okeh was an R'n'B label—a black label. I should have recorded on the Epic label, because I'm not primarily a black artist. It would have done a lot better.

See, in the South the R'n'B stations wouldn't play my stuff because of pressure from the preachers who hated show business and couldn't forgive me for giving up the ministry. We called them the martyrs. They told the D.J.s not to play my records. On the West Coast, especially in L.A. after the Watts riots, the colored D.J.s wouldn't play my stuff because I've always been an artist for all the people and not just the blacks. There was a block, a big wall, and no matter how hard I knocked my head against it they wouldn't let me through. I couldn't get on no TV shows. I had to do it the hard way. I had to work and try to *create* the demand.

*And still the seemingly endless traveling went on. The Hollywood Sunset Hotel, the Beach Ball Club (Boston, Mass.), the Diamond Club (Dayton, Ohio), Isy's Supper Club (Vancouver, Canada), the Red Carpet Lounge (Chicago, Ill.), where Billy Eckstine had just closed, and the Whiskey A-Go-Go (St. Paul, Minn.) following Chubby Checker, playing a six-night week for $750 a night. Then a modest breakthrough. A week at a Las Vegas venue. Not one of the prestigious rooms, just the unpretentious Eden Rock, but a step in the right direction. Then it was back to the grindstone, with a tour of one-nighters in the Southwest.*

EDDIE FLETCHER: Richard opened every show with "Lucille." I guess I played that bass line over a thousand times. Every time he played "Lucille" it had a little bit different impact to it. That's the type of performer he was.

Whenever I started playing one of his songs I could always find something new to do with it. I could always change the bass line around. I'd think, I won't go here this time, I'll go somewhere else. Cos Richard always knew where I was going, so that was the main thing. We played a lot on that, you know, spiritual-type vibes between us. There was very little said on stage. If there was, he did most of the saying and I did most of the laughing. It was like being on a top football or baseball team. You had to build up that adrenaline and get a good flow going. The feeling of "Hey, not only do we enjoy this, we're getting paid for it, too." It got to the point, after so many years of working together, that we became like blood brothers. If one of you had to do a certain thing to make the other stronger you'd try even harder to do that. And that's the way it was with him and I.

*By 1968 life on the road had taken its toll. The tremendously strenuous road tours had left Richard exhausted. He decided to go back home and recuperate. But all the hard work and grass-roots exposure had paid off. The public was finally coming to realize the wonder and amazing talent of Little Richard, the master showman. The big break came when Richard was offered a two-week engagement at the Aladdin Hotel in Las Vegas.*

● It was an unexpected booking, because the big Vegas hotels had refused to book me before. The star that was to open at this time was ill, so they decided they wanted me. I had no time at all for preparation, and there was not much advertising, but I still opened to a full house. The owners of the hotel were a bit skeptical because they had never had a rock act before in this particular room. Well, I was trying to think what I could do to be different. I said "I've gotta be gorgeous." Mind, I'd always do that! I'd stand on stage and tell them how beautiful I was, and they'd agree with me. So I'd had this red jacket made and it had inch-square mirrors sewn all over it. I made 'em put out all the lights except two little baby spots. With those spots jiggling above me, there was light sparkling all over the place, bouncing off the mirrors. Man, they loved it! It was fifteen mintues before I could do my first number! They loved the jacket almost as much as they loved the show. They thought it was fabulous.

For the second show that night there was a line all the

136

way through the casino. People couldn't even get to the gambling tables for the line. Everybody thought the folks were coming to gamble, but they were waiting to go in and see my show. I broke all the house records. Every show they would crowd the room and there would still be a line waiting outside, cos naturally we were loud and rowdy. They would cheer after our numbers, too. They were even dancing all through the casino!

They had originally planned on two shows a night, but we would end up doing three because there was no way to accommodate all those people. I had some fantastic costumes made. A different one for every night and sometimes one for every show. I had this huge cape, white satin outside and red satin inside. When I opened it up I was so gorgeous I couldn't believe it myself. The hotel juggled their dates to keep us for another two weeks, then booked us again for two weeks in June.

*Appearances on the Pat Boone and Joey Bishop TV shows brought Richard further into the public eye. Boone acknowledged Richard as "the man who gave me many hits" and paid tribute to his profound influence on popular music.*

*Just when the road of his career seemed to be taking an upward turn, Richard, with his flair for the unpredictable, shocked everyone who knew him by firing Bumps Blackwell as his manager and appointing J. W. Alexander to do the job.*

● Bumps had started getting heavy with me again, like he always did when I started getting successful, and enjoying the money I was making. He'd get nasty and shout at me. I thought, I don't have to take this stuff. So I fired him. I had known J.W. for a long time. He was cheerful and he had class. He was with it. He had done great things for Sam

Cooke and he really knew the music business. I called him and he said he would manage me.

BUMPS BLACKWELL: Richard's announcement that we were finished came as a stunning blow to me. I had struggled so hard and sacrificed so much to get him on the road to success again. With the booking in Las Vegas and the TV shows, we seemed to be achieving this. Naturally, I was hurt and my first reaction was to enforce my contract, but that would have meant hiring a lawyer and going to court. That would, for all practical purposes, have put Richard out of business. If he didn't work, he wouldn't make any money, which would have been the reason for me to sue him. The only people who would have gained from that action would have been the lawyers, who would get their fee regardless of the outcome. Even if I had won and retained Richard under management, I would not have had him. I know Richard too well. He could never perform to the best of his ability if he were unhappy.

So I decided to accept the situation and concentrate on finding new talent. I couldn't remain angry at Richard. Because of the closeness of the business, I was aware of everything he was doing and where he was appearing. After an awkward period of adjustment, I found we could talk without getting emotional. Richard would call occasionally and we would chat cordially. Then in April Richard called me and said he was very unhappy. He continued to call. In a couple of weeks, there was a closeness that I had never before experienced with him. He said he wanted to come back with me, and though he didn't tell me the whole story, I gathered that Richard had been under a lot of pressure. He had had a problem, and his way out was to sign with J.W.

J. W. ALEXANDER: There had been no discussions.

138

Richard just called me from Vegas and told me he would like me to be his manager. I had my lawyer, Jim Talbot, draw up a manager's contract. I flew up to Las Vegas and I started handling him. One of the first things I did was get him back in the union. He was suspended at the time from some previous problems. I think it cost me a thousand dollars to pay his fines and have him reinstated in the international and join Local 47. So then I started to really try to give a hand to his career. I got him signed up with Associated Booking Corp., of New York, because Lou Rawls and I had worked with them. I had a very good rapport with all their agents, as well as with the owner, Joe Glaser.

*Club appearances in Vancouver, Indiana, Chicago, and Detroit kept Richard busy for most of April and May. Then, on June 1, the eve of another engagement at the Aladdin Hotel, Richard announced that he had fired J. W. Alexander as his manager and reengaged Bumps Blackwell.*

● J.W. had a lot of other artists like Lou Rawls, and I felt I wasn't getting his full attention. I had been talking with Bumps and telling him I was unhappy. He said he would come back with me. J.W.? He didn't mind too much. I guess he didn't like the touring and all that. He liked to drive around in his Rolls-Royce and live in style in his big house in Hollywood, handling his artists from his office.

BUMPS BLACKWELL: Why did he decide to come back? I understand Richard better than anyone and can anticipate his every need, and he knows this. I know that I am the superior manager. I work hard and I have many years of experience that is hard to match. Richard wanted to make it, and it hadn't happened during the period with J.W.

*With their winning partnership once more in operation, Richard and Bumps found everything immediately starting to go right for them. The Aladdin Hotel engagement was a total sell-out on all ten dates from June 2 to 12.*

*Bumps Blackwell was busy negotiating with three record companies, ABC-Paramount, Liberty, and Specialty, and he invited Art Rupe and his new general manager, Mike Akopoff, to Las Vegas, to watch Richard's act at the Aladdin. Rupe had reservations about the overall flavor of Richard's between-song patter. At this time Richard was coming on as "the bronze Liberace" and promoting a determinedly gay image. The music was as exciting as ever, though, with an eleven-piece band led by Eddie Fletcher, including three saxes and two trumpets.*

● Elvis was in the front row on the night Art Rupe came along to hear me. I drew attention to him and he stood up and took a bow. He watched me like a hawk all the way through my act, then afterward there he was waiting for me, a good-looking dude in a white suit with two or three of his boys. After the show he said, "Man, I love your act, you're the greatest."

Elvis was preparing to make a comeback to public performances. But he had a problem. He was due to make his stage comeback at the International Hotel, the biggest in Vegas. After all these years in the movies he had no act. He did not want to go on stage and play his old rock hits. He was into different things now and he couldn't come on in a dress suit and do a Frank Sinatra, even though he would be playing to people old enough to be his parents, instead of screaming teenagers. So Elvis made the rounds of the Las Vegas rooms picking up ideas.

Tom Jones used to come along, too. He took a lot of things from me. When I saw him there in the audience I'd do "I Believe" in a cappella and he'd just marvel. Tom had

140

a great stage act himself, a very sexy act, but his long notes weren't so good and he knew it.

*Ending his run at the Aladdin Hotel, Richard opened the following night at Harrah's Club, in Reno, Nevada, for a seventeen-day engagement that repeated the success he had found in Las Vegas—packed rooms and sold-out shows.*

*August was to be the most important month of Richard's second coming. It opened with two concerts at the Fillmore East, the East Coast sister theater in rock entrepreneur Bill Graham's successful "concept" rock venues in San Francisco and New York. Featuring all the hot bands of the "acid-rock" era, the Fillmore East and the Fillmore West offered a complete entertainment environment, with light shows, films, and poetry readings, as well as rock concerts. In the late sixties, until they closed down in 1971, the Fillmores were the undisputed palaces of the new rock revival.*

*On to Atlantic City, New Jersey, where one of the biggest rock festivals ever seen in the state was in full swing. When Richard arrived on the third and final day to close the event, there was an audience of sixty thousand people. The crowd had already heard bands like Creedence Clearwater Revival, Booker T and the MGs, Three Dog Night, Iron Butterfly, and artists of the caliber of B. B. King, the Chambers Brothers, and Janis Joplin, who went on immediately before Richard.*

● It had started raining and I had to close the show. Janis was screaming. She had been sucking on that Southern Comfort bottle. When she took off her shoes I thought, Oh Lord. And when she started leaping up and down I thought, Look at this woman. And you know, she could scream, too. I thought, Oh, my God. She stopped the whole thing. Got three standing ovations. She was very dangerous, that girl.

141

Well, the promoters came and said they were satisfied that was a fitting ending to the festival and I needn't go on. They would pay me anyway. I said I wanted to go on. They said was I sure I could follow Janis Joplin after she had just finished tearing up the place. I said, "I don't know anyone I can't follow."

My band was scared to death—three standing ovations! But I told 'em, "You don't have to worry," and I went and put on my glass suit. I needed something to make me sparkle! There was dead silence as the band set up on stage. All the other bands had been dressed very casually, as the young groups do. But my band was in formal dress, like when we appeared in the top clubs. I used "Lucille." "Lucille" would always win for me. There's something about that riff that's electrifying. I got them to shine just the spotlights on me. I started gleaming and I just took over the show. The audience was quiet at first. They were so young, they didn't know who I was. Bumps said later, he thought for a minute that we'd bombed, but when they realized what was happening they just went wild. They charged the stage to get close up. The security guards tried to stop them but they just got swallowed up in the crowd. I did all my best songs. Then I threw my shoes to them and ended up throwing away three thousand dollars worth of clothes. It was incredible. The newspapers the next day were full of it. They gave just a little space to Janis, and the headlines said how incredible it was that Little Richard was able to come behind Janis Joplin and eclipse her when she had totally wrecked the audience.

EDDIE FLETCHER: The rain was something fierce and I was worried about getting shocked. When Richard hit that stage it was a turmoil. Can you imagine sixty thousand people just going crazy? Janis had been great and Richard enjoyed seeing her, working with her, and knowing her. But

142

when it came time for Richard to go on, the man just took his place. He had that magic charisma that no one else had or ever has had.

● After Atlantic City we went straight to Central Park, in New York City. There were more older people there, but I did it again. There was nearly a riot. The concert was at the Wollman Skating Rink, and it was packed. Ten thousand people. I opened with "Lucille" again, and already some people in the front row were up and dancing, and by the third number they were all on their feet—even the old people. I had to buy two pairs of shoes the next day cos I'd thrown my others away, along with the clothes.

The following night we played for thirty-two thousand people at Madison Square Garden. That's when I really started getting acclaim, after the Madison Square Garden concert. My costumes. The young people were raving over my outfits. I was way before my time. Back then they were calling me all kinds of sissies and freaks and faggots because I wore these things. Now all the groups are wearing them. Everybody's got a makeup kit in their hand now.

The glass suits—I've thrown a lot of those away! Some of them I designed myself, but I had two fellers to make them for me, Melvyn James, from Detroit, Michigan, and Tommy Ruth, from Los Angeles. I remember on one tour I threw so many away we had to send for Tommy Ruth to come out and make some more for me. He was sewing on the plane before the next show! Sometimes the audience were so crazy to grab them that they cut themselves, trying to rip it apart and get a piece. They *had* to know it was glass. They had to know. On some of the costumes the material alone cost six hundred dollars. I was spending most of my money on costumes, then throwing them out to the audience. But it was worth it because everybody was talking about it and coming to see me do it. They got their money's worth! I always used that old Pancake 31 makeup. My brother used to get it for me from Columbia Drugstore, on the corner of Sunset and Gower.

After New York we went to Mexico City, where I was playing the Forum, which just has to be the most beautiful club in the world. I've seen many, including the best in Las Vegas, but nothing like this. My dressing room was like a small apartment, with a waiting room for guests and another room just for me to lie down and rest! The crowd was made up of the wealthiest people in the city. One night the president of Mexico came with his wife and son. The son stayed for the second show and came back the following night. After the first night we had a terrible time getting around the streets. Crowds kept following us around shouting "Ricardito" and "Pequeno Ricardo." It was a wonderful reaction. A great experience.

We played a few one-nighters in Ohio, then had a few days off to prepare for a big festival in Vancouver. It was a big mess when we arrived there. The other groups on the bill, Canned Heat and Iron Butterfly, were all set to walk out because there was no money. Someone had skipped with it. We always insisted on getting half of our fee in advance, so at least we had that. We took a look at all those thousands of kids out there waiting and decided to give them a show. I put on my glass outfit and went out there and lit up that stage. The kids couldn't move their eyes from it. They jumped out of their sleeping bags and they couldn't believe it. They had expected to see an old man with bags under his eyes and they saw the beautiful Little Richard!

*Associated Booking Corporation, who was handling Richard, suddenly woke up to the fact that they had a gold mine on their hands. They wrote to Bumps Blackwell asserting that Richard was their greatest star and would*

144

*henceforth be treated as such, that once his current commitments were fulfilled they would be booking him in only the best clubs, and that efforts were being made to get him on as many television shows as possible to improve his exposure. They came up with the goods. And Richard didn't disappoint them. His flamboyant behavior on the Johnny Carson show and the Della Reese show led ABC Television to create a Little Richard special in their* Music Scene *series, using clips from 1950s Rock 'n' Roll films and exhilarating footage from the Granada TV special, taped in 1963. Richard's position in the minds of millions of Americans as the man who started it all was established. Little Richard was back... doing it better than ever.*

# *It Ain't What You Do*

here was an atmosphere in Detroit's Cobo Hall that September night that made your hair grab your collar. The electric energy of thirteen thousand people poised on the edge of an experience that they all knew was going to be mind-blowing. Like a world-title fight, Little Richard and Jerry Lee Lewis, those kings of the rocking piano, were about to battle it out onstage.

It was a brilliant piece of promotion—harking back to the excitement of the 1940s and early 50s when the jump bands would get together at the same venue, trying to blow each other off the stage in a battle of the bands. Little Richard and the Killer, both 100 percent full-throttle performers. Both just clawing their way back into the big time after ten years in the doldrums.

There had already been a managerial battle behind the scenes. Both stars had insisted on closing the show and therefore, in the unwritten rule of show business, topping the bill. Richard had lost. Jerry Lee Lewis's smoldering redneck prejudices and monster ego were a byword in the business. In the days of the Alan Freed package shows he had so resented being forced to go on before Chuck Berry in Berry's home city of St. Louis that he played thirty minutes of viciously hard Rock 'n' Roll, then took out a can of *lighter fuel, poured it on the piano, and put a match to it, telling the stage crew as he stomped off, "I'd like to see any son-of-a-bitch follow that." The stage was set for two epic performances, and the crowd couldn't wait.*

● Jerry Lee learned how to Rock 'n' Roll from me. He was just a country singer till he heard my songs and he recorded a lot of them. I hadn't been in the business all these years to let Jerry Lee get top billing over me. So Bumps and me got together to decide what to do. We planned to kill him dead, so to speak. I went out there shining like a diamond with my glass suit, and I really took the house. I gave it all. I used "Lucille" again. I made them lift the piano over to the middle of the stage while they were playing that riff. I sang all my hits. I had that audience right in the palm of my hand. I jumped on the piano and threw them my boots. I did a couple more songs. Then I threw them my glass suit and they tore it to bits for souvenirs. I finished up in just my pants and socks. I sang "Jenny Jenny," "Tutti Frutti," "Ooh Poo Pah Doo," and then "Bony Moronie." I talked to that crowd about how I got started. Then I noticed that Mitch Ryder and the Detroit Wheels were in the front row. Detroit is Mitch's hometown, and he got his break in the business with two of my songs. I got him up to take a bow. The audience really liked that! Then I ended with "Long Tall Sally" and left it to Jerry Lee to try to take them higher.

*Lewis opened with a slow country song, "You Win Again" followed by the similar-tempo "One Has My Name." When the audience, hyped up for Rock 'n' Roll by Richard's set, started to call for "Great Balls of Fire" and "Whole Lotta Shakin'" he blew his top and shouted back at them, "The door is open and there ain't no stop sign on the way out."*
*Jerry Lee is notorious for his treatment of audiences. He*

147

*plays what he wants to play and does not take kindly to suggestions. He told a restive audience in Germany who booed him for playing country music instead of rock, "If you don't like what I'm doing you can kiss my ass! The door swings both ways!"*

*When Lewis did start to play his Rock 'n' Roll hits and looked as though he might be getting the audience on his side, Richard moved in for the kill. Timing his entrance beautifully, he appeared in the center aisle giving away and signing photographs of himself. As people crowded around to take them, he moved slowly out of the auditorium, taking a large part of the audience with him, like the Pied Piper of Hamelin. Jerry Lee was left facing rows of empty seats!*

*Thoroughly psyched up by this triumph, Richard went on to another "battle of the bands" with Ike and Tina Turner at California Western University, in San Diego.*

● Frankly, we were a bit worried because Tina was one of the best performers in competition with us, and Ike had been waiting for a chance to show us up. As we had insisted on 100 percent top billing, we knew that Ike would be cooking up something special to knock us down a few pegs. That's how it had always been in the business, and you expected it.

Tina was one of the most dynamic entertainers of anybody of any race I've ever met. She's electrifying, and very hard to work with. Tina was maid to Ike Turner and his wife when I met her. She looked after the kids. I met them in St. Louis. Then Ike married her, changed her name from Ann Bullock to Tina Turner, and brought her to me to teach her charisma. I used to teach her. I did what I could, but you can't teach it. She's so full of it, anyway. We both are Sagittarius, born in December, and we're both wild, too—the Beauty and the Beast.

Tina and Janis Joplin were some alike, really. But what

148

Tina had, Janis didn't have. Janis could scream and squall just as hard as Tina, but Tina could dance. Janis couldn't. I couldn't. We weren't dancers. Tina is like a female James Brown. She's a mover and she looks good. She'd go on the stage and she'd have nothing on but one of those little things. You'd see all the men sitting down in front. She'd take over the house, with all these men trying to peep and see. That's how she takes the show. Takes the whole place over.

BUMPS BLACKWELL: We had been working constantly and we were all very tired. There was no time to come up with anything special, so we decided we would have to go on with what we had. During the afternoon rehearsal Richard was preoccupied. He listened to the band for a while. Then he walked around the room and did some strange things, like climb on the speakers. I busied myself checking out the sound system and balancing the band for the room. After we were all satisfied that everything was as good as it could be, we waited for the performance. Everyone seemed calm, but I think we were all still a little worried. Even though Richard talked confidently, I knew he was very concerned.

Then the performance was upon us. Ike and Tina were on first. They were trying very hard. But I was elated after the first few numbers. They were getting a tremendous reception and applause. Ike's band was polished and professional and the Ikettes were precision itself and exciting, but I knew we had them beat.

Richard came on to thunderous applause and the crowd got to its feet. It was a typical Little Richard show, each song better than the last. The crowd was unrestrained and Richard was like a wild man. They loved him. Halfway through the show he gave Boogie a tenor solo. Boogie took off his coat and played on his back with his feet in the air.

149

Then Richard got him up on the piano and he repeated the act. Richard called him down, then got up on the piano himself, and took his shoes off and threw them to the audience. They were in a frenzy. It's a wonder no one got injured. Then he took off the top of his costume and gestured as if he was going to throw that, too. The crowd went mad. After a few more numbers he climbed on top of the speakers in midsong, which put him over twenty feet above the floor. It shook me up. Then I remember that earlier in the day he had tested everything to see if it would support his weight. He was on stage for over an hour. The crowd tried for fifteen minutes to get him to come back and do more. The police had to form a line to protect him from the fans trying to touch him as he left the stage. This was one night Richard could say, without any reservations, that he had the best band in the world.

*Six weeks later, Woodstock, hippiedom's finest hour, instilled hope that through the medium of the be-in and Rock 'n' Roll, the young might just be able to pull the world out of the mess the men in suits, the unyoung, and unpoor, had landed it in.*

*The Toronto Peace Festival was held in this rosy aftermath, and Little Richard was on a bill that included John Lennon and the Plastic Ono band, Jim Morrison and the Doors, Chuck Berry, Bo Diddley, Jerry Lee Lewis, and the Chicago Transit Authority. Behind the scenes, however, it was not at all peaceful. Richard, still fighting as always to be the closing act, wanted Lennon to go on before him. The two men spent some time talking together backstage.*

*Lennon realized that he was in the presence of the greatest and most powerful Rock 'n' Roll singer in the world—a natural, whose soul fed on performing in front of a live audience. It must have blown the mind of the lad from Liverpool when he realized that, despite his worldwide adulation and fame, he was a zero as a live musician.*

*A decade before, as a leather-clad beat boy, he had knelt at Richard's feet, pleading to hold his hand.*

*In September 1969 fame had swollen his ego, making him unable to acknowledge that black men like Chuck Berry and Little Richard were the true kings of Rock 'n' Roll—the music he supposedly loved. Under great pressure, as always, from his Svengali, Yoko Ono, to maintain his top billing by going on after Richard, Lennon nevertheless knew that artistically he was hardly fit to tune Richard's piano. The conflict in his mind was insupportable. He left Richard's dressing room and proceeded to throw up. He told* Rolling Stone *magazine two years later: "I just threw up for hours until I went on. I could hardly sing any of the numbers. I was full of shit."*

BUMPS BLACKWELL: John Lennon was so nasty. He was really ridiculous. He insisted on going on last. When Richard hit that stage...oh, man! I had double-miked the guitar and the piano and put the mike right inside the saxophone. Richard hit the stage with the spotlights on him and jumped up on top of the piano. He did everything he knew. He got that crowd just screaming. He invited people onto the stage to dance. He whipped the audience into a frenzy. And boy, when Richard finished, he laid the audience out so much that when Lennon and Yoko came on, they were washed out.

Lennon and his band did some Rock 'n' Roll numbers, but I felt sorry for them trying to follow a giant like Richard. When Yoko started squalling, she sounded like a bull moose in mating season. Horrible. Like she was in pain. The kids started booing and then they started walking out. They bombed totally. After that, Jim Morrison and the Doors wouldn't go on until things had calmed down. They waited sixty minutes before they would come out.

After that, we never had any problems about Richard closing the show.

BRIAN SIMMONS: I was a stagehand at the festival, and I remember they just booed and booed the Lennons, especially Yoko. John helped her off the stage with his arm around her. He said, "Don't worry, baby, I'll make it up to you."

*A film of the festival, entitled* Sweet Toronto, *was released in the United States in December 1971. The sequences showing Richard and Chuck Berry working the crowd are some of the best ever filmed. But reviewers commented on the nervousness of Lennon and the comparative gaucherie of his set. The film was withdrawn for several months, and later reissued entitled* Keep on Rockin' *with the Lennon sequences removed.*

*Why was America suddenly ready for Little Richard and his music? Ten years of exposure to self-conscious, arty rock had left the kids eager for the simple big-beat sound. And their parents, who had danced to "Long Tall Sally" in 1956, were coming in droves to hear Richard live in Vegas, Reno, and L.A. Those factors were at the heart of what became the Rock 'n' Roll revival. Richard's sound had been absorbed so thoroughly into current pop music that every major group, from the Beatles to Creedence Clearwater, were realizing where their roots lay and copying his songs—the original Rock 'n' Roll. But there was another important factor: relaxation of those unwritten rules that had made it so hard for white people to acknowledge black talent.*

● With the emergence of black funk music, and as black-power feelings were starting to come on, a lot of people would try and get me to play for black-power rallies, performances that were strictly for black people. I would

152

never get into that. *People* were always important to me, whatever color they were. I was always supported by white people, but I was never antiblack or antiwhite or anti-anything.

James Brown was different from me. He was big to the black market. When he came to town, you would get ten thousand blacks. When I came to town, you would get ten thousand whites, and about ten blacks. When I would go to Madison Square Garden, I'd have about thirty-five thousand whites and about fifty black people in the audience. In the whole place. But it didn't make me no difference. A scream and a holler's a holler to me. I just love 'em. These were my fans and I loved 'em and they loved me, too. So it was a hand for a hand and a foot for a foot. And a pot on a pot. Bom bom!

*As the decade turned Richard faced his most vital engagement to date. A fortnight at that shrine of American show business, the Cocoanut Grove. The Grove, in Los Angeles's Ambassador Hotel, was where Frank Sinatra, Sammy Davis, Jr., and Lena Horne had crowned their careers. Richard opened there on February 3. The Cocoanut Grove was a very sedate room, catering almost exclusively to the society rich, the tables occupied by dinner-suited businessmen and their carefully coiffed wives drinking champagne and eating the rarest and most expensive foods. Richard's high-energy Rock 'n' Roll show was a drastic change from the mellow middle-of-the-road acts normally featured. With Richard anything was possible, but nothing was predictable.*

● Bumps wanted me to play the Cocoanut Grove because the Las Vegas casinos had started turning me down. They would have me but not in the best lounges. My image was too wild. Everybody thought I was crazy, though I'd pack the places. Our thing was all high energy. And when you bring high energy into a small cram-packed area you can't do nothing but expand, burst out, you know. And that's what we did at the Grove—burst out.

The chandeliers were shaking from the beat, it looked like five points on the Richter scale. I just told the band "Bring that old thing down, boys." There were people eating a nice lobster, you know? And here's "Tutti Frutti" and "Good Golly Miss Molly" coming at 'em while they're trying to crack a crab! We *had* complaints about it being too loud, but really everybody was enjoying it. They really were.

*After the Cocoanut Grove engagement things began to happen very fast. Three days later Richard was in New York appearing on the Dick Cavett show, the David Frost show, and the Mike Douglas show. The newspaper and magazine coverage during his sell-out session at the Cocoanut Grove had suddenly made him a very hot property. The TV talk shows got Richard coast-to-coast exposure. In some ways TV coverage is more important than record sales. And he made sure that no one overlooked his presence, wearing his gaudiest robes. On the Cavett show he broke into a discussion between* Love Story *writer Erich Segal and critic John Simon with a totally unscripted and passionate denunciation of their views on literature. He announced that he was writing a book about his own life to be called* He Got What He Wanted But He Lost What He Had.

*A popular feature of the early 1970s, and an important vehicle for the original rock artists, were revival shows. The most successful impresario was Richard Nader. He had correctly divined that there was a vast audience of music lovers who yearned for the songs and stars of their youth, as well as a lot of kids who were sick of the direction Rock 'n' Roll was taking. Nader's shows harkened back to the hal-*

154

*cyon days of Alan Freed's shows at the Paramount Theater on Broadway. Richard headlined Nader's Rock 'n' Roll Revival Show at the Felt Forum on March 20 and 21, appearing with Gene Vincent, Bo Diddley, the Five Satins, Ruby and the Romantics, and Timi Yuro.*

*It was just like the old days as the massive crowd rose to their feet when Richard took the stage. As the first notes of "Lucille" filled the huge auditorium, people rushed from all over the theater trying to get close and touch him. As he finished the number the Forum police began to hustle the crowd away from the stage. Richard remonstrated the cops over the P.A. system and told the audience, "If you wanna jump up, jump up. If you wanna dance—dance. The Madison Square Garden knows that you're young. Let it all hang out—Oooh, my soul!" He sang nine of his biggest Specialty hits, plus "Midnight Special" and a powerful driving version of the Beatles' "I Saw Her Standing There." The crowd was part of the show, dancing in the aisles, singing along, jiving, and running up to the stage to get autographs.*

● In the second show of the evening, I got my band playing "When the Saints Go Marching In." I sent them out among the audience, up one aisle and down the other, shaking hands with the people. I climbed onto the piano and threw my shoes and diamond ring to the people crowding around with their hands in the air. And they fought over them. I really had no intention of throwing my six-hundred-dollar cape to the crowd, but I was pretending to do it, and teasing them by swinging it around my head, when someone grabbed a corner. They pulled and I pulled. I only just managed to avoid being dragged off the piano and the stage! That was one of the times I was scared of an audience. It's an easy thing to get into.

*They say good things come in threes. First, the Cocoanut*

155

*Grove engagement; second, the TV national coverage; and then the break they had been waiting for—Richard's first hit single in thirteen years. The song, "Freedom Blues," was written by Richard, and came from his first session with Reprise, a subsidiary of Warner Brothers. It appeared on the* Billboard *charts in May and stayed there for nine weeks. The album was called* The Rill Thing, *and Richard went back on the road to promote it.*

● We stayed at the Waldorf Astoria, in New York, for about a month, with Warners picking up the tab. Angel flew in with some other girls and we had a wonderful time. I was getting into drugs by this time, smoking marijuana and using a little cocaine. We used to have orgies all the time. Whenever I was in L.A. we'd book a suite at the Carolina Pines Motel, on La Brea and Sunset. We just let it all hang out. All the hookers, hustlers, and dealers hung around there. I had special people I'd ask along, like Keith Winslow, the best valet I ever had, a guy named Chick, and another guy named Little Jessie. And girls. All kinds of girls. I'd be the one who'd get it started. I'd say, "Everybody take off your clothes. Take 'em all off right now," and sometimes if they were a little slow I would pull them off myself and just lay 'em down. They'd be so shocked they wouldn't know what to say. And they wouldn't know what had happened till it was all over. Some of them girls would be afraid of me, y'know with my look an' all. They were scared to death, thinking, "I don't know what this man's gonna do in this room. Keep the door open so I can run outa here, cos he looks as though he's gonna attack any time!" Some of them would leave before the action started. They'd leave and come back tomorrow, cos they wanted to know what had happened. There were some that even came back in two days. But they all liked to do things...

156

KEITH WINSLOW: I first met Richard when I was a little boy. My mother taught him at Oakwood College. I don't remember too much about him then, but I do remember that he brought his pink and yellow Cadillacs onto the campus.

The next time I met him was nearly ten years later, in San Francisco. He was performing in a very small club on Broadway. He was very nice. He asked me if I was interested in coming out on the road as his valet. I'd just come to live in San Francisco and had a brand-new job, so I declined. Then, about January 1969, I was with a friend on vacation in Reno. We saw on a poster that Richard was appearing in Lake Tahoe, at Harrah's Club. I called him and he seemed glad to hear from me. He said he wanted to pray with us, and could we come over to Lake Tahoe. We didn't have any money and were on our way back to San Francisco; but he told us not to worry, just to catch a taxicab and he'd pay the fare. We went up to his hotel and we spent the afternoon talking to Richard about music and things. Then a couple of girls came up and my friend left because he was a little bit reluctant to be in there with the girls. I don't know why. I decided to stay and that was the first time I had what I guess you'd call an orgy with Richard.

Richard and the girls went to screw, and he told me that if I wanted to get some I could. So I went on and got some. Both of the girls. So he told me that I'd be good on the road and if I ever wanted a job it would be one hundred fifty dollars a week, all expenses paid, to start off as his valet. I told him I would think about it and he gave me money to get back to San Francisco.

In late February Richard called me and said he was on his way to Vancouver, Canada, Isy's Supper Club. He offered me the job again, to start off as valet and work up to road manager. I said, "Okay, fine, I will come on the road."

157

In those days Richard was being managed by J. W. Alexander, who was very sharp. What I had to do was stay in contact with the airport, keep Richard's clothes clean, his hair done, make sure everything was by him, and pretty much not to leave him by himself. I started staying in the room with Richard, always a double suite, so I could make sure his food and everything was taken care of.

I guess the first thing you learned on the road was that show business is a nighttime business. We stayed up all night and did most of our sleeping in the daytime. Richard was also very leery of people being up and around in his room during the daytime. Most of the time he stayed up till about ten and then we'd all pass out together.

The second thing you learned on the road is that nobody's girlfriend is nobody's girlfriend except the one back at home. Any given time a girl can choose you or you choose her and they'll switch up on you. In Canada there was a little girl called Martina who kinda chose me. One of Richard's best friends, Lottie the Body, said that I wasn't experienced enough and I needed to be taught something. So we had a couple of sets with Lottie, who was the first person I had met who wanted to do everything!

Well, we left Vancouver and played several one-nighters on the way to work in the East. We went from Canada through Michigan, to Chicago, and then to Fort Wayne, Indiana. That was the first place I ever left a bag behind. I left the bag at the hotel and had to go all the way back to get it. The bag was still there so I was okay. But I got a twenty-five-dollar fine for leaving the thing. That was Richard's way of controlling musicians. Everybody got fined for doing things that were wrong.

While we were in Fort Wayne this young lady came to the hotel to deliver some food to us. She had a boyfriend who wanted to play trumpet with Richard's band, so Richard had her come back after the show. While her boyfriend was in one room rehearsing with the band, Richard and I had sex with the girl in another room. When Richard left the room to go talk to the band members, the girl got up and closed the door. She got back down with me and Richard got mad at us.

There wasn't but a couple or three guys could get into Richard's room when he was partying. They were Wade Jackson, Eddie Fletcher, and Glen Willings. All of them musicians that had been with him for a time. The horn players, Tricky Lofton and Boogie Daniels, and a couple of other guys were in and out. We did orgies and got high every night after the show—never during the day or before the show.

In Detroit, Little Richard ran into an old girlfriend named Gloria. Gloria says she was the first one that ever gave Richard some pussy. They were really girlfriend and boyfriend. Then Richard sent for a girl named Diane, who was a dancer and singer. She ran around with us for a while and did Richard's hair. She also showed me how to roll Richard's hair myself. So I started doing Richard's hair as well as taking care of his clothes. Diane stayed with us for quite a while. She called me her student. We used to have orgies every day. She used to masturbate in front of everyone and she always wanted to race. Everybody wanted to race. Sex in those days was incredible. I think nowadays it's gotten slower!

This might seem strange after what I've been saying, but Richard has always been a very religious person. He carried a Bible with him all the time. You see, he kept all his important addresses stuck inside the book. Every now and then he'd leave one in a hotel, and we'd lose contact with everyone for about two or three months. Then we'd have to start all over again when we got to the next town, build up the addresses and stuff. I guess religion was the one thing that has always inspired Richard. He believed in God strongly, was continually praying, and continually trying to inspire people toward religion. All his musicians would tease Richard about his being spiritual. But they all appreciated how he kept his troubles down all the time.

It was almost like a miracle the way Richard handled situations. Even when he got angry, he was always able to keep a level head. Like the day of the Los Angeles earthquake.

We were supposed to go on into Los Angeles because some people had called us and sent limousines to the airport. We got to L.A. about eight o'clock, partied all night, and in the morning the earthquake happened. There were several music people in the hotel, like Norman Thrasher of the Temptations, and Smokey Robinson. Of course when this happened everybody got out. I'll never forget how Richard went back into the room and got his Bible.

We had a lot of good times, but Richard, as I say, was still more spiritual than anything else. We'd spend half the time talking about God and religion and what we could all do to make the world a better place to live in. And the other half of the time, we'd be just sitting there humming out tunes and coming up with ideas for music.

*As the heady weeks of 1970 went by it seemed as if events were conspiring to keep Richard in the public eye. He appeared at the Olympic Auditorium in Los Angeles, headlining a show that included California acid-rock heroes Country Joe and the Fish.*

● By the time we got on, the place was in an uproar. The authorities were paranoid after Altamont and they had bussed in about fifteen hundred policemen. Something had happened to cause a delay, and the kids were getting frantic. They were ready for me to come out. With all the publicity I had been getting, they knew I was gonna put on the show of all shows.

And the place was full of police. The band was really pounding it out. I think Truman Thomas was on organ, Bobby Forte on sax, Eddie Fletcher on bass, Wade Jackson on drums, and we had had a whole lot of new equipment, amps and things flown in to really blast this place off the block. Everything was so intense. The crowd did everything I asked 'em to—clapped along, shouted, and sang—and by the third number I'd already thrown my shoes and jacket out to them. The band went out into the audience, then came back on stage.

It was about midway through the show and the crowd was going berserk—about as high as you can get, you know what I mean? Any more and it would have been an earthquake. So I don't know why I did this, but it was something I always did—I asked for two people to come up on stage and dance for me. All right, I got two, I got four, twelve, twenty-four, there must have been a coupla hundred people up there on that man-made stage, dancin' and stompin' and rumpin'. I was on top of the piano and the people were jumping up and down with me and it just started rocking.

The next thing you know there's this huge hole appears in the middle of the stage. Everything standing on the stage slid into it—organ, amplifiers, drums, people, everything. It was just like the earth opening up. And even while the stage was collapsing more people were trying to climb onto it! Everybody thought the piano had fallen on top of me. So they ran up and pulled me out of the hole.

I wasn't hurt. In fact only about four people had little injuries. Eddie Fletcher was at the bottom of the pile. He messed his back up but he wouldn't go to the hospital. We were appearing at Lake Tahoe the following night and he didn't want to miss out on nothing like that! I claimed I was hurt because a lot of people were suing me over it.

People weren't really injured. They just wanted some money...some of them. At the time I told a big lie. A marshmelon lie. I said I had a broken wrist, a deep gash in my neck, a broken leg, three broken ribs, and a fractured skull.

BILL HOUSE: I played lead guitar with Richard's band for several years, up to 1975 (A lot of years, but I remember my first time vividly). At nine o'clock I was on stage playing the opening riff to "Lucille." Suddenly this *madman* comes jumping out of the curtains a few inches away from me, all in mirrors, teeth and eyes flashing! What an incredible way to make an impression. We played the songs the fastest I've ever heard them. Everything double tempo. He was determined to put on a good show every time. For a guitarist the songs played were never complex, but it was so physically demanding. The tempos were so fast I remember my hand cramping up. It just couldn't move anymore. But the drummers were the guys that really had a hard time of it. Richard went through a lot of drummers. He'd just wear them out. The way he would cue the drummer was "Watch my shoulder, drummer!" Not really the best way to be conducted!

Playing with Richard was like a cram course in show business. He was totally spontaneous. You never knew what he was going to do from one day to the next. You could usually tell what you were in for by how wide his eyes were when he came out onto the stage. You might be dead tired, but he'd leap out with his eyes this big. He had one of the wildest looks you've ever seen. He didn't look drug-abused, just wild. He would be about to wear you to a frazzle. He'd just play you into the ground, and then he'd go on for another half-hour. Amazing. I don't think I've ever seen anyone as athletic as he was. He'd lose about six pounds a show, just with sweating. He worked so hard. The only artist who comes anywhere near him for working and not being afraid to move is Springsteen. But Richard worked much harder. And his piano playing! Have you ever tried to play piano like that? It'll give you cramps. It's next to impossible. It's one thing to do it for half a song, but he would do it for song after song, show after show. I've never seen anyone who could do that.

Richard never distinguished between a club and a really big hall. He had a routine where we'd play "When the Saints Go Marching In" and he would say to the sax player, "Okay, jump out in the audience, man." Well, this was okay in a club, but when the stage was fifteen feet high it was a problem. Well, here's Fred Clarke in the middle of a solo, and there's Richard moving toward him shouting "C'mon, c'mon, jump." And he pushed him. And Fred's flying! He was playing all the way down! Fortunately he landed on a bunch of people and they caught him. He got right up and walked through the crowd. He had to come all the way around the building to get back up on the stage. Fred had played with Freddy Gardner's touring band in the fifties and with people like Muddy Waters, Memphis Slim, and John Mayall. He had such a strong ego he pretended he hadn't been hurt. But you could see him walking around all the next week limping, saying, "That don't bother me."

And Richard would never slow down his work rate. Denver now, Denver is at high elevation. But rather than tame the show down, he would ingest large amounts of bottled oxygen between sets to keep his heart going. I said we did the first show at double speed, well, the next show was *triple* speed. He just had to return and better himself. On the road he was very quiet in the daytimes, preceding the shows. It was always like he felt he owed so much to the audience. It was almost like a religion to him, you know. Like he stored up energy all day long and it would burst out on the stage at night.

The care he put into every show was unbelievable. He'd actually rehearse his band every day. It would drive the band crazy, cos we knew the songs so well we could play them in our sleep. The gigs were physically demanding, but he would get us out there every day, whether we'd been on a plane for ten hours or whatever. We'd have to play "Lucille" and "Rip It Up" and everything else over and over again until it was right for him.

The show was very important. You never tuned onstage, cos that was bad. You tuned before you went on. Whether you were going out of tune during a show or not, that was not as important as keeping the energy on and keeping the pace going. There's nothing worse than going ding-ding-ding-ding tuning up. Richard taught me probably everything I know about being onstage. And you were always on time, of course. And no drinking. Absolutely no drinking.

The regimentation was kept up with a system of fines for various things: One of the guitar players showed up in black tennis shoes one time and Richard fined him fifty dollars.

I think in a way Richard was trying to be a mentor to us in the band. Morally. He really did keep us in control. As a result, I don't remember anyone getting into trouble on the road, which is pretty amazing, because it was a pretty motley crew at times.

As for the sex parties he talks about, I never saw any of that. There were a lot of people who wanted to hang out with him. But, as I remember it, he would just go back to his room and sit there. Sometimes I'd go back there and play country songs with him. Richard is an incredible country singer and he loves country music. He knows every Hank Williams song by heart. I never sensed homosexuality in Richard. I think if anyone was ever going to sense it, it would have been me. I was that close to him. And there was no tinge of that, ever. I think he was quite a voyeur. He liked to watch other people—but he always seemed pretty together to me, compared with other people

I've been on the road with. He seemed extraordinarily together. Extraordinarily moral. He really is a moral human being, the most Christ-like character I ever met by a long way. He just is what he is and nothing more. I've known him about ten years and he was always an incredibly kind human being. And that's pretty unusual for a person that important.

It's amazing that he's still alive, living the Rock 'n' Roll life-style for as long as he did. I think that shows how moderate he must have been. He couldn't have been as wild as he says he was and still be alive. Hendrix died and Janis Joplin died and they'd only been doing it for a few years. He'd been doing it for so many years.

● I never know what I'm going to do onstage. We had a regular show, but there was nothing planned like most groups have a set act. I didn't know, the band didn't know. They just had to follow me. I worked according to the people, the impact.

I felt that my singing was like...well, like Billy Graham giving a message. I gave a message in song to help people— to help men, to help women, to help young boys, young girls, to know the way. There was always that little beam of light, of love. I was glad to be back on the Rock 'n' Roll circuit so I could travel around and help bring that little happiness to them. It meant more than money to see those people happy. If a person is in it just for the money they're unreal. If you're in it to do a job and to help, money or no money, that's all there is. And that's what I wanted to do and that's what I did do.

I decided to come back and teach goodness in this business. To teach love, because music is the universal language. We are God's bouquet, and through music we become one.

165

# Slippin' and Slidin'

Ⅰt started in the quiet gloom of a recording studio, at a long session, sandwiched between one-night stands that were three hundred miles apart. They were all tired. Drained. But time was money. So when the man laid the white powder on the table, they sniffed and found instant euphoria and the energy to do four more takes.

Back on the road, cocaine eased the fatigue along boring highways and, better yet, gave everyone a rush of raw energy for the gig. But coke is no joke. The pleasure became the problem—maintaining the habit, and fighting off the mood swings and facing the dark side of the come-downs.

As "Freedom Blues" climbed the charts, the Little Richard bandwagon rolled on, gathering speed by the day. TV exposure was his for the asking. He was never less than outrageous, even taking over Johnny Carson's sacred desk on the Tonight show. Then, in what was considered the supreme accolade of the rock establishment, he made the cover of Rolling Stone magazine as the subject of a perceptive six-page interview by writer David Dalton entitled "Little Richard, Child of God."

Artistic and popular acceptance on this level assured Richard of a good living as a performer forever. But he was coming to depend more and more on a snort of cocaine for *the sparkling energy his shows and TV appearances demanded of him.*

*The drug, combined with record-breaking runs at Caesar's Palace in Las Vegas, and Harrah's in Reno and Tahoe, had put Richard on a new high. He opened a show at New York's Wollman Rink with one of his wildest displays ever. He finished the set dripping with sweat, clad only in a towel. Visually it was very exciting. But he sang only three songs—"Lucille," "The Girl Can't Help It," and "Rip It Up"—and went offstage ignoring the shouts for more. He didn't even sing his current number-one hit, "Freedom Blues." The second show followed the same pattern. For the first time in his career, he was criticized for not giving his best in concert.*

*Coincidentally, rumors began circulating in New York that he had stomach cancer. Richard confirmed this to the press. The story went around the world.*

● I had been working, working. My life-style was taking its toll. I was drinking and taking drugs and partying all the time. I felt really bad with my stomach, so I went to a clinic in New York. They told me there was a strong possibility that I had cancer. The press got hold of the story. But when I got home to L.A. and went into a clinic there, they found that it wasn't that at all. It was all brought on by strain and overworking. I believe the Lord spared me then. He was trying to tell me something, but I wasn't listening at that time. I told the papers about it. I guess they didn't think that was as good a story as my having had cancer. It never ran and people never got to read it. Mother wrote to all my fans in England, so at least they knew the truth there.

*The royal image took precedence over everything. Richard appeared in public with gaudy robes, heavy makeup, and elaborate hairdos. Diners in the best restaurants would watch in amazement as the management cleared space at the choicest table and stood bowing as a crowned and bejeweled Richard, seated on an ornate throne, was carried in by sweating flunkies.*

*Warner Brothers cashed in on the image with an album entitled* The King of Rock 'n' Roll. *"The latest from the greatest" screamed the* Billboard *ads, showing the album cover, an enthroned and berobed Richard kissed by the setting sun. Almost unanimously the critics gave the album rave reviews. But the radio stations failed to give it the country-wide airplay needed to take it into the top fifty.*

● They wouldn't play my stuff, you know? I think they were afraid that I would hit. There was still a lot of prejudice going on. A lot of people in management didn't like it cos I was a white attraction. If I'd been a black attraction, like James Brown or Otis Redding, it would have been different. I think I scared them. I would have had the same stature as the Beatles and Mick Jagger. They'd let some of the songs through. A few black stations played them, but I didn't record for blacks. Blacks didn't want my sound, you know?

Racism has always been so heavy against me in America. Even when I was doing Las Vegas, they somehow never wanted to give me the money they gave the other artists. Yet they all came to see me—Debbie Reynolds, Ann-Margret, Glen Campbell, Elvis Presley, Tom Jones, Dinah Shore, all the top people. And I believe racism was at the head of it all. I was not owned by no white person or by a white management concern. Everybody else would go down and get their check, but mine was always delayed, held up, or something. They'd give everybody else a suite, they wouldn't give me no suite. I had to start demanding. They'd give limousines to all the other artists, but they wouldn't give me no limousine. They'd want me to catch a cab. They were really nasty to me and that was pure racism. I've seen them bring artists that wasn't as popular as me and treat them like a star, even on television shows. An artist of my stature, I should have had my own show. I should have been in commercials. I should have been in movies. But they didn't do it because of racism.

*The pace of Richard's life got even hotter if that was possible. Rock revival shows, TV appearances, and one-night stands crowded together in his mind like a fairground scene from a speeding carousel. And then Richard and Bumps split up again.*

● My fame and acclaim were so wide, I decided to form my own company and bring my brothers in on things, especially Marquette, as a CPA. Robert and Peyton had been working with me for a long time arranging my traveling and personal appearances. I thought it was time for them to move into the business side. We called the company Bud Hole Incorporated because my daddy's nickname had been Bud, and Robert thought it was catchy. It sounded as if you were saying "butt." I didn't like that much, but I went along with it.

I made sure that one of the Bud Hole subsidiaries was a music-publishing company. I put Peyton in charge and called it Peyton Publishing. Robert became my personal manager and Marquette handled the Bud Hole offices and organization.

BUMPS BLACKWELL: I was out. I quit. I had just negotiated a deal with Nader which would have given Richard ten thousand dollars a night for three nights' work. Four weekends a month. That was a hundred and twenty thousand dollars a month and a million in ten months. It would have been his best deal ever, but it fell through.

*Over in England plans were being made for the biggest music festival ever. It was to be held in London's Wembley Stadium, which is twice the size of New York's Shea Stadium. Richard had equal top billing with Jerry Lee Lewis and Chuck Berry. The media had hyped a feud among the three great legends of Rock 'n' Roll. The concert was held to decide who had the right to the title—the King of Rock 'n' Roll!*

*The hassles started as soon as Richard landed at the London airport. He had engaged his former sax player Lee Allen and guitarist George Davis to augment his young backing band. There was trouble over their work permits as they had no formal contracts to show. After an hour-and-a-quarter delay matters were sorted out and Richard and his band drove straight to a press conference at Wembley Stadium. Richard's pancake makeup and bright-green outfit, a topless trouser-suit with supporting straps and puffed sleeves, like a half-finished creation of a demented Dior, attracted a lot of attention from photographers. But most of the media men present wanted to talk about the "feud" with Chuck Berry. Richard was not about to disappoint them.*

● There wasn't *nobody* topping the bill over Little Richard, and the "old black Berry" had to believe it. Why, it would've been Ann-Margret being over Queen Elizabeth. I was the undisputed King of Rock 'n' Roll and that's what the whole world knew.

*Richard slept late the following morning in his suite at the Cumberland Hotel following an appearance on BBC-TV's* Late Night Line-Up *program. When he awoke the hassles continued. A rumor that all was not well with the*

170

*show and that his cash might not be forthcoming sent him
hot-footing over to the offices of the promoters, Ark Concerts. Ark claimed that the agreed advance had been paid
on the thirty-five-thousand-dollar fee that Richard was to
receive for the Wembley show—his biggest paycheck to date
for a single performance—but Richard insisted that he had
not received it.*

● I lost patience with those guys. I told them I'd come
there to let people enjoy themselves, and not to get heisted.
I let them know I wouldn't go onstage till it all got sorted
out.

It was finally settled at 4 A.M. on the day of the concert.
They gave the cash to me in pounds and I packed them in
my shorts and in my socks. I added pounds to my pounds.

The promoters had told me that ticket sales were a bit
sticky. I told them I would start a Cassius Clay–Sonny
Liston–type feud with Chuck Berry. It was all done tongue
in cheek, just to publicize the show, cos Chuck's my friend.
It worked. But it turned some people against me. When we
arrived at the stadium I felt that there was some bad vibes
in the air. The treatment we got at the gate wasn't the
sweetest, and the dressing-room facilities weren't fixed up
for me like they would do for someone like Mick Jagger.

*The concert, which had been going since mid-day in
beautiful sunny weather, really started to rock when Bo
Diddley came on and pulverized the hundred-thousand-
plus people with his beat. Whole families and even the ice-
cream and program sellers were dancing. Jerry Lee Lewis
followed after a long delay, getting the crowd on his side as
easily as if he was entertaining them in his own living
room. After the Killer's superbly professional performance,
a party mood pervaded the stadium, with beer and wine
flowing freely and the more hippie-oriented sections pass-*

171

*ing joints around. Bill Haley and the Comets came up next and surprised everyone with the excitement generated by hits like "Rock Around the Clock" and "See You Later Alligator." The whole arena became a mass of dancing people. Haley was brought back three times to play "Rock Around the Clock" again and again.*

*The sun was beginning to sink, bathing London in a warm orange glow as Richard was introduced. He came out in a yellow suit, the top half covered with mirrors, and received a tremendous ovation. The crowd roared their approval before one note was played or sung.*

*As the applause continued Richard acknowledged the fans with his characteristic peace signs.*

● I believe that somebody had it in for me that night because I said I was the King of Rock 'n' Roll, which is the undisputed truth. When I went on stage the microphones were really high for the other stars, but for me the microphones were down. The lights were down too and didn't show my flamboyant dress with my mirrors and all the other stuff. The microphones were very bad. The sound was terrible in its entirety. The guitar amps, the bass amps, the piano, you couldn't hear nothing, and I believe that someone had it in for me. I had said I was the King, you know, and a lot of people thought to themselves, Well, we'll fix *him*. It was just one of those things which I pray to God will never happen again.

I'm not taking it away from the other artists. They were all tremendous. Jerry Lee Lewis was fantastic and Chuck Berry was out of sight. I was glad to see Bo Diddley getting it across. He's never really had the publicity that should have been given him and he got his chance to get his little spark in, you know. It was beautiful. Bill Haley, too. He was fantastic. He's beautiful. One of the pioneers.

A lot of people didn't know we were doing a movie at Wembley during the concert. The promoter said, "You've got three more minutes"—can you imagine making love and somebody telling you you got another minute? So I went out in the audience for the cameras and the people grabbed me. I had to stay offstage and I didn't get a chance to sing all the songs I wanted to sing.

EDDIE FLETCHER: I was heartbroken. The show was the first we put on while we were in Europe. The sound system went out. I don't know if it was deliberate or just an accident, but it sure messed things up. Richard is a hard-working entertainer. There wasn't one time throughout the ten years I was playing with him that he left the stage and he wasn't dripping wet with sweat—and his band.

DRUMMER ROBIN RUSSELL: I never played so hard in my life as I did that night for Richard.

LEE ALLEN: When all those people rushed forward, I became a little desperate. I was just a skinny feller trying to get away from the crowd, and when you see all that many people coming at you, you don't know just what to do. I just blew my horn and soloed all the way through the chaos.

*In frustration, Richard left the stage by the steps at one side. He was met by a mass of grappling fans and press photographers who pushed him against a wall. Someone grabbed his necklace and pulled it off. The whole scene was being filmed.*

*These events on the side of the stage were apparent only to those close to the stage. People at the far end of the stadium, who could see the performers only as tiny manikin-size dots, heard the sound go off and thought Richard had left the stage, so they started booing.*

*Richard came back onstage as repairs to the microphone had been completed, and concluded his act with "Long Tall*

173

Sally." Accompanied by Bumps, he made his way to his dressing room. A few moments later Chuck Berry came into the room and put his arm around him. He suggested a jam session onstage and Richard said, "When we get back to the States."

Berry took no chances, insisting on a thorough sound check before he went on in front of the tense crowd, who started to boo and demand as soon as he walked onstage. His first number won them over. However, he was in the middle of a classic set when an amazing thing happened. A bowler-hatted, pin-stripe-suited official of Greater London Council came onstage and told Chuck, who had just finished his famous "duck walk," that he was going to switch off the stadium's power because the show was running overtime. Ever in control, Berry informed the crowd of this and asked everybody to light a match. Within seconds the stadium was a sea of small flames as the last rays of the sun left the sky to the wonderful sound of Chuck Berry's guitar. An everlasting memory.

The press, which had widely and gleefully reported Richard's braggadocio in the preconcert interviews, went to town on him, reporting that the whole stadium had booed him. Major Sunday papers carried headlines like "Chuck Berry Bowls Over Little Richard" and "Chuck Is the King," etc. Whatever the reason for the Wembley fiasco, Richard's image was seriously damaged in Europe. The British popular press attempted to do to him what they had done in 1958 to Jerry Lee Lewis, when he arrived in the U.K. with a new bride—his fourteen-year-old cousin.

The film of the concert, which was shown in the U.S. under the title The London Rock 'n' Roll Show, showed Little Richard's performance dwarfing those of Haley, Bo Diddley, and Berry, though he does look tired. His piano playing comes over tremendously.

After playing a date the following night at a new night-

174

spot in Nottingham, showing that his act had lost none of its fire and impact, Richard and his band set off for the Continent. The tour was to have taken in top venues in Europe's major cities. But a clause in the Foulk Brothers' Wembley contract had stipulated that none of these concerts could be advertised before the Wembley event. When the European promoters found this out, they canceled their shows. They felt a few days' publicity was not enough to gather sufficient crowds for such big bookings. With these venues lost to them, Richard and the band wandered around Europe like a lost caravan in the desert, playing only small halls and clubs.

Back in the United States Richard's round of hectic touring and TV appearances continued. Although the Wembley incident had affected his reputation in Europe, it had no effect at all in the States. His living-legend status was still secure and he was able to command fees of up to ten thousand dollars per appearance on the concert circuit.

In November Richard restored his connection with his old friend Quincy Jones, going to the Record Plant in Los Angeles to record two songs for a movie called $ (retitled The Heist for European release). Written and directed by Richard Brooks, with music composed, arranged, and conducted by Quincy Jones, it starred Warren Beatty, Goldie Hawn, Gert Frobe, and Scott Brady. Richard sings the main theme song, "Money Is," and also a gimmicky up-tempo number called "Do It—to It." Richard's delivery suits the occasion perfectly. On the session were bass-man Chuck Rainey, David T. Walker, Billy Preston, and cajun fiddler Doug Kershaw, with other vocals by Roberta Flack.

Richard's dissatisfaction with the material Warner Brothers had come up with and the company's lack of interest in promoting his disks brought a parting of the ways.

● I left Reprise because I felt that the producers didn't

175

have me at heart. *The Rill Thing* was a good album. All the Reprise albums were, but they didn't push them. It was almost like someone had said "Hold Richard back." So I left them. It was not mutual. I went to Reprise because I felt the company could do something. Mo Austin, who was president of the company, seemed to really have my interests at heart. His son and I were very dear friends, but I think the producers and people who worked there thought I wasn't their main singer.

A lot of record companies wanted me to do certain things that I wouldn't do. Warner Brothers wanted me to record a terrible version of "Midnight Hour" right after it became a big hit for Wilson Pickett. I wouldn't do it. I was as good as, or better than, any of those fellers in the top ten, but I couldn't hit because I wasn't with the right people. I might have been with the right record company, but I didn't have the right producer. The producer doesn't necessarily have to be the most talented, but he does have to be in the clique. When the right name appears on the sleeve, it's a signal.

I would record a song that was good, and if a white boy didn't produce it, it wouldn't get any airplay. I wouldn't go along with the system. I refused. I would have let a white guy produce it, if it didn't make no difference. But it wasn't like that. If a record was produced by a black man it wouldn't get played. I didn't like that. If a man was good it was all the same to me. If he's black or if he's white, whatever, I don't care. So I refused to go along with it and I insisted on using the producer who I thought would get the best result.

I found out very fast that the radio stations *are* controlled. And television *is* controlled. It's almost like families. It's a thing going on, you see. Certain people are let on television to be seen, and certain people they don't want. They won't let them on cos they're not in their little clique.

176

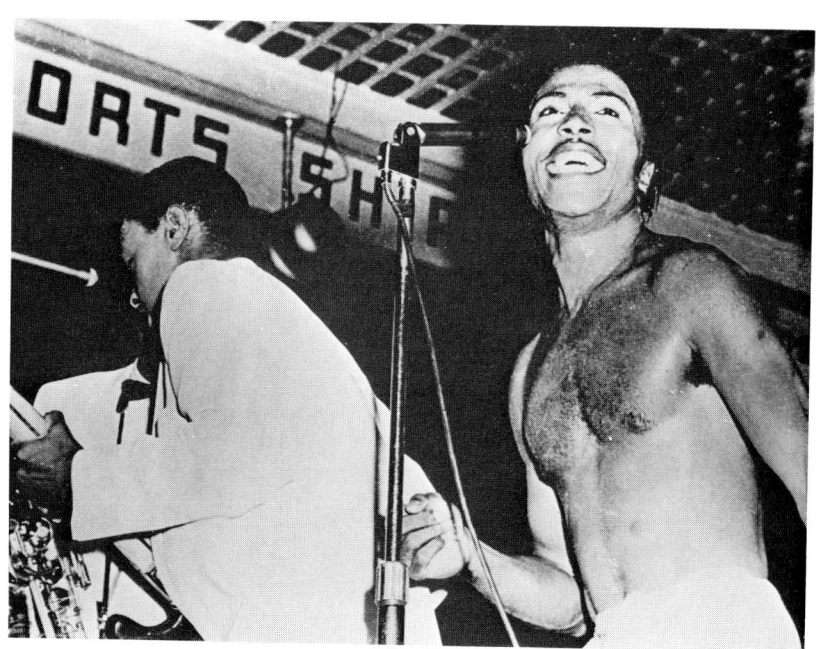

Brisbane, Australia, 1957. The King of Rock 'n' Roll sheds his robes and
retires after this record-breaking tour.

1

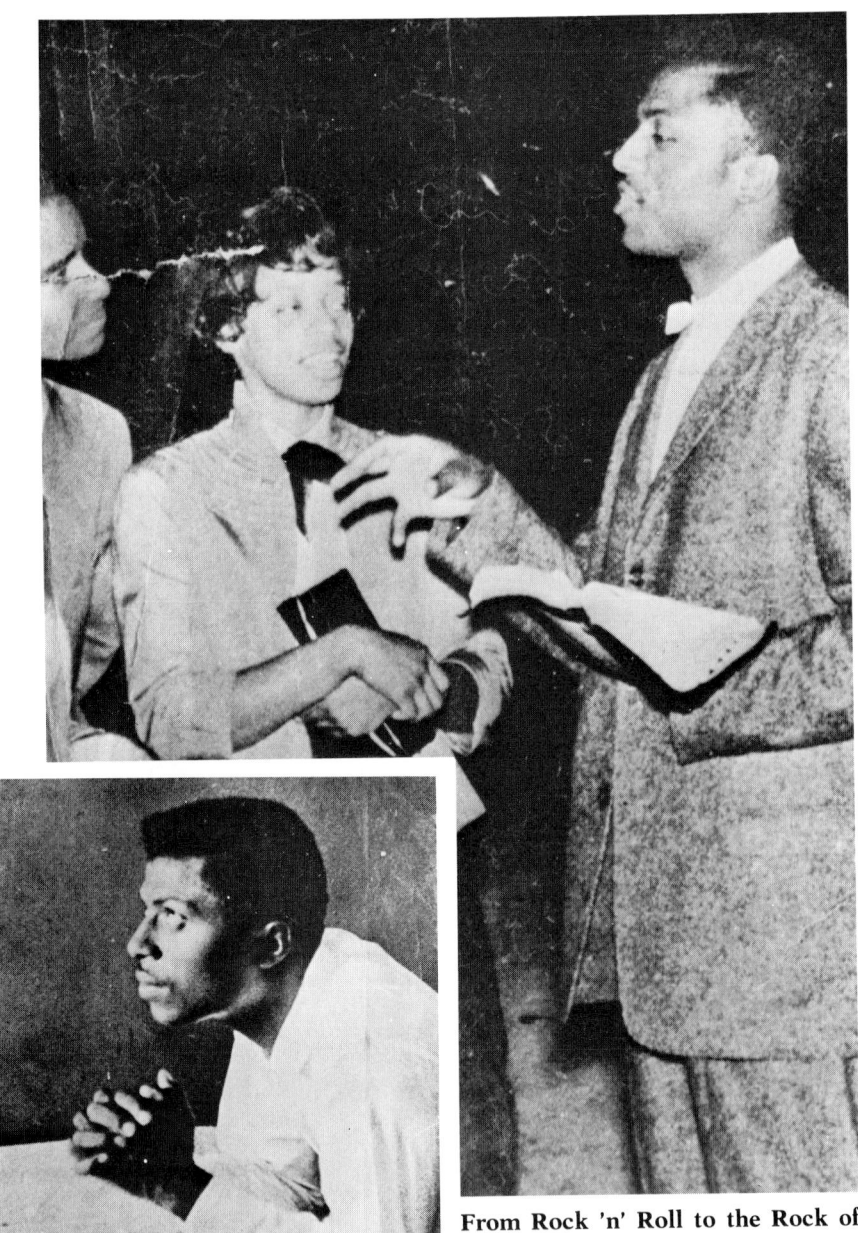

From Rock 'n' Roll to the Rock of Ages. Born again, Richard spreads the Gospel.

Little Richard, the preacher man, outside his home in California, 1958.

Pressing his new-found sounds.

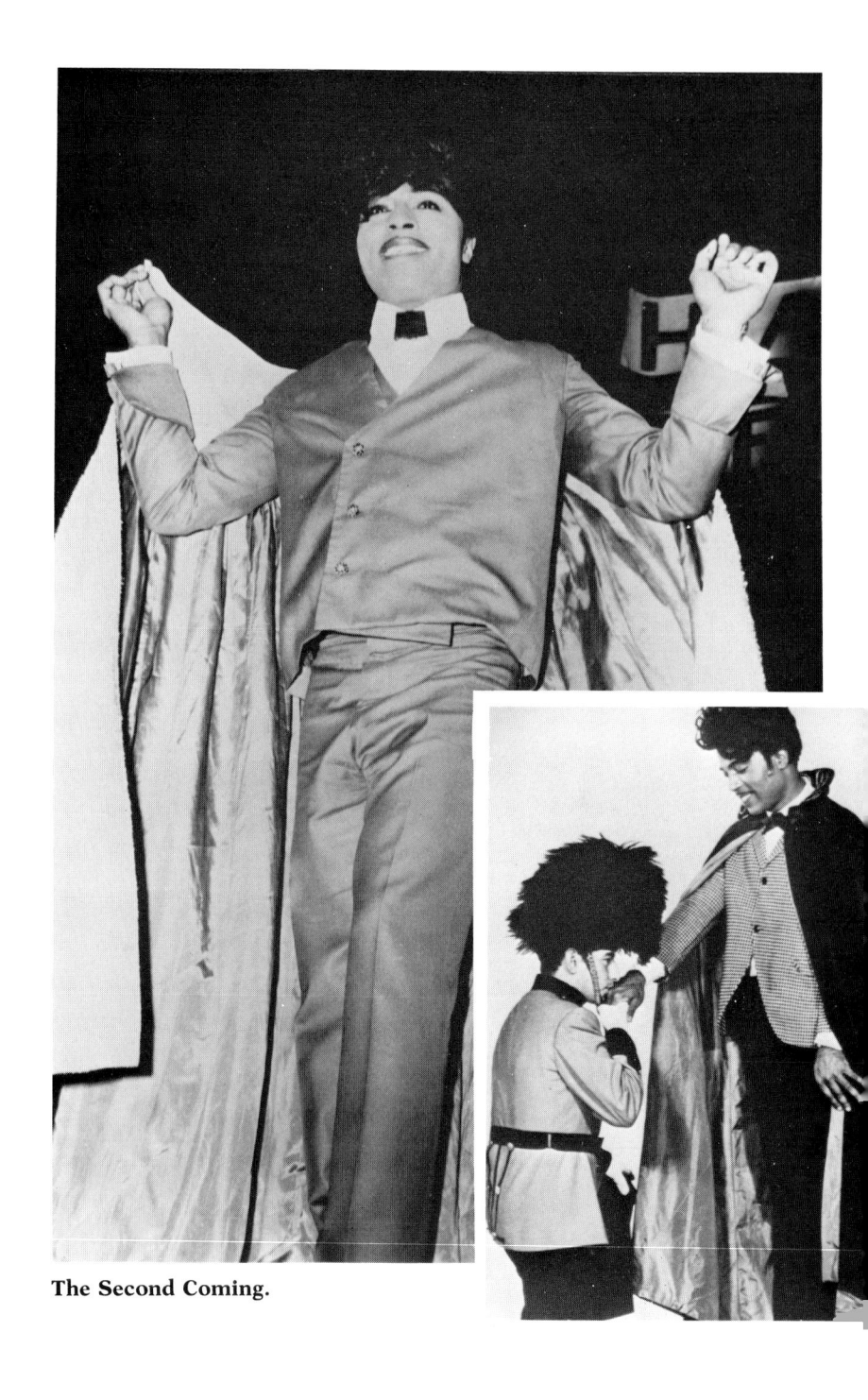

The Second Coming.

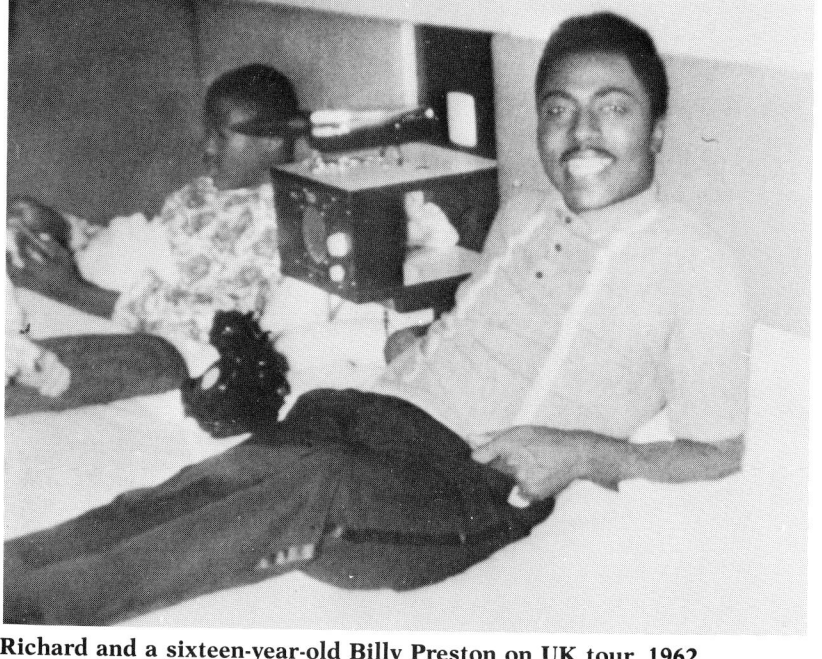

Backstage with Sam Cooke on UK tour, 1962.

Richard and a sixteen-year-old Billy Preston on UK tour, 1962.

The Boys from Liverpool pay homage to the King.

The 1963 Granada TV spectacular, "It's Little Richard," costarred The Shirelles. More than 60,000 letters poured in from thrilled fans.

Bo Diddley and Richard tuning up backstage. The opening act that night in 1963 was a mean young band known as The Rolling Stones.

Jimi Hendrix, Little Richard, and The King Curtis Band at the Apollo Theater, 1965. A night the Stars came out!

Little Richard and The Royal Company in Sacramento, California, 1966.

9

10

Raising the roof at the Oasis Club in Manchester, England, 1964.

**Little Richard in 1969.**

Happy Birthday
To The King
Of Rock & Roll
Little Richard & Ivan

Raving rockers kiss Richard's feet in Hamburg, Germany.

At the Wembley Stadium concert in England, an exhilarated Richard acknowledges an adoring crowd.

**Jerry Lee Lewis, Bumps Blackwell, and Richard. Modern Times.**

**H. B. Barnum, wailing sax player; Charles White; and J. W. Alexander, Richard's old friend and Sam Cooke's manager.**

"The most exciting moment of my life was appearing on the same stage as Little Richard."

*From left to right:* Little Richard, Stevie Wonder's mother, Stevie Wonder, and Chuck Berry at the Grammy Awards.

The Quasar.

Rock music may be just a bunch of noise to some people, but to me it was the music of love. My music brought togetherness, happiness. My music broke barriers that had seemed unbreakable. It drove tunnels through walls that no one had been able to get through. My music did that. It was called "race music" till I came on the scene. I'm grateful for that.

But it's still a racial thing. Even today in 1983, on MTV, the videos are 90 percent white groups... mediocre at best. Even a star like Michael Jackson has trouble getting airplay unless he teams up with Paul McCartney ("Say, Say, Say"). And radio stations are the worst offenders. Radio is race-biased targeting certain markets. If you turn on the radio and there's a black artist singing you immediately associate with disco. It's crazy, but that's what's going on here. The *Billboard* "Hot 100" is like a Ku Klux Klan meeting. You do have a few black records in the top one hundred, but they're just easy-listening kind of stuff for the most part. It's such an unhealthy thing.

*Richard was able to hit the spot nearly every time he appeared live in concert, but he just couldn't find the right formula in the recording studio. The big hits remained out of reach. And that was where the real money lay. Touring brought in the ready cash, but after everyone had been paid off—the drivers, the road crew, the airlines, the girls, the drug dealers—there was often little left to maintain the standard of living that Richard was getting used to. True, the big concerts, such as the Nader shows, brought in a lot of money, but the bigger the payoff the bigger the parties, the bigger the numbers of hangers-on, and the bigger the cocaine tab.*

EDDIE FLETCHER: These would not necessarily be groupies. I'm talking about your top nurses, doctors, your top newspaper writers, the people who're in heavy power. These people loved to be around Richard, and once they made contact, sorta broke the barrier, we couldn't get rid of them. They would just want to stay with us. Here we are traveling all over the country putting on shows, working, y'know, and we got people just neglecting work. I've heard doctors say, "I don't think I'll go in the hospital this week. I'll just travel back East with y'all."

● We were about to start a tour and we needed some money. So Bumps and me got a deal for one album with an advance of ten thousand dollars from Kent Modern. We went into the studio and did it in one night. I did material we had worked out together. I prefer recording at night, my voice is in better shape then.

*The single from the session was "In the Name." The album was called* Little Richard Right Now! *It was issued as a low-budget LP with no promotion, relying for sales purely on Richard's name.*
*The film* Let the Good Times Roll *was released in April. A colorful documentary of the Richard Nader rock revival shows, it was made up of footage from the Nassau Coliseum and the Cobo Hall concerts, mixed with 1950s newsreel items and skillfully chosen clips from vintage cult films like* The Wild One *and* I Was a Teenage Werewolf. *Richard's performance of "Lucille" at Cobo Hall is juxtaposed with the same number in the film* Mr. Rock 'n' Roll *in 1957. It gives an insight into Richard's preperformance neurosis: "That drummer is too loud. We colored people don't make that kinda noise," he complains about one of his (black) back-up percussionists. "Move the piano and amplifiers closer to the people. I wanna be closer to the people," he demands before going onstage. A polite stage manager explains that this is impossible because the leads are too*

*short. Richard repeats his demands over and over again. "I've gotta be closer to the people. It'll ruin my impact. It's a trick on me," he declares. His performance in the event was dynamic.* Let the Good Times Roll *used a multiscreen technique, thereby making it unsuitable for television, and so the movie didn't get much exposure. In fact, very few people have ever seen it in its entirety. A two-record soundtrack album was issued on the Bell label. Richard, changing record companies at whim, recorded two tracks for Charles Greene's L.A. company, Green Mountain. Richard said, "He never even gave me a green apple." They were penned by Jimmy Holiday and called "In the Middle of the Night," a soul number, and "Where Will I Find a Place to Sleep This Evening," in gospel-soul. The songs made the top ten on WWRL in New York, and reached number fifty-two on the* Record World *"Soul Singles" chart. They were also featured on the* Billboard *and* Cashbox *national charts. The disk was without a doubt one of Richard's finest. His singing is superbly controlled and the backing masterly. But the in-thing was soul and Richard's* King of Rock 'n' Roll *image kept preventing him from being accepted as a maker of contemporary music.*

*As a glamorous personality, though, his appearances were always sought after, and on August 16 Richard hosted the Saturday-night rock show,* Midnight Special, *introducing Kool and the Gang, Scandinavian rockers Golden Earring, Eddie Kendricks, Aerosmith, and Blood Sweat and Tears vocalist David Clayton Thomas. Richard sang five songs himself.*

● So many entertainers became addicts, you know. Sitting around the dressing rooms with the musicians, in the bedrooms with the guys, they want to try something different. Something to keep them on that high. They use all types of narcotics. They go from marijuana to angel dust;

179

from angel dust to barbiturates; to liquors; to cocaine; to heroin and acid. I was getting deeper and deeper into drugs. All I wanted was to have sex with the most beautiful women and get high.

My girlfriend, Angel, she wasn't my only girlfriend. I used to have lots of girls. We would go into a city and we would get three or four girls. We would get high and take off all our clothes and do anything—anything. I used to like to watch girls be with girls, you know? I thought that was the most beautiful thing I'd ever seen. I always looked for girls that wouldn't mind doing that. I'm telling you the truth! That was my thing. I would watch. In different cities I would have my people. In New York I had a girl called Chris and another girl called Evil. Angel would come in on these things. And they would bring people to me, cos they wanted to see them, too.

I was the one that was bold. The new people would be scared. But I would tell 'em "Hey, c'mon," you know, and that was it. I liked to see guys with girls, too. Guys that were really big.

Angel would do it, she never minded another man watching. She didn't mind having sex with two or three men while I was in the room. It didn't bother her. You didn't have to hide, cos she didn't care. That's the way it was.

So I had this boy with fifteen inches and I watched him turning into a homosexual through that. I tried to have sex with him in my rectum. It was like to have killed me. Oh, I think I know how women feel when they are having a baby. I thought my liver, my intestines, whatever, was going to come out.

I've watched him get people to be gay who weren't gay. But I never dealt with little boys. I was always against that. Young men, yes. But never little boys. Many homosexuals are attracted to children because they can control them. A man will want to have sex with a little boy because he can

180

make him do all the things he wants, all the way, and most men won't.

A man that will do everything that a homosexual wants is homosexual himself. But a little boy that's innocent, that has never had a woman in his life, the only thing he does is masturbate. Let's say a guy comes along and gets friendly with the little boy and says he's going to french him. The boy has never had that sensation before. He will fall in love with that guy and start hanging around with him. It's a thrill he never had. And that guy will take possession of the little boy. Control him. And he becomes a homosexual, too. That's what happened to me. It takes over your whole life. It demoralizes you. It got so that I didn't want to be around my own family because I knew that they wouldn't accept me.

# PART IV
# BACK IN THE ARMS
# OF THE LORD

# Call My Name

espite the high life, or because of it, there were definite signs in Richard's behavior that the ever-present conflict between the delights of the flesh and the needs of his soul were coming to the surface.

He cut a gospel track, "Try to Help Your Brother," which was released on the Mainstream label. Then he departed for a major tour of Europe, arriving in Brussels on June 6, 1975. He was signed to play venues in the major cities of Holland, Denmark, Sweden, and France. He arrived in the U.K. to find that the promoter, somewhat out of his depth with a star of Richard's magnitude, had failed to give the tour the publicity it should have had. (He had actually arranged for Richard to travel 350 miles from London to Newcastle by British Rail!)

The opening concert, in London, was only half full, and was equipped with a lousy system. The Teddy boys in the audience, part of a peculiarly British subculture that idolized the 1950s and considered anything later as not worth a hill of beans, were not at all pleased by Richard's new image. Although the kids in the United States were turned on by Richard's outrageous flaunting of sexual and racial taboos, their English counterparts were not ready for him at all. They jeered the band in their Afro wigs and slashed-

185

*to-the-navel jumpsuits, and they missed the honking sound of the tenor sax—a trademark of Rock 'n' Roll in the 1950s.*

*Richard himself seemed like a being from another planet in his pixie-pink jumpsuit with its glittering collar and plunging neckline. The volume was cranked up so high it pressed the pain threshold, and the glazed-eyed band looked as though they were in a drug-induced trance. There were memorable moments, though.*

*Richard's piano playing was, when he wanted it to be, the best, and "Be-Bop-a-Lula," "Blueberry Hill," and "Good Golly Miss Molly" with its "What'd I Say"-type introduction, were themselves worth the price of admission. Richard was at his most manic, shouting and screaming at the audience, "Take my picture, I'm real—I don't feel real, but I am real."*

*The promoter of the concert complained to the press about the extracontractual expenses he had had to pay. He said that Richard had threatened to pull out of the tour unless his hotels and first-class travel were paid for—a sum that he estimated at eighteen thousand dollars on top of the eighty thousand dollars for the fifteen days of performances. In an attempt to recoup some of his losses, he canceled Richard's airline tickets back to America, forcing Richard to pay four thousand dollars in cash to fly home.*

● When I found out that man was gay, I knew that he was going to work against me. He was really mean, one of those closet gays who resent the gays like me who are open about it. They wish they could be that way so they resent the ones who are. He was fooling about with one of the boys in my group. He wanted his room to be next to mine and I resented it. At night when I was asleep, he would ease himself in with those guys. I caught him putting a towel around himself and leaving with his penis hanging out.

186

And then he got so he wouldn't pay me. He hid the money and wouldn't pay me. He was *bad.*

*While in Britain Richard was arrested for nonpayment of income tax. He was forced to appear at a private hearing before a Registrar in Chambers on the petition for bankruptcy filed against him after the Wembley concert. He was told to return to Britain in August for a full hearing of the question of his still-outstanding bill of eight thousand dollars. He claimed that the taxes were withheld from his paycheck, but never handed over to the Inland Revenue by the promoters.*

*Promoters have frequently found Richard difficult to deal with. He regards them with distrust because of the ripoffs and maltreatment he has been subjected to throughout his career.*

BUMPS BLACKWELL: Richard was owed some money by a promoter, so he arrived at his office for payment. The dialogue went like this: "I have called to see Mr. X about my tour money." Mr. X's secretary: "I'm sorry, Mr. X is away in Paris." Richard: "Thank you." As secretary disappears into main office Richard hides under desk. Some time later, in from the main office comes Mr. X and secretary. Out jumps Richard: "Why, Mr. X, you sure got back from Paris pretty quick. Now about my money..."

● Concert promoters were always trying to rip us off. But we learned a lot of things. When I was first in my fame, the ripoffs were really heavy. Really blatant. At some places we'd be given only half of what we were supposed to get. Then suddenly there'd be guns around and we'd be told, "You niggers, get outa town." So the second time around we always had to have a deposit up front of fifty

187

percent on signing the contract. Then we'd take the other fifty percent before we would go on. We had to get paid in full. There were still some hassles sometimes, but not so many.

*Back in the States, Richard allowed his life to be taken over by alcohol and drugs. They completely dominated and altered his personality. His work was seriously affected.*

● I spent thousands and thousands of dollars getting high. I missed a lot of engagements being laid up. I got behind financially. I got behind in my life.

I got so heavily into drugs that for a year I never went to Riverside to see my mother. I was in a bad way. I didn't want her to see some of the ways my life had come into. I had deteriorated. I came so low that I only weighed about a hundred and fifteen pounds. All I was interested in was getting high. I'd be riding all over the city of Los Angeles looking for cocaine. I just had to be froze. I wanted to be one on one. They shoulda called me Little Cocaine, I was sniffing so much of the stuff! My nose got big enough to back a diesel truck in, unload it, and drive it right out again. Every time I blew my nose there was flesh and blood on my handkerchief, where it had eaten out my membranes.

A habit like mine cost a lot of money. I was smoking marijuana and angel dust and I was mixing heroin with coke. I felt funny when I didn't have anything. It was costing me around a thousand dollars a day—and there was always trouble with the dealers. Larry Williams, a guy I started in show business, came to my house with a gun to shoot me. I had got some cocaine from him, arranged to pay later, and didn't show up—because I was high. Larry and I were good friends. He had been with me at Specialty Records. I brought him to fame. We were very good friends—but he came to shoot me! That was probably the most fearful moment in my life. That is what drugs do to you. He said, "Richard, I'm gonna kill you. Ain't no one going to mess around with my money." I knew he loved me—I hoped he did! But he had this pistol right there and he would have shot me if I hadn't paid him.

I became very nasty, which I never used to be. Cocaine made me paranoid. It made me think evil. It made me feel sorry for myself. When I got real high I couldn't sleep. I couldn't get tired enough to sleep. With everybody else asleep I couldn't find nothing to do. It was so boring that I started drinking as well. See, I had bodyguards around me constantly. There were so many people around me that when I wanted to raise my hand there was someone there to raise it for me. They would bring me cocaine and I'd take it all the time. I spent my time locked up in a hotel room. I'd go to New York City, get a suite in the Waldorf Astoria and stay there for days, just sitting in a room with the television on all the time. The chauffeur would come to take me to the show with the bodyguards, manager, valet, and bookkeeper....

The drugs brought me to realize what homosexuality had made me. When I felt that, I wanted to hurt. I wanted to kill. I had never been like that before. I wanted to fight those boys who didn't want to do what I wanted them to do. I had guys working for me who were scared to come into the room to get paid! They were *scared* of me cos my homosexuality was so heavy they could see it in my eyes.

Homosexuality takes over your whole mind, but it's an illusion. It's not really any excitement. It's like masturbation, it's false. It's not a completeness. When you hug and kiss a man you feel like something is missing afterward. Even when you've got your rocks off, you still got your rock. When you're with a girl the rock has gone. I've been with guys that have sucked me and eaten my breasts and neck. Guys that have done everything. Guys that have actually believed they were in love with me. I was famous. Then as soon as they see a girl they forget you. Because their mind wasn't there. It was false.

Then I started to get so demanding that the cats working for me, Ken Dahanna and Keith Winslow, were getting me whisky. They were getting me drunk so that they could be free. They didn't have no time for themselves. So I became an alcoholic. I would drink every day, drinking without eating. Now when you're like this, high all the time, you don't really know what's going on. I lost a lot of money because people stole from me.

LEE ANGEL: He was a different man. He was totally different toward me and everybody. He'd gotten into drinking, smoking, and drugs in a big way. He just wasn't himself. To me he wasn't. It was funny. It wasn't him. He didn't know how to hold a cigarette, yet he was smoking!

MARQUETTE: His habits had changed. He was becoming withdrawn from us. Kinda distant. He kept away from us. He'd stay in one place while we stayed in another. You could tell he was getting tired of the business, because he had picked up his Bible. Not that he had ever really put it down. He carried it everywhere. You would go by his room and he'd be reading it...

How did he get into drugs? I don't really know. He'd been around these hip session musicians and arrangers when he was at the Record Plant making a soundtrack for a movie. That's when he started to change. Maybe he was trying to change his image, to be more hip like them, instead of just being a Rock 'n' Roll revival. But he got really heavily into it.

At first it didn't affect his performances except that he perspired more. He was always a heavy perspirer. I think

190

near the end it slowed him down, wasted his talents. He was always a hard worker, and he didn't work so hard at the end. We were worried. We talked to him about it, got a little heavy. And that's when he started to get distant from us.

● A lot of tragedies happened around that time. The first was when a very close friend of mine, a very very close personal friend, who had traveled with me as a valet, called. He wanted to hear me sing and play at Magic Mountain, in L.A. I fixed it up for him to come. My brothers and sisters and my mother were coming—but he never did arrive. He got shot in the head that very night. Twenty-one years old. He got shot at the heroin man's house.

Another close friend of mine, called Curly Knight, was coming out of an apartment building one night and some fifteen-year-old boys beat him and put him in the trunk of his car. Fifteen-year-old boys. They drove him around the city, then they cut him up with a butcher knife. They broke the knife off in his body, put him between two houses, and called the police to say they had found a dead man. They had killed him! When they asked those boys why they had killed him, they said, "We thought he was white." He was a light-complexioned man. But isn't that pitiful. He was a man God made and died for.

What happened next happened to my brother Tony. Tony and his wife, Nita, were both schoolteachers. They had a little boy, also called Tony. Well, my brother called me and asked me to let him have two hundred dollars to get a station wagon. I was just about to leave for Miami, Florida, to appear at the Americana Hotel in place of Tina Turner, who was sick. I told him that I would let him have the money when I got back.

Well, when I got back to Los Angeles, instead of going to see Tony, I picked up some people. We checked into a little hotel out in Hollywood and got high and had a good time and let it all hang out. I had made a lot of money. There were three or four of us and this beautiful girl. We put cocaine all over the girl's body and we were licking it off. We were crawling about on the floor naked, like animals. With some people cocaine kills the sex feeling, while some people say it makes them feel *more*. It makes me feel more, usually. But this time we had overdone it. None of us could get erected, we were so high. It was probably just as well, cos we probably would have killed that girl.

The next morning everybody was looking for me. My brother had got up and watered his lawn and took little Tony for a walk. Then he felt a pain in his chest. He went to lie down for a few moments. He died. He died of a heart attack. I never did get over there to see him.

Then I knew that God was no respector of persons. God had permitted all these things—maybe to save Little Richard—to open my eyes, to let me know that it could have been me, to let people know that the Rock of Ages is present and the world is getting ready to end. I knew then I was called to be an evangelist for his Gospel.

Then something happened that really shook my mind. Ricky, Deanie's little boy, who I loved just like I would have loved my own son, got shot dead. He was fooling around with some friends in the street. One of them had a gun and he got shot in the head. It nearly killed Deanie. She was a sister to our family. It shook my mind even more than it was already shook. I thought it might be my turn to die next. I was afraid I was going to die. I always did believe I would die before I was forty and though I was still at the top nothing would satisfy me.

Tony's death was the saddest moment of my life. But it was also one of the happiest. I knew after Tony died that I was going to come out of show business. I felt that it would be a *joy* to come out. Tony's death was a door that I didn't want to be opened, but it *was* opened. And I walked through it. To come out of show business and take my stand on God's side. To be an evangelist for all denominations, for all races, creeds, and colors.

I had heard God speaking to me to go out and tell the people of the goodness and how He had snatched me from the burning. And it gave me a peace, a serenity, a tranquillity that I never knew existed. It was as if something came over my whole being. I didn't care about money. I didn't care about popularity. I didn't care about fame or fortune or any of those things. All I wanted was God in my life. I knew that I needed to tell and to share that with everybody. I wanted people to know that the only rock they needed was *the* Rock, Christ Jesus. The only roll they needed was the Roll of Glory, the Roll of Heaven. That's the only rock and roll they need. All the other can rock and roll away. It's transitory.

*Many rock stars enmeshed in the life-style of unlimited drink, sex, and self-indulgence have found it impossible to give it all up and change their ways. Now they are getting high in the sky. But behind Richard's projected image as a wild, gay, ultrasexual screwball has always been a strong-willed and shrewd earthiness and strength of character. And so he changed to the religious and abstemious life-style with the ease of a chameleon changing color.*

# God's Beautiful City

**L**ittle Richard was back in the arms of the Lord. And so Richard stepped out of the Rock 'n' Roll spotlights for the last time. He had a thousand-dollar-a-day drug habit to kick. But he had two things to help him. The first and most important was his deep conviction that God was speaking to him. "I was living like a dog, and God was telling me I was losing my soul." And the second was the warm haven of his home and family at Riverside. He had always preserved its sanctity even when his excesses were at their height.

Underweight, ill, and ravaged by dark thoughts and fears of damnation, Richard retreated to Riverside to fight his battle with addiction and sweat the drugs out of his system.

LEVA MAE: When he came out of show business this last time it was a shock to me. I didn't know he was coming out until he walked into the dining room and said to me, "Mother, I'm out of show business. I'm going back to the church. I believe that Jesus is coming soon, and I'm just goin' to get prepared." Well, there wasn't too much to say: "What you think we gonna do? You think God's gonna throw money out of the sky for us?" But he said the Lord would provide. And he's been right.

You know, over the years I never saw Richard in drugs. I

194

always stay home. I've never been a person who likes to go out, not like Richard. He was on the road all the time. When he was at home, it was only for a few days or so. You know, he'd be at hotels and things. Well, I wasn't at the hotels, and I didn't know what he was doing. But when he was in my company, and around of us, he always respected us and treated us right.

When he came out of show business he stayed at home for weeks in his room just reading his Bible. Then he went out on the road again with Elder Rainey. Joe Lutcher was afraid to come back preaching in a tent.

JOE LUTCHER: The thing I like about Richard's ministry, and what he's in, is that he never pushes a person or tries to make him different. He just shows them what God has done for him. And that's a beautiful philosophy.

Richard has never been fanatic. He's a very sincere person. There are a lot of people who do not accept his way. But, you see, they didn't accept Jesus' way, neither. Now he's helping so many people, and especially young people. Richard's ministry is a dignified ministry. You know, people think that you've got to go to school or college and get a master's degree to preach, but you can have what is called common mother wit or common wisdom. Richard uses that. Richard reaches the person on a level that maybe the man from Oxford University could not. A lot of people are scared to go to church. A lot of people seem to think that if you haven't been to a university you don't know anything. But it's what's in your heart.

MARQUETTE: He didn't have any trouble giving up drugs and all that. He just decided that was it. He's one of those people who is so strong. He's like that with everything. If he decides to do something he can do it.

195

*In 1977 Richard became a traveling salesman for a Nashville company called Memorial Bibles International, Inc. They published an annotated edition of the Good Book aimed at the burgeoning black-consciousness market. The* Black Heritage Bible *was a special edition that showed how many major figures in biblical history had been black. It came in a cedar box and sold for $24.95.*

*Dressed in a sober gray three-piece suit, Richard, quiet-spoken and dignified, visited churches and religious conventions singing religious songs and taking orders for* The Black Heritage Bible.

● I had been making ten thousand dollars for an hour's work. Getting used to the big drop in my income was very hard for me at first. But at least I had been able to give my family a good start in life. They were all taken care of, married and working in good jobs, you know, and my mother lived in a nice home. My family, especially my sisters, were raised to a very extravagant life. They had gotten used to living with riches. We didn't believe in sparing anything. We never had nothing in the early days, but when I became famous, I made sure that none of them ever wanted for anything. Yes, there was a big drop in my life-style. But there was another thing happening in my life which made up for that—the joy of being with God. The contentment of having peace. You know, the Bible tells us in John 14:27 "Jesus says: 'Peace I leave with you. Peace I give unto you.'" Not as the world gives it. The world gives you a piece of this and a piece of that—a piece of rock, a piece of blues, a piece of jazz, a piece of Bach, a piece of Beethoven. The world gives you pieces. God gives you a whole life eternal. A peace which passeth all understanding. God gives you tranquillity, that little thing that money can't buy you. I have God to thank that I'm a living legend and not a dead one.

I have rejected homosexuality. I have rejected sex. Now I get my thrills from the ministry. When I meet people who I have changed through my presentation of God's words, that makes me feel good. Guys that were thieves, guys that were murderers who are not murderers anymore after hearing me present Christ. I have met black guys that hated white people, who thought all whites were devils. And I have met white people trained to hate blacks, people who turned away from their hatred by my ministry from Jesus. That's rewarding to me. You know, I don't care how far a man has fallen, or what he has done. Jesus loves him, God guides him, and he's still His son.

My true belief about Rock 'n' Roll—and there have been a lot of phrases attributed to me over the years—is this: I believe this kind of music is demonic. I have seen the rock groups and the punk-rock people in this country. And some of their lyrics is demonic. They talk against God. A lot of the beats in music today are taken from voodoo, from the voodoo drums. If you study music in rhythms, like I have, you'll see that is true.

I believe that kind of music is driving people from Christ. It is contagious. I believe that God wants people to turn from Rock 'n' Roll to the Rock of Ages—to get ready for eternal life. And I believe that I am supposed to walk the way that God says to walk. I believe that God permitted me to be famous for a reason. That my teachings in rock now, as God has showed me, might be believed.

*Johnny Otis is a seminal influence on American R'n'B and rock music. He discovered Little Esther, Jackie Wilson, Big Mama Thornton, Little Willie John, and Hank Ballard. Ethnically white, he is nominally black, with a fierce pro-tectiveness toward black music, which he sees as the only significant move forward in music since the classical mas-ters of the eighteenth century. Otis, like Richard, has em-*

*braced religion. The pastor of the Landmark Community Church in Los Angeles, he is, however, still active musically.*

JOHNNY OTIS: I think it's a terrible shame. Creative artists like Richard are rare. We can't afford to lose them. Look at him. He's in his prime right now. He's very vital and in good shape. And we have lost this part of his creative life. That's too bad. I would tell Richard as one minister to another that there's nothing to be ashamed of. In fact there is much to be very proud of in what he's done for music. I don't mean what he's done in his personal life. The musician may not lead a holy life, but there's nothing wrong with the music. It *does* square with Christianity.

We did a thing, a Gospel festival, at the Shrine Auditorium. I thought, What if I had brought my band as part of the show and Richard got up there and did his "Awop-Bop-a-Loo-Mop Alop-Bam-Boom." Did his thing. Then those kids would listen to him. There's no need to be ashamed of "Awop-Bob-a-Loo-Mop Alop-Bam-Boom" because it was a blessing to the whole world. I love it now! When I hear it, it makes me feel good.

I would like for us to put a thing together and take it around. We would do rhythm-and-blues music. Take an intermission, go and put our robes on, and then come back and do gospel music. That would be great. Blues and gospel music. Not only would Richard rock that stage with his great rhythm-and-blues, but he would rock it with his great gospel soul. After all, that's where rhythm-and-blues comes from. The blues are beautiful. It's a distillation of black America. It's a cultural heart. It says so much for Afro-Americans, North American Afro people. And it must have something, cos it swept the world in many forms, including country-and-western, which I love.

I want to tell Richard: White folks stole or appropriated all your art in the rhythm-and-blues field. Took it and made

198

all the money. They took all the bows as though they invented it. Now you're letting them steal your gospel soul. Now you're giving them that. Jesus is the final authority with me. Someone will say, "Well, Paul said..." I say, "Tell me what Jesus said." Paul may have been reciting the mores of the day when he said that women should shut up in church and wear something on their face and that homosexuality is an abomination. Jesus told me only one thing—love ye one another. And don't judge each other. That's what Jesus said.

● God told me, "Little Richard, let the world know that they need to go back and study the Bible." The Old Testament speaks and the New Testament says "Amen, hallelujah." God told me to teach it as it is. Don't add nothing to it. Don't take nothing away from it. To preach the unadulterated Gospel. People may not like it. But it's the truth. At times like these we need the Bible. At times like these we need a Savior. God told me to teach that all the races are His bouquet—the black, the white, the red, the brown, and the yeller. We're just like the lily, the rose, the sunflower, and the medallion. That's what I'm doing now. I'm trying to do that.

There are so many preachers in this country that are teaching fake religions. There are preachers who preach only for dollars. That is a common old *racket*. Instead of teaching people to read and study their Bible, they have their own conceptions. Their own terms, their own playing with God's word. And that's a sin in the sight of God.

My church is the Universal Remnant Church of God, meaning the last. We believe that you have to keep all ten of God's Commandments. We believe that it has to be stressed in this generation that all ten of the Commandments have to be kept. Any man that says he loves God and doesn't keep his Commandments is telling a lie. God said so.

From a little boy I wanted to be a preacher. I always did, cos I was raised around them. And I loved God. I always wanted to be a prophet for the Lord. But I didn't know this was going to happen to me. It came. It wasn't nothing my people planned. They didn't have no money to plan anything.

It's not many preachers today that stand up and tell the truth as it is. That will stand up and say "I've been a homosexual and God changed me." There's not many people would say "I've been a dope addict." I believe that God permitted me to become these things so that I could be a witness and an evangelist for all denominations, for all races, colors, and creeds. That God is a loving God. He can save from the guttermost to the uttermost. He is a mighty Savior. And, if He can save Little Richard, He can save anybody, of any denomination or any church.

My income now is way down there. But I've found out that it don't take as much money to live as I'm making. When I get a hundred dollars now it's a million to me. I feel like a person that never made a quarter. It's a joy. I found out what money really is. It meets your needs. It's just a necessity.

MARQUETTE: I wouldn't like to see him back in Rock 'n' Roll. I figure he's happiest at what he's doing now. And after all, he is fifty-one. Richard is not ashamed. When he gives his testimony it's true. He really gives it out. And that's the smartest thing that anybody in his position could do. Now he's in religion. Nobody can come up and say, "I remember when he did such and such a thing. I knew him when…" because he's already put it to the world. He's testified about it. When he was on television telling about being a homosexual and using dope, my wife said, "Do you think the kids should be seeing this?" And I said, "Yes, because one day they're going to read it anyway, or some-body's going to say, 'That uncle of yours did this and that...' He's told it."

*Richard made an album of gospel songs, entitled* God's Beautiful City. *In early 1979 he set out on a country-wide evangelical campaign, traveling wherever a group of people wanted to hear his testimony. His message has remained the same over the past five years. Whether it is given to 250 people in a small church one night or a packed 21,000-seat auditorium the next, it is a call for a return to holiness of living, based upon a strict obedience to the Ten Command-ments, all couched in an earthy street language that he admits offends some people—particularly the frank way he deals with the sexual hangups of both the older and youn-ger generations.*

● I don't charge no guarantee to go no place. It's free. If I go anywhere it's on a free-will offering. If I come to speak in your town, we do not allow any tickets to be sold. You pay my fare and my hotel. The night's offering comes to me, but we do not charge admission.

Sometimes the honest way I preach offends some folks. I don't know any other way to talk to people. I am unedu-cated. I haven't even got a high-school education. But I'm doing it the way the Lord has impressed me. I talk about my life as a homosexual and drug addict because I think it is right to tell people what God has done for me. That the same God who saved Peter, who saved Mary Magdalene, a prostitute, saved Little Richard.

It bothers some people, but some of these people are guilty. They say they wish I were more educated so I could use some big words and cover up some things. But if I used big words the simple people that God has sent me to to teach would not be helped. They'd go away saying, "What did he mean?" God has called me to an open and frank ministry.

There's a lot of entertainers today going on about being born again. But they're only being born from scotch to bourbon. I like Pat Boone as a friend, but he's trying to serve two masters. He can't light the candles at both ends. Pat believes he can go to Las Vegas and do his thing, then preach on Sunday. I don't believe we can do that. God has not called us to do that.

I can never see myself going back to Rock 'n' Roll. I have no desire to do it. I enjoy preaching the gospel. I enjoy living the gospel. What makes the gospel so dearly endearing to me is that you have to live what you preach. If I was living a double life you couldn't respect me. And I couldn't respect myself. But when a man *believes* what he believes, then whether he's right or wrong you have to respect him.

Yes, I feel I still have the charisma and magnetism that I had when I was in show business. But I believe it is more so now. Because it is holy. But I think, when people come to hear me now, they are coming to hear my story. I wish I had the gift in the Scriptures that people like H. M. S. Richards, George Vandeman, E. E. Cleveland have. But I'm not a preacher. I'm just a messenger for Christ.

*Richard's preaching techniques are in a direct line with his Rock 'n' Roll showmanship. He is mesmerizing, gaining total control over the listener, using the call-and-response pattern, the black gospel formula which is so much a part of his life and his music, bringing his audience together into one entity. His energy taps a mystic source of mental power which is available only to the greatest preachers and shamans. The body and soul speaking as one.*

*One of his many engagements across the United States was his visit to the Jesus 79 Campaign at Mount Morris*

*Park in Harlem. Coincidentally near the Apollo Theater, where he had headlined the big Rock 'n' Roll spectaculars of the 1950s, the event was sponsored by the Soul Saving Station for Every Nation, Christ Crusaders of America, Inc.*

*A packed church waited expectantly for Richard, who was ninety minutes late. Most of those present had waited four hours in the park the previous day, only to be told by Bishop Jesse H. Winley that Richard's plane had had difficulties and he would not be appearing.*

*All this was forgotten in the welcoming applause. The immaculately suited figure of Richard Penniman strode down the aisle of the church. His build was that of an athlete. His face was the face of a man nearer his twenties than his fifties. Could this be the posturing, flamboyant Little Richard of just three years before who dressed in gaudy satin jumpsuits and garish, glittering robes? Who peacocked around the stage in pancake makeup, mascara, and a foot-high wig? Who threw his clothes to fighting audiences after reducing them to a frenzy with his mind-crunching Rock 'n' Roll?*

*Yes. Those large flashing eyes that had mesmerized screaming audiences for more than twenty years were not dimmed at all. The charisma was still there. And above all, that magnificent voice was in better form than ever as it soared above the congregation singing the introductory hymn, "He Is Lord."*

● I am sorry I did not arrive at Mount Morris Park yesterday. I missed my plane. The Lord did not want me to get on that plane. If he had wanted me on it he would have put me on it.

*Praise the Lord, responded the congregation.*

All you women, listen to me. Do you give your man what he wants? Do you? Some of you here today, comin' to church together, and you don't even speak to each other at home. The wife sleepin' in one room and the husband in the other. Your children don't understand that. God doesn't understand that. If you don't give your man what he wants there is always a Jezebel around the corner who will. He'll go around the corner and get himself a Jezebel.

*Cries of That's the truth! and Hallelujah!*

And you men. You treat your wife right. Make her feel like the lady she is, and the children will see the light of holiness in the home. I want you men to remember this. You have not got a roller-coaster in your house. Your wife is not your roller-coaster.

*Hysterical approval from the congregation.*

# From Rock'n'Roll to the Rock of Ages

he sermon that follows is a compilation of Little Richard's testimony presented to hundreds of thousands of people all over the world. I have culled what I feel are the most powerful pieces— for he is always spontaneous and his speech can change from meeting to meeting.

● I want to say hello out there. I'm so glad to be with you today. My name is Little Richard. I'm the Rock 'n' Roll singer that you've heard about through the years. I'm the one that sang "Long Tall Sally," "Good Golly Miss Molly," "Rip It Up," "Ready Teddy," "Lucille," "Keep a-Knockin' But You Can't Come in," and "The Girl Can't Help It." I was making ten thousand dollars for one hour's work. Going from place to place, singing—just jumping all up in the air with all of the makeup and the eyelashes on. With all of the mirrored suits and the sequins and the stones, going all over the place. I had forgotten all about God—going from town to town, city to city, and from country to country, not knowing that I was directed and commanded by another

205

power. The power of darkness. The power that you've heard so much about. The power that a lot of people don't believe exists. The power of the Devil. Satan. We must realize that there's a force that is fighting against us in this world.

The Bible says in Luke, the fourth chapter, verse 6, if you have your Bible read it with me. It says: "And the Devil said unto Jesus, 'All this power will I give thee, and the glory of them, for that is delivered unto me, and to whomsoever I will I give it.'" If you worship me I will give you this power. If you worship me you can have this power. But Jesus said, "It is written, thou shalt worship the Lord, thy God. And Him only shalt thou serve."

Jesus spoke one of the Ten Commandments. So many people say they're no good today. But I want you to know that the Ten Commandments is a spiritual mirror. The same as when you look in the mirror at home. The mirror shows you that you need to shave, but it can't shave you. The Ten Commandments shows you that you are a sinner. But the gift of God is eternal life, through Jesus Christ our Lord and our Savior.

What can take away my sins? Nothing but the blood of Jesus. Jesus said that "If you love Me, you'll keep My commandments." I gave up Rock 'n' Roll for the Rock of Ages. I cut off my crown of hair for a crown of life.

When I was in show business I got heavy into narcotics. I started taking drugs. Some people call it pot, some people call it reefer, some people call it weed, some people call it grass, but I call it dope. I got hooked into dope. I started smoking marijuana, I went from marijuana to angel dust. Some people think angel dust is new. Angel dust is old. There is nothing new under the sun, people. I started using this angel dust. Me and a young lady one night was having a big orgy. We got naked. Me, the young lady, and three other fellers. We took off all our clothes. We smoked this angel dust. We was crawling about on the floor like dogs, naked. We got dusty from the angel dust. We were afraid to answer the phone. We were afraid to answer the door. Our bodies was numb. We was paranoid. I found out that the Devil was controlling our minds, directing our lives, just like it is with so many young people today.

I went from there to cocaine, paying a thousand dollars an ounce and sometimes more than that. I want you to know it didn't stop there. I went from there to heroin. I needed Jesus in my life. You need Jesus in your life. You need to give up drugs and let Jesus have His way in your life. What the world needs today is Jesus. What the world needs today is the Ten Commandments. What the world needs today is the Bible from Genesis to Revelation. What am I supposed to do without Jesus?

Before I go on to my testimony tonight, how many Bibles do we have with us tonight? Let me see the Bibles tonight. You know, a little boy walked over to his momma, and he picked up his Bible and he said, "Momma, Momma, tell me, whose book is this?" His mother looked at him and said, "Son, it's God's book." He said, "Momma, don't you think we ought to give it back to Him, because we never use it here." There's so many of you got Bibles and you never use them at your home. Some of you have hidden your Bibles in your trunk. Because your age is in your Bible. Your mother has written it in there. So you lock it in your trunk. Because you been telling everybody you're thirty and you know you're fifty!

Take that Bible out of your trunk, and get up from those soap operas! Stop trying to watch *Search for Tomorrow* and search your Bible. Jesus says, "Search the Scriptures. In the Scriptures is life eternal. In the Scriptures is life everlasting. The only way you can learn about Me and know Me is through My holy word." So you got to study, ladies and gentlemen. I didn't know that homosexuality was wrong until I read it in the Bible. I didn't know that it was a sin until I read it in the Bible. I'd been going that way for so many years. I want to tell you something, I enjoyed being a homosexual. I didn't give up something that I hated. I enjoyed being gay. I enjoyed being unnatural. It was fun to me. It was the in-thing to be. Everybody wants to be gay today. Everywhere people are gay. That's what people think. But I want to tell you tonight, that's from Hell. I want to let you know tonight that God never intended for no man to be gay. God never intended for no woman to be no lesbian. God never intended for no man, woman, boy, girl, black, white, red, brown, and yellow, to be bisexual. That's not the way God planned it.

I want you to watch me closely tonight. So many of you've been used to people moaning and groaning, and not telling you nothing. Listen. When a man don't moan and groan, you say he can't preach! And that's a lie! Do you know what preaching is? Preaching is the good news of the Savior.

The Bible says in Matthew 4:4 that man shall not live by bread alone, but by every word that proceedeth out of the mouth of God. Do you believe that? The Bible says in Psalms 119, verse 105, "Thy word is a lamp unto my feet, and a light unto my path." Without the word I can't see where I'm going. There's so many people, they look at the Bible and they say, "Hallelujah! I like that! (Who they think going to live like that?) Ooh, that's good. Praise the Lord! (I ain't gonna do that.) Praise God! Hallelujah! (Not in this life.)" Man don't want the word of God today. The Bible says, because iniquity shall abound, the love of man shall wax cold. And God says, there will come a time when they shall not endure sound doctrines. He says, but they're gonna have itching ears. They're gonna like fables. They gonna like lies. They gonna like to hear soothing things, to soothe their conscience. To make them feel free.

208

There's a lot of people hollering they're saved. You ain't saved. You're brave. If you're saved you'll live for Jesus. If you are saved you will do His will. If you are saved you will keep His commandments. If you are saved you will have His love in your heart. If you are saved you read your Bible. If you are saved you will love to hear people talk about Jesus. Can you say Amen to that? Jesus loves you. Now we're going to get down to the nitty-gritty. I want everybody to be quiet and listen.

What I'm gonna tell you now, you're not gonna shout. You're not gonna holler. You're gonna hear something that you never heard in your life. I want you to listen carefully. If the Bible don't teach it, I don't preach it. Everything I tell you is coming from the Scriptures. I'm gonna bring it from there. If I don't bring it from there don't you accept it. Can't you say Amen? You know how I got gay? My momma wasn't paying attention at the time. You know, if she had said "homosexual" when I was a little boy I wouldn't have known what she was talking about. I didn't even know what it was. They called you "sissy" back then. Or "freak." Or "faggot." That's the common name for it. All those other names are beautiful names that the old Devil done fixed up. Trying to put class to it. There ain't no class in it. Ain't no class in sin. And God said that the wages of sin is death. Listen carefully.

You can't point your finger at no homosexual. You know people love to point their finger. But you forgot, look how your thumb comes back at you. You point at one of them, your thumb hits back at you. Did you know that Jesus died for them? Did you know Jesus went on the cross for 'em? Did you know that Jesus spilled His precious blood for them? And the Bible says, "Without the shedding of blood there is no remission of sin." And listen carefully, ladies and gentlemen, I was a homosexual.

When I was a little boy, I was a man. I used to play playhouse. I was the daddy and my cousin was always the momma. Don't laugh, cos there's a whole lot of 'em here tonight. And all of you secret servers and closet folk, I'm gonna tell you. So you won't have to go back in the closet. I'm letting you stay out tonight. You can just lock it up and throw away the key. Some of you that has been shackin', you can just go packin'. Now. We're gonna have to get you straight. I wanna tell you something.

I was so wrapped up in my homosexuality, I didn't like no women. I didn't want no woman. The only woman that I loved was my momma, I thought. God spoke everything that He made into existence. He just spoke and it came. The Bible says He spake and it was done. He commanded and it stood fast. He spoke the moon, the stars, the sun, the rivers, the lakes, the trees, the birds, the bees, the oceans, the mountains—everything! But when it came to man, He *made* him. And not only did He make him, but He made *us.* The whole Trinity got together and made man in the image of the Holy God. Breathed into his nostrils the breath of life. Man became a living soul, in the image of the great God of the universe. See, the Devil can't make no man. The Devil can't make no woman. He knew that He made Adam and Eve. Not Adam and Steve. God knew that. God never intended me to go with nobody but a woman. I don't care what I get cut off. I don't care what I add on. I don't care what I get sewed to. In Heaven my name is still Richard Penniman. I may call myself Marie down here, but in Glory I'm still a man. I want you to listen carefully, ladies and gentlemen.

I read in my Bible what God says in Leviticus 18:22, "Thou shalt not lie with mankind as with womankind; it is an abomination." The Bible says in First Corinthians— what book I say? First Corinthians, the sixth chapter, verse 9, let's read it. Come on, let's read it together... everybody turn to it. It says, "Know ye not that the unrighteous shall not inherit the kingdom of God? Be not deceived: neither fornicators, nor effeminate, nor abusers of themselves with mankind." God says you cannot go to Heaven that way. Do you believe it?

I'm your brother, you're my brother. But the woman, your wife, is the one to love and be intimate with. God tells us in the Book of Romans, chapter one—the whole first chapter deals with unnatural affection. God lets us know that the Bible is more up-to-date than the *New York Times,* in America, and the *Daily Mirror,* in England, or any newspaper in any country. The Bible is the truth. God has given us rules and guidelines to go by.

I don't care how far you've fallen in sin, God can lift you out. God is willing to take you out. God is willing to take your hand. He's willing to make you a man. You know what? God don't do no repair work. God don't do no remodeling. God just builds it all over. That's what the Bible says in Second Corinthians 5:7, "If any man be in Christ, he's a new creation." Let everybody say that. How many of you believe it? Not only does he say you're a new creation, but he says all things are become new. If you're still doing the same thing it means you haven't met Him. If you're still lusting after the flesh, you haven't met Jesus.

The Bible says in first John 2:15–17, "Love not the world, nor the things that are in the world. If any man love the world, the love of the Father is not in him. For all that is in the world, the lust of the flesh, and the lust of the eyes, and the pride of life, is not of the Father, but of the world. And the world passeth away, and the lust thereof, but he that doeth the will of God abideth for ever." Do you believe that? There's three roads to Hell, ladies and gentlemen. The lust of the flesh, the lust of the eyes, and the pride of life. But there is only one road to glory. That's found in John, 14:6, Jesus saith, "I am the way..." Do you believe that?

You think you're flying high but I'm going to bring you

low. Listen. The Bible says in the book of Romans, "Wherefore God also gave them up to uncleanness, to the lusts of their own hearts, to dishonor their own bodies between themselves," listen what God is saying, ladies and gentlemen, "Who changed the truth of God into a lie?" God said, "Little Richard, you're a man." I said, "I'm a woman." God said, "You lie." He said, "You lie. I made you a man. When your momma brought you home she brought a boy. If you hadda been a girl she would have named you Martha. You are a boy." My daddy wanted seven boys, and I was messing it up. He had six and a part. My daddy used to put me in a boxing ring with my brother. He was trying to get my brother to beat it out of me. And my brother would try to kill me. I couldn't box. And my brother would just hit me in the nose. And I would go to bleeding. And I would go to hollering. And Dad would say, "Take him out. The round is over."

I told you, some preachers don't preach it, cos they'd lose their whole choir. Some of 'em don't preach it cos they'd have no pianist and no organist! No lead director and no lead vocalist! But I want you to know, don't you forget, that the Devil himself was a master musician. Don't forget that. He was also a director of the choir. He was also a composer and a conductor. And the Bible says he's down here with his evil angels. He's down here getting you and you and you and me and all of us, to break God's law. To condemn the word of the living God. It's time for preachers, it's time for deacons, it's time for people, it's time for members in the churches to preach God's word as it is written. Listen. Don't clap, just listen.

The world is getting ready to end.

Let me tell you something. You leave your children with too many different people. You leave your children with too many strange people. You leave your little boys and your little girls crying "Momma, please don't leave me." "Shut

212

your mouth and get on in there." You don't know what your little boy's trying to tell you. God has left those children with you for a reason. He has entrusted you with those precious lives. And you've got to take care of your children. You are in charge of them for Jesus.

Jesus showed me something. He said, "Little Richard, listen. Adam saw that everything God had made had a mate, but him. Even if God had sent the angels from glory, it could not have satisfied or pacified Adam, cos it had to be bone of his bone. It had to be flesh of his flesh. That's the reason God took woman from man, so man would desire her. He wants her back cos she's a part of him."

You know, a whole lot of you women got your husbands on punishment, 'cos you're mad with him and "Old Jim, I'll fix him." And "I'll put him in the room with Bobby tonight. You go back there with Bobby." See, you're crazy. She's the one that ought to move, she should go back there. It's your house, you're the head of the house. God made you the head of it. And so you can't put your husband on no punishment. Your body belong to your husband. And his body belong to you. You're not supposed to put your husband on punishment and then sit around and call yourself a Christian. Christians don't punish their husbands. He's not your little boy. That's your husband. Can't you say Amen to that? I see a whole lot of men saying thank God for that! A lot of men are so glad. I used to watch my sister, how she'd take her husband's whole check. She'd take the whole check from him and give him ten dollars. I used to feel so sorry for him: I'd say, "How you doing, Sam? Good morning." He'd say, "What's good about it?" He had a bad night. And he didn't like it. Finally Sam left my sister. I wouldn't have married her in the first place. See, I knew my own sister. And when I saw him taking her away I thought, Oh, Lord. And my momma knew too. We knew that she wasn't going to cook him nothing, cos she didn't cook her own self nothing. She was eating at our house!

I want to tell you something. The Devil don't want me to tell you what I've been telling you. I've been telling you the naked truth. What you call the unadulterated gospel. This is the kind of preaching it's gonna take for you to walk in the kingdom. You're gonna have to go back to primitive godliness. You're gonna have to go back to find the old pathway. God is calling for holiness or Hell. You got to do it. Some of you got so modern you done changed the ways around, 'cos you don't want to live clean no more. You got one foot in the church and you got one in sin. You're trying to have God and the Devil. But you can't drink out of God's cup and the Devil's cup. Did you know that? Jesus can save you tonight. Jesus wants to help you tonight. Jesus saved Little Richard, a homosexual all my life.

I never knew that I could like women. I never knew there'd be a day when I didn't want to have a man. And my desire. A young lady asked me, "Did He change your feelings?" I said, "No, He changed my *desire*. You have a desire before you get a feeling." That old feeling can fool you. He sanctified my desire and gave me a new heart and a new mind. See, the Bible says, "Let this mind be in you that is also in Christ Jesus. Greater is he that is in you than he that is in the world."

I'd rather have Jesus than anything the world could afford today. Jesus took me. And when I went back home, my curls was gone. I didn't have no more curls. My eyelashes was gone. I didn't have no makeup on. The only makeup I had on was the day when I went on television, and they put that on to keep me from coming up a-shining. You know, black folks shine. They had to stop me from shining. God changed me around. He gave me a new walk. Somebody said... "You don't walk the way you used to walk." I said, "Cos I don't go where I used to go." Somebody said, "Well, you sure can't talk the way you used to

214

talk." I said, "I don't say what I used to say." Because Jesus has given me a new song. He's given me a new life. At this time, I want to sing a song for you. I want you to bow your heads while I sing this song.

I want to let you know that there is nothing too hard for the Lord. If you have an unnatural problem Jesus can change it. Won't you try Him? If you have a drinking problem, if you have a dope problem, the Bible says in Hebrews 13:8, that Jesus Christ is the same yesterday, today, and forever. I want to sing for you about a city that Jesus has prepared for me and you can go to. It's a city where are no more funeral homes, no more hospitals, no more crying, no more dying; Jesus is gonna take all our tears and He's gonna put 'em in a bottle and He will remember them. No more loneliness. That's the reason a lot of people go to homosexuality, because of loneliness. They're so lonely, they want people to love 'em. Homosexuals are the nicest people that you can ever meet. They're kind, they're artistic, they are lonely people. You can't hate 'em to Jesus, you got to love 'em to Jesus. You've got to remember that's *you* without Jesus. That's me, that's your brother, that's your sister. You got to remember that. At this time I want to sing for you "God's Beautiful City."

Every head is bowed. In the name of Jesus, Lord, we thank You tonight. We thank You for what our ears have heard tonight, dear God. We thank You for the power of the Holy Ghost, dear Lord. We thank You for the direction of Your spirit and Your dear Son, dear God. We thank You for the word, dear Lord, for the stamping and the writing of it on our hearts. We pray tonight that we'll be new creatures, O Lord, in Christ Jesus. We pray tonight that we will see that God can do anything. We thank You tonight, O Lord, that Your arms are not too short. We thank You that Your ears are not too heavy. Be with us tonight, O Lord, and bring us back to study Your word. We thank You, O Lord, in Jesus' name. In Jesus' holy name. Amen.

215

# TESTIMONIALS

ELVIS PRESLEY: Your music has inspired me—you are the greatest.                                                —1969

JOHN LENNON: Elvis was bigger than religion in my life. Then this boy at school said he'd got this record by somebody called Little Richard who was better than Elvis—we used to go to this boy's house after school and listen to Elvis on 78s: we'd buy five ciggies loose and some chips and go along. The new record was Little Richard's "Long Tall Sally." When I heard it, it was so great I couldn't speak. You know how you are torn. I didn't want to leave Elvis, but this was so much better. We all looked at each other, but I didn't want to say anything against Elvis, even in my mind. How could they *both* be happening in my life? And then someone said, "It's a nigger singing." I didn't know Negroes sang. So Elvis was white and Little Richard was black. This was a great relief. "Thank you, God," I said. "There is a difference between them." But I thought about it for days at school, of the labels on the records of Elvis and Little Richard. One was yellow and the other was blue, and I thought of the yellow against the blue.        —1970

MUHAMMAD ALI: Little Richard is my favorite singer.

ELTON JOHN: Little Richard's records were the best Rock 'n' Roll records."

JIMI HENDRIX: I want to do with my guitar what Little Richard does with his voice.                    —1966

DAVID BOWIE: After hearing Little Richard on record I bought a saxophone and came into the music business. Little Richard was my inspiration.

SMOKEY ROBINSON: Little Richard is the beginning of Rock 'n' Roll.

BO DIDDLEY: Little Richard was one of a kind, a show-biz genius. He influenced so many people in the business, I was afraid to follow him onstage.

SAM COOKE: I love Little Richard, he is a great entertainer and he has done so much for our music.     —1962

JANIS JOPLIN: I'd fly across the country to see Otis; I'd go see Little Richard anywhere. They work, they happen, they're electric, they're exciting, they sweat for you.—1969

SCREAMIN' LORD SUTCH: The best rock voice in the world.

GENE VINCENT: The very first time I saw Little Richard work I couldn't believe my own eyes or ears! But I'll tell you one thing, I made up my mind from that moment on that I would never be able to follow this man onstage. My good friend Jerry Lee Lewis came to the same conclusion! Now that's no mean admission, for Jerry and I both rate ourselves pretty wild performers, but neither of us could keep up the excitement that Richard generates.

EDWIN STARR: Little Richard is probably the father of Rock 'n' Roll, along with the immortally famous Chuck

Berry. Little Richard is the most dynamite man that you will ever meet.

WOLFMAN JACK: In the spiritual poll of Rock 'n' Roll Little Richard is a tried and true original. Since his beginning others have all picked up from his style and his music, from the early Beatles to Mick Jagger today. At one time it was all Little Richard's original raving craving thing.

MITCH RYDER: I have the best musicians in the world in my band, but I am not the best singer in the world. Little Richard is.

BUDDY HOLLY: You can't keep,vs still when you hear the great Little Richard. He's the wildest act in Rock 'n' Roll, and you cannot beat his act onstage.  —1958

JOHNNY OTIS: Little Richard is twice as important as the Beatles and the Stones put together.

MICKEY MOST: Little Richard's records were the most dynamic records of the Rock 'n' Roll era and his voice was the best Rock 'n' Roll voice ever.

DON COVAY: Little Richard rep,vsresented what I wanted to be. He was, and still is, my idol.

DICK CLARK: Once you have seen this man you know instantly you have seen the greatest Rock 'n' Roll legend of our time.

DEWEY TERRY: Little Richard has been one of the guiding lights in American music as we know it. Little Richard can take you and just stand up by himself and make you cry. He is the master at captivating an audience.

JOHNNY GUITAR WATSON: He *is* the King of Rock 'n' Roll.

CHUCK BERRY: Little Richard is a great originator. He was right there at the start, a thrilling performer.

RY COODER: The first 45 I ever played was by Little Richard, even today I constantly listen to Little Richard.

PROFESSOR LONGHAIR: Little Richard? Now he is something else. A fantastic, powerful voice and the wildest act I've seen anywhere.

DAVID ESSEX: Little Richard is my favorite singer. As a man and a performer he is larger than life, with a singing voice charged with emotion. A terrific singer.

JON LORD: There would have been no Deep,vs Purple if there had been no Little Richard.

KENNY EVERETT: The greatest singer of all time.

PAUL SIMON: When I was in high school I wanted to be like Little Richard.

MIKE READ: Little Richard is the mostest, the utmost.

BILLY FURY: The greatest rough-edge powerhouse singer of them all.

JACQUES BARASAMIAN: Truly the Muhammad Ali of pop.

MARTY BALIN: Little Richard, man, was the God. I grew up on Little Richard in the rocking fifties.

PHIL EVERLY: We first met Richard in New York in 1957, the Steve Allen show. We were straight out of Tennessee and we loved Richard's music, and it was quite a revelation to see how beautifully he could handle a crowd. He could really make 'em come alive. He could do that better than anybody. It was impossible to follow him. When Richard was on the show he was it. Richard is an original, and the songs that he's written and the songs that he's done and made famous are just one of a kind. He was just a master showman.

JAMES BROWN: Little Richard is my idol.

OTIS REDDING: If it hadn't been for Little Richard I would not be here. I entered the music business because of Richard—he is my inspiration. I used to sing like Little Richard, his Rock 'n' Roll stuff, you know. Richard has soul, too. My present music has a lot of him in it. He did a number way back called "Directly from My Heart to You" which was the personification of soul, and he had one out—I heard it in L.A. a lot—called "I Don't Know What You've Got But It's Got Me." Yes, sir. Little Richard has done a lot for me and my soul brothers in the music business.                                        —1966

PAT BOONE: No one person has been imitated more than Little Richard.

# THE LITTLE RICHARD
# CHRONICLES

# RECORDING SESSIONS

*The following section attempts to chronicle the various recording sessions that led to the hundreds of Little Richard records that have been available since 1951. A sessionography lists recordings in the order they were recorded, not the order in which they were released to the public (which often has little to do with when they were cut!).*

*The format used herein is pretty standard.* Personnel and Instrumentation: voc = vocal, pno = piano, bs = bass, gtr = guitar, vln = violin, tpt = trumpet, tbn = trombone, dms = drums, voc gp = vocal group

**Date Of Recording (Recording location)**

Master No.   Song Title . . . . . . . .   Record No.

*Whenever possible, information was taken from either the original session notes or company files; at other times we were forced to use the personal recollections of musicians from the given sessions—and that data, frankly, is not 100 percent certain.*

*The record numbers we have listed for each song represent the* first *appearance of a given song on 45 rpm (or 78 rpm) single, 45 rpm EP (extended-play single, four songs instead of two), and 33 rpm LP (long-playing album). In a few cases where clarification was necessary, we have expanded the record-number listing to include all releases within an appropriate time frame to contain the given song; these instances are so noted preceding the sessions involved.*

*We have not included recordings of live performances that have appeared on various bootlegs, since (a) they were never intended for recording, much less release, and (b) the inclusion of every known tape in the hands of collectors would defeat the purpose of the listing.*

*Master numbers are assigned by a record company to differentiate each recording made; the problem arises when a company assigns the master number at the time of release, instead of at the time of actual recording. Hence some of the master numbers are meaningful (Okeh,*

223

*Reprise), while some are just confusing (Specialty). We have used the master numbers from the original singles whenever possible, and then referred to company files for confirmation. Where master numbers were not assigned, or have proven untraceable, we have used ----.*
*Abbreviations used for the numerous record labels involved are:*

| Abbreviation | Record Label | Parent Company |
|---|---|---|
| ALA | ALA | —— |
| Atl | Atlantic | WEA |
| Bell | Bell* | Arista |
| Brun | Brunswick* | Columbia & MCA |
| Camd | Camden | RCA |
| CBS (UK) | CBS | Columbia |
| Demand | Demand (bootleg) | —— |
| End | End* | Roulette |
| Gld | Goldisc* | Roulette |
| GM | Greene Mountain | —— |
| GsSt | Guest Star* | Roulette? |
| Joy | Joy | —— |
| K-Tel | K-Tel | —— |
| LS | Little Star* | —— |
| Main | Mainstream | Audio Fidelity |
| Mant | Manticore | Motown |
| Merc | Mercury | Polygram |
| Modern | Modern* | United |
| Okeh | Okeh | Columbia |
| Pea | Peacock* | MCA |
| RCA | RCA | —— |
| Redita | Redita (bootleg) | —— |
| Rep | Reprise | WEA |
| SenS | Sensational Sounds* | —— |
| Spec | Specialty | —— |
| Spin | Spin-O-Rama* | Roulette |
| Sum | Summit | —— |
| 20th | 20th Century-Fox | Polygram |
| United | United | —— |
| VJ | Vee Jay | —— |
| World | World | —— |

*Label is defunct.

## THE PRE-SPECIALTY SESSIONS

*Little Richard's first recordings, done in a radio-station studio, were mostly urban piano blues in the style of Billy Wright, featuring his band.*

*The releases met with little success. RCA has reissued the recordings in album form at least twice, but at the present time they are out of print.*

## October 16, 1951 (WGST Studio, Atlanta)

PERSONNEL: Little Richard (voc, pno) with Tom Patton (pno), George Holloway (bs), Albert Dobbins (alto sax), Carlos Bermudaz (alto sax), Willie Mays (tpt), Fred Jackson (tenor sax), Donald Clarke (dms).

| | | |
|---|---|---|
| 3773 | Get Rich Quick . . . . . . . . . . | RCA 4582, Camd LP-420 |
| 3774 | Why Did You Leave Me . . . . | RCA 4772, Camd LP-420 |
| 3775 | Taxi Blues . . . . . . . . . . . . . | RCA 4372, Camd LP-420 |
| 3776 | Every Hour . . . . . . . . . . . . | RCA 4372, Camd LP-420 |

## January 12, 1952 (WGST Studio, Atlanta)

PERSONNEL: Same as above.

| | | |
|---|---|---|
| 5034 | I Brought It All on Myself . . | RCA 5052, Camd LP-420 |
| 5035 | Ain't Nothin' Happening . . . | RCA 4772, Camd LP-420 |
| 5036 | Thinkin' 'bout My Mother . . | RCA 4582, Camd LP-420 |
| 5037 | Please Have Mercy | |
| | on Me . . . . . . . . . . . . . . . . . . . | RCA 5052, Camd LP-420 |

*Richard's Peacock recordings leaned more toward Rhythm 'n' Blues than outright Rock 'n' Roll. As a member of the Tempo Toppers, he toured with the Duces of Rhythm, making enough of an impression to warrant an article in a popular music magazine of the era (1954, Rhythm & Blues Songs). Even so, his records sold poorly, and for his second session, Peacock owner Don Robey brought in the Johnny Otis band. The numbers recorded at this later session were not released until three years later, when Richard's Specialty cuts were climbing the charts.*

*The Peacock recordings have never appeared on a legitimate album and are currently out of print. It has been said, though never confirmed, that an additional eight sides were cut at another session with the Otis orchestra. Alternate takes of at least two of the October 1953 songs have recently been found at MCA and might be included in an upcoming reissue.*

## February 25, 1953 (Houston)

PERSONNEL: Little Richard (voc), with the Tempo Toppers (Billy Brooks, Barry Lee Gilmore, Jimmy Swan, voc gp) and the Duces of Rhythm (Raymond Taylor, org, Mildred Taylor, dms), Eddie Lee Williams (gtr), Roy Montrell Orch.

| | | |
|---|---|---|
| 2422 | Always . . . . . . . . . . . . . . . . . | Peac 1628 |
| 2423 | Ain't That Good News . . . . . | Peac 1616 |
| 2424 | Fool at the Wheel . . . . . . . . | Peac 1616 |

2425 Rice, Red Beans and Turnip
    Greens ................... Peac 1628

**October 5, 1953 (Houston)**

PERSONNEL: Little Richard (voc) with the Johnny Otis Orchestra: Johnny Otis (vibes), Devonia Williams (pno), Pete Lewis (gtr), George Washington (tbn), Walter Henry or Fred Ford (baritone sax), Lorenzo Holden or James Van Streeter (tpt), Don Johnson (tpt), Albert Winston (bs), Leard "Kansas City" Bell (dms).

2698 Maybe I'm Right.......... Peac 1673
2699 Directly from My Heart to
    You ...................... Peac 1658
2700 I Love My Baby.......... Peac 1673
2701 Little Richard's Boogie .... Peac 1658

## THE SPECIALTY SESSIONS

*The recording sessions Little Richard cut for Specialty Records between 1955 and 1957 are among the most important (and enjoyable) in the history of pop music. They have also, unfortunately, been among the hardest to accurately chronicle. Teased by the sporadic appearance of underground tapes and exotic bootlegs containing fragments and previously unreleased takes from those legendary sessions—and without access to company files—the erstwhile Richard fanatic could quickly go crazy trying to sort it all out.*

*Piecing our information together from the recollections of Richard himself, Bumps Blackwell, John Marascalco, and finally our own ears, we were still not satisfied with our reconstruction of the sessions.*

*Just before presstime, Specialty Records in Los Angeles graciously opened their files to us, after more than a year of requests, enabling us to publish this information for the first time anywhere. Our heartfelt thanks are extended to Mr. Joseph Mattia and all the rest at Specialty who helped with this critical part of the session listings.*

*We have annotated the following session listing with the superscripts o (to indicate overdubbed version) and e (to indicate edited or truncated versions). When Richard abdicated from Rock 'n' Roll in late 1957, Specialty was forced to go back to earlier, less rock-oriented recordings they had rejected initially to make future releases. In an effort to make these bluesy recordings sound "current," they added a female chorus (and in at least one instance, extra instrumentation) to the basic track; hence the special annotation.*

*The original three Specialty albums, as well as the "Well Alright!" compilation, are all in print and readily available.*

## February 9, 1955 (WBML Studio, Macon)

PERSONNEL: Little Richard (voc, pno?)

| | | |
|---|---|---|
| ---- | He's My Star............ | UNRELEASED |
| ---- | Wonderin'.............. | UNRELEASED |

*This was the demonstration tape Richard submitted to Specialty in early 1955 at Lloyd Price's suggestion. Tapes also exist of Richard performing "She's My Star" (a cappella) and "Baby" (with a spoken introduction by Richard addressing Mr. Rupe, owner of Specialty).*

## September 13 & 14, 1955 (J & M Studio, New Orleans)

PERSONNEL: Little Richard (voc, pno-1), Melvin Dowden (pno except -1), Justin Adams (gtr), Frank Fields (bs), Lee Allen (tenor sax), Alvin "Red" Tyler (baritone sax), Earl Palmer (dms).

*Although not listed in the Specialty files, Huey "Piano" Smith was almost certainly present and probably played at some point during the September 14th session.*

| | | |
|---|---|---|
| ---- | Lonesome And Blue....... | Spec 664, LP-2104 |
| 5182 | Wonderin'.............. | Spec 699, LP-2136 |
| 5215 | All Night Long .......... | Spec 670, LP-2104 |
| ---- | Kansas City............. | Spec LP-2104 |
| ---- | Tutti Frutti -1 ........... | Spec 561, EP-402, LP-100 |
| ---- | All Alone .............. | UNRELEASED |
| ---- | I'm Just a Lonely Guy..... | Spec 561, LP-2104° |
| ---- | Baby.................. | UNRELEASED |
| 5250 | Directly from My Heart to You...................... | Spec 686°, LP-2104°, LP-2136 |
| 5249 | The Most I Can Offer...... | Spec 686°, LP-2104° |
| 5237 | Maybe I'm Right......... | Spec 680°, LP-2104° |
| ---- | Chicken Little Baby -1..... | Spec 734, LP-2104° |

*A tape exists (in fragments) of "Chicken Little Baby" featuring Richard alone at the piano; it was this recording that supposedly was engineered to construct the released version. Perhaps the band on the released single was overdubbed later.*

## November 29, 1955 (Radio Recorders, Hollywood)

PERSONNEL: Little Richard (voc, pno?), Lloyd Lambert (bs), Joseph Tillman (sax), Oscar Moore (dms), William Pyles, Renald Richard, Clarence Ford (Guitar Slim's band).

| | | |
|---|---|---|
| 5182 | Wonderin'.............. | Spec 660°, LP-2104° |
| ---- | Slippin' and Slidin' ....... | UNRELEASED |
| ---- | Miss Ann .............. | UNRELEASED |

5240  Baby.................... Spec 681, EP-401, LP-100
––––  The Thing ( = Long Tall
  Sally) ..................... Redita LP-101 (bootleg)
5101  True Fine Mama.......... Spec 633, EP-402, LP-100
5200  Kansas City............. Spec 664, LP-2136
  (alternate take) ............. Redita LP-101 (bootleg)

**February 10, 1956 (J & M Studio, New Orleans)**

PERSONNEL: Little Richard (voc, pno), Edgar Blanchard (gtr), Frank Fields (bs), Lee Allen (tenor sax), Alvin "Red" Tyler (baritone sax), Earl Palmer (dms).

––––  Slippin' and Slidin' ....... Spec 572$^e$, EP-401, LP-100
––––  The Thing ( = Long Tall
  Sally) .................... Spec 572, EP-400, LP-100
5069  Miss Ann ............... Spec 606, EP-400, LP-100
5239  I Got It................. Spec 681
––––  Ready Teddy ............ UNRELEASED
5103  Birmingham ( = Hey-Hey-
  Hey-Hey) ................. Spec 624, EP-403, LP-2103
––––  Rip It Up .............. Spec 579, EP-402, LP-100

**May 9 & 15, 1956 (J & M Studio, New Orleans)**

PERSONNEL: Little Richard (voc, pno), Edgar Blanchard (gtr), Frank Fields (bs), Lee Allen (tenor sax), Alvin "Red" Tyler (baritone sax), Ernest McLean, Paul Palmer.

––––  Ready Teddy ............. Spec 579, EP-401, LP-100
––––  Heeby-Jeebies............ UNRELEASED

**July 30 & August 1, 1956 (J & M Studio, New Orleans)**

PERSONNEL: Little Richard (voc, pno), Raymond Montrell (gtr?), Frank Fields (bs), Lee Allen (tenor sax), Alvin "Red" Tyler (baritone sax), Earl Palmer (dms).

––––  Oh Why ................ Spec 734, EP-401, LP-100
5000  Heeby-Jeebies............ Spec 584, EP-405, LP-2103
––––  Good Golly Miss Molly .... UNRELEASED
5015  All Around the World...... Spec 591, EP-404, LP-2103
5075  Can't Believe You Wanna
  Leave ................... Spec 611, EP-400, LP-100
5213  Shake a Hand ........... Spec 670°, LP-2104°, LP-2136°

*The version of "Shake a Hand" on Specialty LP-2136 contains overdubbing different from that used on the LP-2104 version, including instrumentation and a different female chorus.*

228

**September 6, 1956 (Master Recorders, Los Angeles)**

PERSONNEL: Little Richard (voc, pno), Nathaniel Douglas (gtr), Olsie Robinson (bs), Clifford Burks (tenor sax), Wilbert Smith (tenor sax), Grady Gaines (tenor sax), Jewell Grant (baritone sax), Charles Connor (dms).

| | | |
|---|---|---|
| ---- | I Got It . . . . . . . . . . . . . . . . . | Redita LP-101 (bootleg) |
| ---- | Send Me Some Lovin'. . . . . . | Redita LP-101 (bootleg) |
| 5005 | She's Got It . . . . . . . . . . . . . | Spec 584$^e$, EP-400, LP-100 |

**October 15 & 16, 1956 (J & M Studio, New Orleans)**

PERSONNEL: Little Richard (voc, pno), Ray Montrell (gtr?), Frank Fields (bs), Lee Allen (tenor sax), Alvin "Red" Tyler (baritone sax), Earl Palmer (dms), The Robins (voc gp -1).

| | | |
|---|---|---|
| 5067 | Jenny Jenny . . . . . . . . . . . . | Spec 606, EP-402, LP-100 |
| 5099 | Good Golly Miss Molly . . . . | Spec 624, EP-404, LP-2103 |
| | (alternate take) . . . . . . . . . . . . . | Redita LP-101 (bootleg) |
| 5147 | Baby Face . . . . . . . . . . . . . . | Spec 645, EP-404, LP-2103 |
| | (alternate take) . . . . . . . . . . . . | Redita LP-114 (bootleg) |
| 5016 | By the Light of the Silvery Moon . . . . . . . . . . . . . . . . . . . . | Spec 660, EP-403, LP-2103 |
| 5019 | The Girl Can't Help It -1 . . . | Spec 591, EP-405, LP-2103 |
| | (alternate take, from film) . . . . . | Redita LP-114 (bootleg) |
| 5043 | Send Me Some Lovin'. . . . . . | Spec 598, EP-405, LP-2103 |

**January 16, 1957 (Washington D.C.)**

PERSONNEL: Little Richard (voc, pno), Nathaniel Douglas (gtr), Olsie Robinson (bs), Clifford Burks (tenor sax), Wilbert Smith (tenor sax), Grady Gaines (tenor sax), Samuel Parker Jr. (baritone sax), Charles Connor (dms).

| | | |
|---|---|---|
| 5045 | Lucille . . . . . . . . . . . . . . . . . | Spec 598, EP-403, LP-2103 |
| 5072 | Keep a-Knockin'. . . . . . . . . . | Spec 611$^e$, EP-403$^e$, LP-2103$^e$, LP-2136 |

*The released version of "Lucille" does not sound like it came from this session (Specialty files notwithstanding) and might come from the 9/6/56 session instead. The complete version of "Keep a-Knockin'" has never been released. Originally only 57 seconds long, the basic track was doubled and redoubled to engineer it to single-record length. One verse with the words "I'm drinkin' gin and you can't come in" was also deleted from the final release. Finally, it is believed that two songs by Don Covay (with Little Richard on piano) and the Upsetters were recorded at this session (Atlantic 1147—"Bip Bop Bip" b/w "Paper Dollar," as by Pretty Boy).*

**October 18, 1957 (Master Recorders, Los Angeles)**

PERSONNEL: Little Richard (voc, pno), Nathaniel Douglas (gtr), Olsie Robinson (bs), Clifford Burks (tenor sax), Wilbert Smith (tenor sax), Grady Gaines (tenor sax), Charles Connor (dms).

| | |
|---|---|
| 5149 I'll Never Let You Go (Boo Hoo Hoo Hoo) . . . . . . . . . . . . . . | Spec 645, EP-405, LP-2103 |
| 5125 Ooh! My Soul . . . . . . . . . . | Spec 633$^e$, EP-404, LP-2103$^e$ |
| 5164 Blues (= Early One Morning) . . . . . . . . . . . . . . . . . | Spec 652, LP-2104 |
| 5162 She Knows How to Rock . . . | Spec 652, LP-2104, LP-2136$^e$ |
| (alternate take) . . . . . . . . . . . . . | Redita LP-101 (bootleg) |
| 5238 Whole Lotta Shakin' Goin' On . . . . . . . . . . . . . . . . . . . . . | Spec 680$^e$, LP-2104 |
| (alternate take) . . . . . . . . . . . . . | Redita LP-101 (bootleg) |
| ––––– Hound Dog . . . . . . . . . . . . . | Redita LP-101 (bootleg) |
| ––––– Good Morning Little Schoolgirl . . . . . . . . . . . . . . . . . | UNRELEASED |

*The released version of "Ooh! My Soul" does not sound like it comes from this session but rather from the "Keep a-Knockin'" session. On a private tape containing this final session for Specialty, mention is made of another title Richard was to record: "Hoochie Coochie."*

## THE GOLDNER SESSIONS

*The first religious cuts Little Richard made for public consumption were for long-time record industry mogul George Goldner. Goldner, who owned or worked with a number of somewhat interrelated record labels in the 1950s (End, Gone, Rama, Gee, Roulette, Goldisc, et al.), released the twenty songs on a number of different albums and leased the cuts to other companies almost simultaneously! Sorting out the release pattern of the many budget LPs that appeared between 1959 and 1963 is a job worthy of Sherlock Holmes, and for that reason we have expanded the normal release listing for this section to include all the albums from this period.*

*The recordings themselves are pretty miserable, and three record labels with access to the "dirgelike" cuts overdubbed drums and miscellaneous percussion to fill out the sound. These have been annotated in the release listing with the superscript O.*

**c. September 1959 (New York City)**

PERSONNEL: Little Richard (voc) with Herman Stevens (organ).

| | |
|---|---|
| 569 Save Me Lord . . . . . . . . . . . . | End 1057, Gld LP-4002 |

---- Jesus Walked This
Lonesome Valley . . . . . . . . . . . .    Gld LP-4001, Cor LP-57446°,
GsSt LP-1429
Add unk. voc gp
567 Milky White Way . . . . . . . . .    End 1058, Gld LP-4001, Cor LP-
57446°, 20th LP-5010
568 Troubles of the World . . . . . .    End 1057, Gld LP-4002, 20th LP-
5010, Spin LP-119
570 I've Just Come from the
Fountain . . . . . . . . . . . . . . . . . .    End 1058, Gld LP-4001, 20th LP-
5010, GsSt LP-1429
---- Certainly Lord . . . . . . . . . . .    Gld LP-4002, 20th LP-5010, GsSt
LP-1429, Spin LP-119, Sum LP-
4029
Add unk. pno
---- Need Him . . . . . . . . . . . . . .    Cor 62366°, LP-57446°, Gld LP-
4001
---- Just a Closer Walk with
Thee . . . . . . . . . . . . . . . . . . . . .    Gld LP-4001, GsSt LP-1429, Cor
LP-57446°
---- Comin' Home . . . . . . . . . . .    Gld LP-4001, 20th LP-5010, Cor
LP-57446
---- Every Time I Feel the Spirit    Gld LP-4002, Cor LP-57446°,
20th LP-5010, Spin LP-119
---- I'm Tramping . . . . . . . . . . .    Gld LP-4001, Cor LP-57446°,
20th LP-5010
---- God Is Real . . . . . . . . . . . . .    Gld LP-4001, Cor LP-57446°,
20th LP-5010, Sum LP-4029
   *as "He Is Real"* . . . . . . . . . . .    *Spin LP-119*
---- In My Heart . . . . . . . . . . . .    Gld LP-4002, Spin LP-119
Omit unk. voc gp.
---- Walk with Me . . . . . . . . . . .    Spin LP-119
   *as "I Want Jesus to Walk
   with Me"* . . . . . . . . . . . . . . . . .    *Cor LP-57446, Sum LP-4029*
---- Search Me Lord . . . . . . . . . .    Gld LP-4002, Spin LP-119, Cor
LP-57446°
---- Does Jesus Care . . . . . . . . . .    Gld LP-4001, Cor LP-57446°,
20th LP-5010, GsSt LP-1429
---- Precious Lord . . . . . . . . . . .    Gld LP-4001, Cor LP-57446, GsSt
LP-1429, 20th LP-5010
   *as "Take My Hand"* . . . . . . . .    *Sum LP-4029*
---- I Know the Lord . . . . . . . . .    Gld LP-4002, 20th LP-5010, Spin
LP-119
   Tell God My Troubles . . . . . .    Gld LP-4002, GsSt LP-1429, 20th
LP-5010

as "All About It" .......... *Spin LP-119*
as "I'm Going to Tell God".. *Sum LP-1429*
———— I'm Quittin' Show Business   Gld LP-4002, Spin LP-119

*Crown LP-5362 and Custom LP-2061 are identical to Goldisc LP-4001, and 20th Century-Fox LP-5010 has the Crown LP number scratched out in the run-off wax.*

## THE LITTLE STAR SESSION

*In 1962–63, two 45 rpm singles were released on the Little Star label that contained what was Richard's first Rock 'n' Roll since 1957, backed by his former band the Upsetters. The recordings are out of print. Musicians involved say that enough tracks were recorded for an album, but the rest cannot be traced.*

### c. 1960 (New York)

PERSONNEL: Little Richard (voc, pno) with Joe Hughes (gtr), Grady Gaines (sax), Olsie Robinson (bs), Milton Hopkins (gtr), Richard Roy (sax), Cliff Burks (sax), unk. (dms).

———— I'm in Love Again ......... LS 123
———— Every Night about This
Time...................... LS 123
———— Valley of Tears .......... LS 128
Omit vocal.
———— Freedom Ride........... LS 128

*Around this time, Richard recorded two gospel tunes that appeared on a demo bearing the Sensational Sounds (New York City) label; as far as we know, they were never officially released and are certainly unavailable. Richard has no memory of this session.*

### Unk. date (New York City)

PERSONNEL: Little Richard (voc, pno?) with Jessie McDaniel (organ), Kay Weather (pno), Gospel Spiritualettes (voc gp).

———— I Found God ............ UNRELEASED?
———— Fly Away Jesus .......... UNRELEASED?

*It is possible that another four songs were recorded at this session, although details are lacking.*

## THE MERCURY SESSIONS

*Quincy Jones, of recent Grammy fame, produced these excellent recordings that wear well more than twenty years later... if you can find them. They are, unfortunately, out of print.*

## c. June 1961 (New York City)

PERSONNEL: Little Richard (voc) with the Quincy Jones Orchestra, unk. dms, bs, pno -1, gtr -2, brass -3, organ -4, and the Howard Roberts Chorale.

6056  The Captain Calls for You
   -1-3 . . . . . . . . . . . . . . . . . . . . . . .  Merc LP-60656
6057  Do You Care -1 . . . . . . . . . . .  Merc 71911, LP-60656
6058  He's Not Just a Soldier -3 . .  Merc 71884, LP-60656
Add harp.
6059  In Times Like These -1-4 . . .  Merc LP-60656
Omit Chorale, dms, bs.
6060  He's My Star -4 . . . . . . . . . .  Merc LP-60656
Add Chorale, dms.
6061  My Desire -2-4-7 . . . . . . . . .  Merc LP-60656
Add bs.
6062  It Takes Everything to
   Serve the Lord. . . . . . . . . . . . . .  Merc LP-60656
Omit strings, harp.
6063  Ride on King Jesus -1 . . . . .  Merc 71911, LP-60656
6064  Peace in the Valley -1-2-4 . . .  Merc LP-60656
6065  Joy Joy Joy -1 . . . . . . . . . . .  Merc 71884, LP-60656
6066  It's Real -1-4 . . . . . . . . . . . .  Merc LP-60656
6067  Do Lord, Remember Me -1
   -2-4 . . . . . . . . . . . . . . . . . . . . . .  Merc LP-60656

## March 1962 (Unk. location)

PERSONNEL: Little Richard (voc) with unk. personnel.

24081  Old Ship of Zion . . . . . . . . .  Demand LP-25 (bootleg)
24082  I Keep on Living . . . . . . . . .  Demand LP-25 (bootleg)
24083  Change Your Ways . . . . . . .  Merc 71965
24087  Walking through the
   Valley in Peace . . . . . . . . . . . . .  Demand LP-25 (bootleg)
24088  Let's Pray for Peace . . . . . .  Demand LP-25 (bootleg)
24089  He Got What He Wanted . .  Merc 71965
   (alternate take) . . . . . . . . . . . . .  Merc LP-20019
24400  I Asked the Lord . . . . . . . .  Demand LP-25 (bootleg)
24401  It's a Miracle. . . . . . . . . . .  Demand LP-25 (bootleg)

## Unk. date (Los Angeles)

338293  What Has the World
   Done to My Heart. . . . . . . . . . .  UNRELEASED
338294  Love's Stronger Than Me.  UNRELEASED

338295 Her Hurt Upon My
  Hands. . . . . . . . . . . . . . . . . . . . .  UNRELEASED
338296 Wheels. . . . . . . . . . . . . . .  UNRELEASED

*Assuming that Mercury assigned master numbers in a somewhat chronological order, it would make sense to assume that these four recordings were made in 1966.*

## THE ATLANTIC SESSIONS

*These recordings, continuing Richard's commitment to religious material, are out of print.*

**June 14, 1962 (Conway Studios, Los Angeles)**

PERSONNEL: Little Richard (voc, pno) with unk. personnel.

—— Hole in the Wall . . . . . . . . .  UNRELEASED
—— You'll Never Walk Alone . . .  UNRELEASED
—— Eliger Rock . . . . . . . . . . . . .  UNRELEASED
—— Jericho. . . . . . . . . . . . . . . .  UNRELEASED
—— If You Can't Take It, You
  Can't Make It. . . . . . . . . . . . . .  UNRELEASED

**February 14, 1963 (Los Angeles)**

PERSONNEL: Little Richard (voc, pno) with unk. gtr, bs, dms, strings, brass, female chorus.

6770 Hole in the Wall . . . . . . . . .  Atl 2181
6771 Crying in the Chapel . . . . . .  Atl 2181
—— My Mother's Eyes. . . . . . . . .  UNRELEASED
—— He Gave . . . . . . . . . . . . . . . .  UNRELEASED

**April 2, 1963 (New York City)**

PERSONNEL: Little Richard (voc) with unk. bs, dms, female chorus, organ, miscellaneous percussion, steel gtr -1.

6913 Traveling Shoes . . . . . . . . . .  Atl 2192
6914 It Is No Secret -1. . . . . . . . . .  Atl 2192

## THE RETURN TO SPECIALTY

*In the wake of the "British Invasion" and following a very successful tour of England, Richard collected his current guitarist (Glen Willings), the drummer from his New Orleans sessions (Palmer), and old labelmates Don and Dewey (who had a number of hits on their own) and returned to Specialty to start his comeback. Most of these recordings are still in print.*

**April 1963 (Sam Cooke's Studio, L.A.)**

PERSONNEL: Little Richard (voc, pno) with unk. personnel.

---- Well . . . . . . . . . . . . . . . . . . .    Spec LP-2136

**April 1964 (Los Angeles)**

PERSONNEL: Little Richard (voc, pno) with Glen Willings (gtr), Don "Sugarcane" Harris (bs), Dewey Terry (gtr), Earl Palmer (dms).

| | |
|---|---|
| ---- Bama Lama Bama Loo . . . . | Spec 692, 697°, LP-2136° |
| ---- Annie Is Back . . . . . . . . . . . | Spec 692 |
| (alternate take) . . . . . . . . . . . . . | Spec LP-2136 |
| ---- Poor Boy Paul . . . . . . . . . . . | Spec 699, LP-2136 |
| ---- Miss Ann . . . . . . . . . . . . . . . | UNRELEASED |

## THE VEE JAY SESSIONS

*Even with access to the Vee Jay files, information is a bit uncertain in some areas of this listing. Of most importance to latter-day rock fans are the cuts that Jimi Hendrix played on, as a member of Richard's touring band. We have singled out those tracks we are relatively sure have Hendrix involvement, although he may have appeared on others. Nearly all the Vee Jay recordings are available, though split up among numerous (and often misleadingly labeled) albums.*

**June 1964 (Los Angeles)**

PERSONNEL: Little Richard (voc, pno) with Dewey Terry (gtr), Glen Willings (gtr), Jimi Hendrix (gtr), Don "Sugarcane" Harris (bs, vln), 2 unk. (dms), unk. female voc gp -1.

| | | |
|---|---|---|
| 4405 | Whole Lotta Shakin' -1 . . . . | VJ 612, LP-1107 |
| 4406 | Hound Dog . . . . . . . . . . . . . | VJ LP-1107 |
| 4407 | Going Home Tomorrow . . . . | VJ LP-1107 |
| 4408 | Goodnight Irene -1 . . . . . . . . | VJ 612, LP-1107 |
| 4409 | Money Honey . . . . . . . . . . . | VJ LP-1107 |
| 4410 | Lawdy Miss Clawdy . . . . . . . | VJ LP-1107 |

**1964 (Unk. location)**

PERSONNEL: Little Richard (voc, pno) with unk. bs, dms, gtrs, voc gp, brass.

| | | |
|---|---|---|
| 6636 | Blueberry Hill . . . . . . . . . . | VJ 625, LP-1107 |
| 6637 | Cherry Red . . . . . . . . . . . . . | VJ 625, LP-1107 |

Omit voc gp.

| | | |
|---|---|---|
| 6801 | Only You . . . . . . . . . . . . . . . | VJ LP-1107 |

235

Omit gtr. Add voc gp.
6802  Memories Are Made of This    VJ LP-1107
Omit brass. Add gtr.
6803  Groovy Little Suzie . . . . . . .    VJ LP-1107
6804  Short Fat Fanny . . . . . . . . . .    VJ LP-1107

## c. December 1964 (Los Angeles)

PERSONNEL: Little Richard (voc, pno) with unk. gtrs, bs, dms, brass.

6916  Send Me Some Lovin'. . . . . .    VJ LP-1124
6917  She's Got It . . . . . . . . . . . . .    UNRELEASED
6918  Keep a-Knockin'. . . . . . . . . .    VJ LP-1124
6919  Baby Face . . . . . . . . . . . . . .    VJ LP-1124
6920  Lucille . . . . . . . . . . . . . . . .    VJ LP-1124
6921  Slippin' and Slidin' . . . . . . .    VJ LP-1124
6922  She's Got It . . . . . . . . . . . . .    VJ LP-1124
6923  Good Golly Miss Molly . . . .    VJ LP-1124
6924  Tutti Frutti . . . . . . . . . . . . .    VJ LP-1124
6925  Long Tall Sally . . . . . . . . . .    VJ LP-1124
6926  Cross Over. . . . . . . . . . . . . .    VJ 652
Add unk. voc gp.
6927  Jenny Jenny -1  . . . . . . . . . .    Joy (UK) LP-260
Omit pno, brass.
6928  The Girl Can't Help It . . . . .    VJ LP-1124
Add pno. Omit voc gp.
6929  Ooh! My Soul . . . . . . . . . . .    VJ LP-1124
Omit pno.
6930  My Wheel's Been Slippin'
     All the Way . . . . . . . . . . . . . . .    Joy (UK) LP-195
6931  It Ain't What You Do . . . . . .    VJ 652
––––  Rip It Up . . . . . . . . . . . . . . .    VJ LP-1124

## January 1965 (Los Angeles)

PERSONNEL: Little Richard (voc, pno) with Clyde Johnson (sax), William
Green (sax), Buddy Collette (sax), Earl Palmer (dms), and unk. strings
-1, voc gp -2, percussion.

7844  Something Moves in My
     Heart . . . . . . . . . . . . . . . . . . . .    Dynasty LP-7304
7844a  I Don't Come from
     England . . . . . . . . . . . . . . . . . .    UNRELEASED
Omit brass, pno.
7845  Without Love -1. . . . . . . . . .    VJ 665
Add brass, pno.
7846  Dance What You Wanna -2 .    VJ 665
7847  Talking 'bout Soul . . . . . . . .    Joy (UK) LP-195

236

**1965 (Unk. location)**

PERSONNEL: Little Richard (voc, pno) with unk. dms, bs, gtr, brass, voc gp -1.

| 8537 | Dance What You Wanna -1 . | Joy (UK) LP-195 |
|---|---|---|
| 8538 | Thank You . . . . . . . . . . . . . . | UNRELEASED |

**Unk. date (Unk. location)**

PERSONNEL: Little Richard (voc, pno -1) with Jimi Hendrix (gtr), unk. dms, bs, brass, organ.

| 8652 | Dancin' All Around the World . . . . . . . . . . . . . . . . . . . . . | Joy (UK) LP-195 |
|---|---|---|
| 8655 | You Better Stop . . . . . . . . . . | Dynasty LP-7304 |
| 8657 | I Don't Know What You've Got But It's Got Me (Part 1) . . . . | VJ 698 |
| 8658 | I Don't Know What You've Got But It's Got Me (Part 2) . . . . | VJ 698 |
| | (alternate take, both parts) . . . . | Joy (UK) LP-195 |
| ———— | Every Time I Think about You -1 . . . . . . . . . . . . . . . . . . . . | Joy (UK) LP-195 |

*"Dancin' All Around the World" is listed in Vee Jay files as "Dance A-Go-Go."*

**Unk. date (Unk. location)**

PERSONNEL: Little Richard (voc -1, pno, organ -4) with Jimi Hendrix (gtr -2), Black Arthur (gtr), Henry Oden (bs), unk. dms, brass, electric bottleneck gtr -3.

| ———— | Belle Stars -2. . . . . . . . . . . . . | ALA LP-1972 |
|---|---|---|
| ———— | Funky Dish Rag -4 . . . . . . . . | ALA LP-1972 |
| ———— | Why Don't You Love Me -1-3 | ALA LP-1972 |

*"Funky Dish Rag" sounds like little more than a very loose rehearsal of "Lucille." It and the other two titles from the ALA LP are quite suspect with regard to their origin and personnel. The album was packaged to capitalize on Hendrix's post-mortem popularity (1972).*

## THE BIT AND MODERN SESSIONS

*"Bit" was a record label Richard was going to set up for releasing his own recordings, but apparently it never went beyond cutting the two songs below.*

**c. 1965 (Los Angeles)**

PERSONNEL: Little Richard (voc, pno?) with unk. personnel.

```
―――― Scuba Party. . . . . . . . . . . . .    UNRELEASED
―――― My Mother's Eyes. . . . . . . .    UNRELEASED
```

*He might have done better had he continued with the label, as his next association, Modern Records, was fruitless from almost every standpoint. It is next to impossible to sort out the Modern recordings, since they are comprised of demos, studio warm-ups, tapes supplied by Richard, and actual Modern sessions. These recordings, for what they're worth, are still available on numerous compilations. According to Richard, Jimi Hendrix played on some of these Modern recordings.*

**December 1965 (Domino Club, Atlanta)**

PERSONNEL: Little Richard (voc, pno-1) with the Upsetters.

```
―――― Medley: Tutti Frutti/Keep a-
Knockin'/Rip It Up/Jenny
Jenny/Bama Lama Bama Loo . .    Modern LP-100
―――― Medley: Long Tall Sally/
Ready Teddy . . . . . . . . . . . . . .    Modern LP-100
―――― True Fine Mama. . . . . . . . .    Modern LP-100
―――― Bony Moronie. . . . . . . . . . .    Modern LP-100
―――― Lucille . . . . . . . . . . . . . . . .    Modern LP-100
―――― Slippin' and Slidin' . . . . . . .    Modern 1030, LP-100
―――― Miss Ann . . . . . . . . . . . . . .    Modern LP-103
―――― Send Me Some Lovin'. . . . . .    Modern LP-103
―――― Good Golly Miss Molly . . . .    Modern LP-103
Add female voc gp.
―――― Baby What You Want Me to
Do (Part 1) . . . . . . . . . . . . . . . .    Modern 1043, LP-103
―――― Baby What You Want Me to
Do (Part 2) . . . . . . . . . . . . . . . .    Modern 1043, LP-103
```

*"Slippin' and Slidin' " was supposedly just a studio warm-up, never intended for release!*

**Unk. date (Unk. location [Domino club?])**

PERSONNEL: Little Richard (voc, pno) with unk. personnel (Upsetters?).

```
―――― Whole Lotta Shakin' . . . . . .    Modern LP-100
―――― Bring It Back Home. . . . . . .    Modern LP-100
―――― Do You Feel It (Part 1) . . . . .    Modern 1019, LP-100
―――― Do You Feel It (Part 2) . . . . .    Modern 1019, LP-100
```

*All tracks on Modern LP-100 have an overdubbed audience to enhance what sounds like a poor "live" recording.*

238

## c. Spring 1966 (Sun Studio, Memphis)

PERSONNEL: Little Richard (voc, pno-1), with Stax session musicians (unk. gtr, bs, dms, brass) and unk. voc gp-1.

| | | |
|---|---|---|
| ---- | Holy Mackerel .......... | Modern 1018, LP-103 |
| ---- | Baby................. | Modern 1018, LP-103 |
| ---- | I'm Back .............. | Modern 1022, LP-103 |
| ---- | Directly from My Heart to | |
| | You..................... | Modern 1022, LP-103 |
| ---- | Bring It on Home to Me. ... | Modern 1030 |
| ---- | Groovy Little Suzie -1 ..... | Modern LP-103 |
| ---- | Do the Jerk ............. | Modern LP-103 |

*"Groovy Little Suzie" appears to be the original Vee Jay recording.*

### THE OKEH SESSIONS

*Excellent, soul-oriented recordings and a superb, in-studio-with-audience live set highlight Richard's Okeh period. The best of these recordings are available on an import (British) LP.*

### February 5, 1966 (Hollywood)

PERSONNEL: Little Richard (voc, pno) with Johnny "Guitar" Watson (gtr) and unk. personnel.

| | | |
|---|---|---|
| 89976 | Poor Dog .............. | Okeh 7251°, LP-14117 |
| 89977 | Well ................. | Okeh 7251, LP-14117 |

### August 30, 1966 (Hollywood)

Omit Johnny "Guitar" Watson (gtr).

| | | |
|---|---|---|
| 88099 | A Little Bit of Something . | Okeh 7286 |
| 88100 | I Don't Want to Discuss It. | Okeh 7271, LP-14117 |
| 88101 | The Commandments of | |
| | Love ..................... | Okeh 7262, LP-14117 |
| 88102 | Never Gonna Let You Go.. | Okeh 7278, LP-14117 |

### September 2, 1966 (Hollywood)

| | | |
|---|---|---|
| 88114 | I Need Love ............ | Okeh 7262, LP-14117 |
| 88115 | Land of a Thousand | |
| | Dances................... | Okeh LP-14117 |
| 88116-2 | Don't Deceive Me....... | Okeh 7278, LP-14117 |
| 88117 | Money ................ | Okeh 7286, LP-14117 |

### September 15, 1966 (Hollywood)

| | | |
|---|---|---|
| 88144 | Function at the Junction.. | Okeh LP-14117 |
| 88145 | Hurry Sundown ......... | Okeh 7271, LP-14117 |

239

### December 1966 (Abbey Road, London)

PERSONNEL: Little Richard (voc, pno), Big Jim Sullivan (gtr) with unk. bs, brass, dms. (Bluesology?)

| | | |
|---|---|---|
| ―――― | Get Down with It | CBS (UK) 8116 |
| ―――― | Rosemary | CBS (UK) 8116 |
| ―――― | Hound Dog | UNRELEASED |
| ―――― | The Rocking Chair | UNRELEASED |

### January 25, 1967 (CBS Studio, Hollywood)

PERSONNEL: Little Richard (voc, pno) with Billy Preston (organ), Eddie Fletcher (bs), Glenn Willings (gtr), Johnny "Guitar" Watson (gtr), unk. dms.

| | | |
|---|---|---|
| 94627 | Lucille | Okeh 7325, LP-14121 |
| 94628 | The Girl Can't Help It | Okeh LP-14121 |
| 94629 | Tutti Frutti | Okeh LP-14121 |
| 94630 | Send Me Some Lovin' | Okeh LP-14121 |
| 94631 | Long Tall Sally | Okeh LP-14121 |
| 94632 | True Fine Mama | Okeh LP-14121 |
| 94633 | Jenny Jenny | Okeh LP-14121 |
| 94634 | Good Golly Miss Molly | Okeh LP-14121 |
| 94635 | Whole Lotta Shakin' | Okeh 7325, LP-14121 |
| 94636 | Anyway You Want Me | Okeh LP-14121 |
| 94637 | You Gotta Feel It | Okeh LP-14121 |
| 94638 | Get Down with It | Okeh LP-14121 |
| ―――― | I'm in Love Again | UNRELEASED |
| ―――― | Rip It Up | UNRELEASED |
| ―――― | Keep a-Knockin' | UNRELEASED |

### May 17, 1967 (Hollywood)

| | | |
|---|---|---|
| 94808 | Something Moves Me | UNRELEASED |
| 94809 | Golden Arrow | UNRELEASED |
| 94834 | World Of Love | UNRELEASED |

## THE BRUNSWICK SESSIONS

*These recordings did not sell for good reason—they're quite mediocre and now out of print.*

### 1967 (New York City)

PERSONNEL: Little Richard (voc, pno-1) with unk. gtr, bs, brass -2, dms, female voc gp -3, organ -4, Bert Decoteaux Orchestra.

| | | |
|---|---|---|
| 119521 | Try Some of Mine -2-3 | Brun 55362 |

240

119522  She's Together -2-3 . . . . . .    Brun 55362
120195  Baby Don't You Tear My
       Clothes -1-4 . . . . . . . . . . . . . . .    Brun 55377
120196  Stingy Jenny . . . . . . . . . .    Brun 55377

**1967 (Chicago)**

120761  Soul Train -2-3-4 . . . . . . . .    Brun 55386
120762  Can I Count on You -2 . . .    Brun 55386

## THE REPRISE SESSION

*The Reprise era was the peak of Richard's comeback, highlighted by numerous television talk-show appearances. These recordings are also out of print.*

**March 11, 1970 (Record Plant, Los Angeles)**

PERSONNEL: Little Richard (voc, pno) with unk. personnel.

18375  Greenwood, Mississippi . .    Rep 0942, LP-6406
18376  Dew Drop Inn . . . . . . . . . . .    Rep 0907, LP-6406
18377  Freedom Blues . . . . . . . . .    Rep 0907, LP-6406
18378  Spreadin' Natta What's
      the Matter . . . . . . . . . . . . . . . .    Rep LP-6406

**June 1 & 2, 1970 (Wishbone Studio, Sheffield, Alabama)**

PERSONNEL: Little Richard (voc, pno, clv-1) with Harrison Callay (tpt), Ronnie Eader (baritone sax), Harry Thompson (tenor sax), Charles Rose (tbn), Clayton Ivey (pno), Jerry Masters (bs), Travis Womack (gtr), Albert Lowe (gtr), Roger Hawkins (dms), Eddie Fletcher (bs), Wade Jackson (tenor sax).

18700  The Rill Thing -1 . . . . . . . .    Rep LP-6406
18701  Somebody Saw You . . . . . .    Rep 1005, LP-6406
18702  Lovesick Blues . . . . . . . . . .    Rep LP-6406
18703  Two Time Loser . . . . . . . . .    Rep LP-6406
18704  I Saw Her Standing There.    Rep 0942, LP-6406

**January 14, 1971 (Criterion Studio, Miami, Florida)**

PERSONNEL: Little Richard (voc, pno) with unk. bs, 2 gtrs, brass, female voc gp, dms.

0001 Shake a Hand. . . . . . . . . . . .    Rep 1005

**May 25, 1971 (Hollywood)**

PERSONNEL: Little Richard (voc, pno) with unk. personnel.

0389  The Way You Do the Things
     You Do . . . . . . . . . . . . . . . . . . . .    Rep LP-6462

241

0390 Green Power . . . . . . . . . . . .   Rep 1043, LP-6462
0391 Midnight Special . . . . . . . .   Rep LP-6462
0392 Settin' the Woods on Fire . .   Rep LP-6462
0394 Dancing in the Street. . . . . .   Rep 1043, LP-6462
0395 Born on the Bayou . . . . . . . .   Rep LP-6462
0396 I Don't Love You No More . .   UNRELEASED
0397 I'm So Lonesome I Could
    Cry . . . . . . . . . . . . . . . . . . . . . .   Rep LP-6462
0398 King of Rock and Roll . . . . .   Rep LP-6462
0403 In the Name . . . . . . . . . . . .   Rep LP-6462

**July 2, 1971 (Record Plant, Hollywood)**

PERSONNEL: Little Richard (voc, pno) with unk. personnel.

0507 Joy to the World . . . . . . . . .   Rep LP-6462
0508 Brown Sugar. . . . . . . . . . . .   Rep LP-6462

**March 27 & April 12, 1972 (Record Plant, Los Angeles)**

PERSONNEL: Little Richard (voc, electric pno, clv) with Lee Allen (tenor sax), Bill Hemmons (tenor sax), Jim Horn (baritone sax), Chuck Rainey (bs), Sneaky Pete Kleinow (pedal steel gtr), Mike Deasey (gtr), George Davis (gtr), Earl Palmer (dms).

3097 Mockinbird Sally . . . . . . . .   Rep 1130, LP-2107
3099 The Saints. . . . . . . . . . . . . .   Rep LP-2107
3102 Thomasine . . . . . . . . . . . . .   Rep LP-2107
3103 Nuki Suki . . . . . . . . . . . . . .   Rep 1130, LP-2107
3104 Sanctified Satisfied
    Toetapper. . . . . . . . . . . . . . . . .   Rep LP-2107
3331 Rockin' Rockin' Boogie . . . .   Rep LP-2107
3348 It Ain't What You Do . . . . . .   Rep LP-2107
3350 Second Line . . . . . . . . . . . .   Rep LP-2107
3351 Prophet of Peace. . . . . . . . .   Rep LP-2107
–––– Good Golly Miss Molly . . . .   UNRELEASED
–––– In the Name . . . . . . . . . . . .   UNRELEASED
–––– Slippin' and Slidin' . . . . . . .   UNRELEASED
–––– Sneak the Freak . . . . . . . . . .   UNRELEASED

**April 1972 (Record Plant, Los Angeles)**

PERSONNEL: Little Richard (voc, pno) with Lee Allen (tenor sax), Jim Horn (sax), Sneaky Pete Kleinow (pedal steel gtr), Earl Palmer (dms), Bob Love (?).

–––– Southern Child. . . . . . . . . . .   UNRELEASED
–––– I Git a Little Lonely . . . . . . .   UNRELEASED
–––– Last Year's Racehorse . . . . .   UNRELEASED

```
———  Ain't No Tellin' . . . . . . . . . .   UNRELEASED
———  Burning Up with Love . . . . .   UNRELEASED
———  If You Pick Her Too Hard . .   UNRELEASED
———  Puppy Dogs. . . . . . . . . . . . .   UNRELEASED
———  Over Yonder . . . . . . . . . . . .   UNRELEASED
———  California . . . . . . . . . . . . . .   UNRELEASED
```

*There are possibly another seven titles from this session that cannot be traced.*

## October & November 1972 (Unk. location)

PERSONNEL: Little Richard (voc) with Billy Preston (kybd), David T. Walker (gtr), Chuck Rainey (gtr), Doug Kershaw (fiddle), Bill Plummer and/or Eric Gale and/or Elek Bacsik and/or Arthur Adams (gtrs), Ray Brown (bs), Paul Humphrey or Ronnie Tutt (dms), Victor Feldman and Milt Holland (percussion).

```
0977  Money Is . . . . . . . . . . . . . . .   Rep 1062, LP-2051
———   Do It—to It . . . . . . . . . . . . .   Rep LP-2051
0983  Money Runner . . . . . . . . . .   UNRELEASED
```

*A long, multidubbed track named "Brooks 50¢ Tour" appears on Reprise LP-2051 and uses excerpts from "Money Is."*

### MISCELLANEOUS SESSIONS

*We have divided this section of miscellaneous recordings from the 1970s into two parts: those sessions which revolved around Little Richard as the featured performer, and those for which he "sat in" with other artists of the era for an odd song or two. In those cases where personnel is listed, they are "probable," i.e. they were present for most of if not all of the sessions with the particular artist at the time.*

### PART ONE

#### c. late 1972 (Nassau Coliseum, Long Island, and Cobo Hall, Detroit)

PERSONNEL: Little Richard (voc, pno) with Eddie Fletcher (bs, overdubbed later) and unk. personnel.

```
———  Lucille . . . . . . . . . . . . . . . . .   Bell LP-9002
———  Good Golly Miss Molly . . . .   Bell LP-9002
———  Rip It Up . . . . . . . . . . . . . . .   Bell LP-9002
```

Omit Eddie Fletcher (bs).

#### January 1973 (Muscle Shoals, Alabama)

PERSONNEL: Little Richard (voc, pno) with unk. personnel.

```
———  In the Name . . . . . . . . . . . .   United LP-7791
```

243

| | | |
|---|---|---|
| ———— | Mississippi . . . . . . . . . . . . . | United LP-7791 |
| ———— | Don't You Know . . . . . . . . . . | United LP-7791 |
| ———— | Chain Chain Chain . . . . . . . . | United LP-7791 |
| ———— | Geraldine Jones . . . . . . . . . . | United LP-7791 |
| ———— | Dock of the Bay . . . . . . . . . . | United LP-7791 |
| ———— | Chains of Love . . . . . . . . . . . | United LP-7791 |
| ———— | Hot Nuts . . . . . . . . . . . . . . . | United LP-7791 |

**May 1973 (Atlanta)**

PERSONNEL: Little Richard (voc, electric pno), Eddie Fletcher (bs), and unk. gtr, dms, female voc gp.

| 413A | In the Middle of the Night . | GM 413 |
|---|---|---|
| 413B | Where Will I Find a Place to Sleep This Evening . . . . . . . . | GM 413 |

**1975 (Unk. location)**

PERSONNEL: Little Richard (voc, pno -1) with Billy Preston (organ -2), unk. gtr, bs, electric pno, voc gp -3.

| 50015 | Call My Name -1 . . . . . . . . . | Mant 7007 |
|---|---|---|
| 50016 | Steal Miss Liza -2-3 . . . . . . | Mant 7007 |

**1975 (Unk. location)**

PERSONNEL: Little Richard (voc, pno) with unk. personnel.

| ———— | Try to Help Your Brother . . | Main 5572 |
|---|---|---|
| ———— | Funk Proof . . . . . . . . . . . . . | Main 5572 |

**1976 (Jack Clement Studio, Nashville)**

PERSONNEL: Little Richard (voc, pno?) with Denis Brownside (pno), Eddie Bayers (dms), Jack Jackson (bs), Paul Wormley (gtr), Pat Patnik (gtr).

| | | |
|---|---|---|
| ———— | The Girl Can't Help It . . . . . | K-Tel LP-462 |
| ———— | Rip It Up . . . . . . . . . . . . . . . | K-Tel LP-462 |
| ———— | Send Me Some Lovin'. . . . . . | K-Tel LP-462 |
| ———— | Bama Lama Bama Loo . . . . | K-Tel LP-462 |
| ———— | She's Got It . . . . . . . . . . . . . | K-Tel LP-462 |
| ———— | Can't Believe You Wanna Leave . . . . . . . . . . . . . . . . . . | K-Tel LP-462 |
| ———— | Long Tall Sally . . . . . . . . . . | K-Tel LP-462 |
| ———— | Jenny Jenny . . . . . . . . . . . . | K-Tel LP-462 |
| ———— | Good Golly Miss Molly . . . . | K-Tel LP-462 |
| ———— | Lucille . . . . . . . . . . . . . . . . | K-Tel LP-462 |
| ———— | Keep a-Knockin' . . . . . . . . . | K-Tel LP-462 |

|  |  |
|---|---|
| ──── All Around the World...... | K-Tel LP-462 |
| ──── True Fine Mama.......... | K-Tel LP-462 |
| ──── Ready Teddy............. | K-Tel LP-462 |
| ──── By the Light of the Silvery Moon..................... | K-Tel LP-462 |
| ──── Slippin' and Slidin'....... | K-Tel LP-462 |
| ──── Baby Face.............. | K-Tel LP-462 |
| ──── Ooh! My Soul........... | K-Tel LP-462 |
| ──── Miss Ann............... | K-Tel LP-462 |
| ──── Tutti Frutti............. | K-Tel LP-462 |

**1979 (Nashville)**

PERSONNEL: Little Richard (voc) with unk. pno, bs, organ, voc gp, dms.

|  |  |
|---|---|
| ──── There Is Someone Worse Off Than I Am.............. | World LP-1001 |
| ──── If You Got the Lord on Your Side..................... | World LP-1001 |
| ──── It's No Secret........... | World LP-1001 |
| ──── I Surrender All.......... | World LP-1001 |
| ──── Come by Here, My Lord.... | World LP-1001 |
| ──── God's Beautiful City....... | World LP-1001 |

Omit all but voc, gtr.

|  |  |
|---|---|
| ──── What Am I Supposed to Do without Jesus.............. | World LP-1001 |

Omit gtr. Add organ.

|  |  |
|---|---|
| ──── Little Richard's Testimony (Part 1).................... | World LP-1001 |
| ──── Little Richard's Testimony (Part 2).................... | World LP-1001 |

**June 17, 1981 (Cash Studios, Los Angeles)**

PERSONNEL: Little Richard (voc) with Bill House (pedal steel gtr), Ron Jones (pno), Rini Kramer (percussion), Eddie Fletcher (voc, bs), Michael Jackson, Mary Love, Semia (voc gp).

|  |  |
|---|---|
| ──── One Day at a Time........ | UNRELEASED |
| ──── Where Will I Go without the Lord.................. | UNRELEASED |

**PART TWO**

**1971 (Masters Studios, Atlanta)**

PERSONNEL: Little Richard (voc) with Mylon LeFevre (gtr, voc), Marty Simon (dms), Tina Blount, Renay Marvin, Pat Cummings (voc gp), Auburn Burrell and/or J. P. Lauzon and/or Leslie West and/or Barry

245

Bailey (gtrs), Mac Rebennack ("Dr. John") and/or Lester Langdale and/
or Allen Toussaint (kybd), Steve Sanders (voc), Tom Robb (bs).

―――― He's Not Just a Soldier . . . .   Columbia LP-31472

**1971 (Florida)**

PERSONNEL: Little Richard (pno) with Delaney Bramlett (gtr, voc),
Bonnie Bramlett (voc), Ben Benay and/or Duane Allman and/or Charlie
Freeman (gtrs), Kenny Gradney and/or Tom McClure and/or Jerry
Scheff (bs), Ronnie Tutt and/or Chuck Morgan and/or Sammy Creason
(dms), Jerry Jumonville, Frank Mayes, King Curtis, Ed Logan, Floyd
Newman, Andrew Love (sax), Sam Clayton (conga), Darryl Leonard,
Wayne Jackson (tpts), Alan Estes (percussion), Sneaky Pete Kleinow
(steel gtr), Bobby Whitlock (kybd, voc), Jack Hale (tbn).

―――― Miss Ann . . . . . . . . . . . . . . .   Atco 6788, LP-341

**1971 (Cleveland Recording Studio)**

PERSONNEL: Little Richard (voc?, pno?) with Jim Fox (dms, voc), Dale
Peters (bs, voc), Glen Schwartz (gtr), and other unk. personnel.

―――― Black Man—White Man . . .   ABC 11312

**1971 (Unk. location)**

PERSONNEL: Little Richard (voc?, pno?) with Paul Kantner (gtr, voc),
Grace Slick (kybd, voc), Jack Casady (bs), Joey Covington (dms), Jorma
Kaukonen (gtr), John Creach (vln), David Crosby? (gtr, voc), Graham
Nash (voc), Jerry Garcia? (gtr, banjo), Spencer Dryden (voc, percussion).

―――― Bludgeon of a Bluecoat . . . .   Grunt LP-1002

**1971 (Los Angeles)**

PERSONNEL: Little Richard (pno) with Bob Hite (voc), Henry Vestine
(gtr), Fito de la Parra (dms), Antonio Barreda (bs), Harvey Mandel (gtr),
Joel Scott Hill (voc, gtr), Ernest Lane (kybd), Clifford Solomon (sax),
Charles Lloyd (flute), Kevin Burton? (organ).

―――― Rockin' with the King . . . . .   United Artists 50892, LP-5557

**1974/75 (Los Angeles)**

PERSONNEL: Little Richard (voc?, pno?) with Randy Bachman (gtr, voc),
Fred Turner (bs, voc), Blair Thornton (gtr, voc), and unk. personnel.

52542 Take It Like a Man . . . . . . .   Merc LP-1-1067
52545 Stay Alive . . . . . . . . . . . . .   Merc LP-1-1067

# DISCOGRAPHY/FILMOGRAPHY

*The recordings and films of Little Richard appear in the order they were released or presented to the public.*

*To keep the discography relevant, a few procedures have been used to simplify matters. For the LPs, only those cuts appearing for the first time are listed. The numerous repackagings that appeared in the 1960s for the gospel recordings and 1970s for the Specialty and Vee Jay recordings, among others, would, if listed completely, make this section equal in size to the main text!*

*All record numbers that do not bear the prefix LP are single, 45 rpm (or 78 rpm) records.*

*Peak chart positions are indicated as follows:*

◇ = highest ranking on *Billboard* "Hot 100" chart
□ = highest ranking on *Cashbox* "Top 100" chart
○ = highest ranking on *Billboard* "Rhythm & Blues" chart

*Film dates indicate time of first world showing, and only those films in which Richard is seen on screen are listed.*

**1951**

| | | |
|---|---|---|
| November | Taxi Blues/Every Hour | RCA 4372 |

**1952**

| | | |
|---|---|---|
| February | Get Rich Quick/Thinkin' 'bout My Mother | RCA 4582 |
| May | Why Did You Leave Me/Ain't Nothing Happening | RCA 4772 |
| November | I Brought It All on Myself/Please Have Mercy on Me | RCA 5052 |

247

**1953**

April      Ain't That Good News/Fool at the      Peacock 1616
Wheel

**1954**

March      Always/Rice, Red Beans and      Peacock 1628
Turnip Greens

**1955**

October      Tutti Frutti ⟨21⟩⟨2⟩/I'm Just a      Specialty 561
Lonely Guy

**1956**

March      Long Tall Sally ⟨13⟩[7]⟨1⟩/Slippin'      Specialty 572
and Slidin' ⟨33⟩⟨1⟩

April      Directly from My Heart to You/      Peacock 1658
Little Richard's Boogie

June      Rip It Up ⟨27⟩[21]⟨1⟩/Ready Teddy      Specialty 579
⟨44⟩[32]⟨1⟩

October      Heeby-Jeebies [50] ⟨15⟩/She's Got It      Specialty 584
⟨15⟩

December      The Girl Can't Help It ⟨49⟩⟨11⟩/All      Specialty 591
Around the World

December      *FILM: The Girl Can't Help It (20th Century Fox)*
SONGS: Ready Teddy; She's Got It; The Girl Can't Help It (alternate take)

**1957**

January      *FILM: Don't Knock the Rock (Columbia Pictures)*
SONGS: Tutti Frutti; Long Tall Sally

February      Lucille ⟨27⟩[22]⟨2⟩/Send Me Some      Specialty 598
Lovin' ⟨54⟩⟨2⟩

March      *LP: Here's Little Richard*      Specialty LP-
100 (2100)

NEW SONGS: Oh Why; True Fine Mama; Baby; Miss Ann; Jenny Jenny; Can't Believe You Wanna Leave

June      Jenny Jenny ⟨14⟩[17]⟨1⟩/Miss Ann      Specialty 606
⟨56⟩⟨2⟩

June      Bip Bop Bip/Paper Dollar      Atlantic 1147

July      Maybe I'm Right/I Love My Baby      Peacock 1673

August      Keep a-Knockin' ⟨8⟩[12]⟨5⟩/Can't      Specialty 611
Believe You Wanna Leave

September     *FILM: Mr. Rock and Roll (Paramount Pictures)*
SONGS: Lucille; Keep a-Knockin'

## 1958

| | | |
|---|---|---|
| January | Good Golly Miss Molly ◇⑩ ⑱ ⑥/ Hey-Hey-Hey-Hey | Specialty 624 |
| April | *LP: Little Richard* | Camden LP-420 |
| NEW SONGS: none | | |
| May | Ooh! My Soul ◇㉟ ⑤② ⑮/True Fine Mama ◇⑥⑧ ⑮ | Specialty 633 |
| July | Baby Face ◇㊶ ⑫/I'll Never Let You Go (Boo Hoo Hoo Hoo) | Specialty 645 |
| July | *LP: Little Richard* | Specialty LP-2103 |

NEW SONGS: By the Light of the Silvery Moon

| | | |
|---|---|---|
| November | Early One Morning/She Knows How to Rock | Specialty 652 |

## 1959

| | | |
|---|---|---|
| March | Wonderin'/By the Light of the Silvery Moon | Specialty 660 |
| March | *LP: The Fabulous Little Richard* | Specialty LP-2104 |

NEW SONGS: All Night Long; Kansas City; Lonesome and Blue; The Most I Can Offer; Maybe I'm Right; Shake a Hand; Chicken Little Baby; Directly from My Heart to You

| | | |
|---|---|---|
| April | Kansas City/Lonesome and Blue | Specialty 664 |
| Summer | Shake a Hand/All Night Long | Specialty 670 |
| August | Whole Lotta Shakin'/Maybe I'm Right | Specialty 680 |
| August | I Got It/Baby | Specialty 681 |
| September | Save Me Lord/Troubles of the World | End 1057 |
| September | Milky White Way/I've Just Come from the Fountain | End 1058 |
| ? | Directly from My Heart to You/ The Most I Can Offer | Specialty 686 |

## 1960

| | | |
|---|---|---|
| ? | *LP: Pray Along with Little Richard* (Volume 1) | Goldisc LP-4001 |

NEW SONGS: Need Him; Comin' Home; I'm Tramping; Just a Closer Walk with Thee; Does Jesus Care; God Is Real; Jesus Walked This Lonesome Valley; Precious Lord

| ? | *LP: Pray Along with Little Richard* (Volume 2) | Goldisc LP-4002 |

NEW SONGS: Search Me Lord; I Know the Lord; Every Time I Feel the Spirit; Certainly Lord; Tell God My Troubles; In My Heart; I'm Quittin' Show Business

| ? | *LP: Clap Your Hands* | Spin-O-Rama LP-119 |

NEW SONGS: none

## 1961

| September | He's Not Just a Soldier ⟨13⟩ 91 / Joy Joy Joy | Mercury 71884 |
| December | Do You Care/Ride on King Jesus | Mercury 71911 |

## 1962

| c. January | *LP: The King of Gospel Singers* | Mercury LP-60656 |

NEW SONGS: The Captain Calls for You; In Times Like These; He's My Star; It's Real; Peace in the Valley; It Takes Everything to Serve the Lord; Do Lord, Remember Me

| April | Change Your Ways/He Got What He Wanted | Mercury 71965 |
| ? | I'm in Love Again/Every Night about This Time | Little Star 123 |

## 1963

| February | Crying in the Chapel ⟨19⟩/Hole in the Wall | Atlantic 2181 |
| May | Traveling Shoes/It Is No Secret | Atlantic 2192 |
| Summer | *LP: Little Richard Sings Gospel* | 20th Century-Fox LP-5010 |

NEW SONGS: none

| c. October | Milky White Way/Need Him | Coral 62366 |
| November | *LP: Little Richard's Biggest Hits* | Specialty LP-2111 |

NEW SONGS: none

| c. December | *LP: Comin' Home* | Coral LP-57446 |

NEW SONGS: none

| ? | Valley of Tears/Freedom Ride | Little Star 128 |

| ? | LP: *Little Richard Sings* | Summit LP-4029 |
|---|---|---|

NEW SONGS: none

| ? | LP: *Little Richard Sings Freedom Songs* | Crown LP-5362 |
|---|---|---|

NEW SONGS: none

| ? | LP: *Little Richard with Sister Rosetta Tharpe* | Guest Star LP-1429 |
|---|---|---|

NEW SONGS: none

## 1964

| April | Bama Lama Bama Loo ⟨82⟩/Annie Is Back | Specialty 692 |
|---|---|---|
| August | Whole Lotta Shakin' ⟨126⟩/ Goodnight Irene ⟨124⟩ | Vee Jay 612 |
| c. August | LP: *Little Richard Is Back* | Vee Jay LP-1107 |

NEW SONGS: Hound Dog; Money Honey; Going Home Tomorrow; Lawdy Miss Clawdy; Short Fat Fannie; Only You; Groovy Little Suzie; Memories Are Made of This

| October | Blueberry Hill/Cherry Red | Vee Jay 625 |
|---|---|---|
| c. December | LP: *Little Richard's Greatest Hits* | Vee Jay LP-1124 |

NEW SONGS: Send Me Some Lovin'; Lucille; She's Got It; Keep a-Knockin'; Slippin' and Slidin'; Good Golly Miss Molly; Tutti Frutti; Long Tall Sally; Rip It Up; Baby Face; The Girl Can't Help It; Ooh! My Soul

## 1965

| February | Cross Over/It Ain't What You Do | Vee Jay 652 |
|---|---|---|
| May | Without Love/Dance What You Wanna | Vee Jay 665 |
| October | I Don't Know What You've Got But It's Got Me (Parts 1 & 2) ⟨92⟩ [83] (12) | Vee Jay 698 |

## 1966

| early | Holy Mackerel/Baby | Modern 1018 |
|---|---|---|
| c. January | LP: *The Incredible Little Richard Sings His Greatest Hits—Live!* | Modern LP-1000 |

NEW SONGS: Tutti Frutti; Keep a-Knockin'; Rip It Up; Jenny Jenny; Lucille; Bama Lama Bama Loo; Long Tall Sally; Ready Teddy; True Fine Mama; Whole Lotta Shakin'; Slippin' and Slidin'; Bring It on

Home to Me; Bony Moronie; Do You Feel It (Parts 1 & 2)

| | | |
|---|---|---|
| c. June | Do You Feel It, Parts 1 & 2 | Modern 1019 |
| June | Poor Dog ㉑ ㊶/Well | Okeh 7251 |
| c. September | I'm Back/Directly from My Heart to You | Modern 1022 |
| October | I Need Love/Commandments of Love | Okeh 7262 |
| ? | LP: The Wild and Frantic Little Richard | Modern LP-1003 |

NEW SONGS: Miss Ann; Good Golly Miss Molly; Send Me Some Lovin'; Groovy Little Suzie; Do the Jerk; Baby What You Want Me to Do (Parts 1 & 2)

## 1967

| | | |
|---|---|---|
| January | I Don't Want to Discuss It/Hurry Sundown | Okeh 7271 |
| January | LP: The Explosive Little Richard | Okeh LP-14117 |

NEW SONGS: Function at the Junction; Never Gonna Let You Go; Land of a Thousand Dances; Don't Deceive Me; Money

| | | |
|---|---|---|
| early | Get Down with It/Rosemary | CBS (UK) 8116 |
| March | Don't Deceive Me/Never Gonna Let You Go | Okeh 7278 |
| June | A Little Bit of Something/Money | Okeh 7286 |
| July | LP: Little Richard's Greatest Hits—Recorded Live! | Okeh LP-14121 |

NEW SONGS: Lucille; Long Tall Sally; The Girl Can't Help It; Send Me Some Lovin'; Jenny Jenny; Tutti Frutti; True Fine Mama; Whole Lotta Shakin'; Good Golly Miss Molly; Anyway You Want Me; You Gotta Feel It; Get Down with It

| | | |
|---|---|---|
| December | Try Some of Mine/She's Together | Brunswick 55362 |

## 1968

| | | |
|---|---|---|
| April | LP: Little Richard's Grooviest 17 Original Hits | Specialty LP-2113 |

NEW SONGS: none

| | | |
|---|---|---|
| Spring | LP: Forever Yours | Roulette LP-42007 |

NEW SONGS: none

| | | |
|---|---|---|
| June | Baby, Don't You Tear My Clothes/ Stingy Jenny | Brunswick 55377 |

| | | |
|---|---|---|
| September | Soul Train/Can I Count on You | Brunswick 55386 |

**1969**

| | | |
|---|---|---|
| February | Lucille/Whole Lotta Shakin' | Okeh 7325 |
| ? | *LP: Little Richard Sings Spirituals* | Custom LP-2061 |

NEW SONGS: none

**1970**

| | | |
|---|---|---|
| April | Bama Lama Bama Loo/Keep a-Knockin' | Specialty 697 |
| April | Freedom Blues ◇47 62 28◇/Dew Drop Inn | Reprise 0907 |
| August | Greenwood, Mississippi ◇85 96◇/I Saw Her Standing There | Reprise 0942 |
| August | *LP: The Rill Thing* | Reprise LP-6406 |

NEW SONGS: Spreadin' Natta What's the Matter; Lovesick Blues; The Rill Thing; Somebody Saw You; Two Time Loser

| | | |
|---|---|---|
| November | Poor Boy Paul/Wonderin' | Specialty 699 |
| November | *LP: Well Alright!* | Specialty LP-2136 |

NEW SONG: Well Alright!

**1971**

| | | |
|---|---|---|
| March | Shake a Hand/Somebody Saw You | Reprise 1005 |
| May | *LP: Over the Influence (Mylon Le Fevre)* | Columbia LP-31472 |

NEW SONG: He's Not Just a Soldier

| | | |
|---|---|---|
| c. June | *LP: Mr. Big* | Joy (UK) LP-195 |

NEW SONGS: My Wheel's Been Slipping All the Way; Talking 'bout Soul; Dance What You Wanna

| | | |
|---|---|---|
| September | *LP: To Delaney from Bonnie* | Atco LP-341 |

NEW SONG: Miss Ann

| | | |
|---|---|---|
| September | Black Man—White Man/ Midnight Man ◇80◇ | ABC 11312 |
| October | *LP: The King of Rock 'n' Roll* | Reprise LP-6462 |

253

NEW SONGS: Green Power; Settin' the Woods on Fire; Dancing in the Street; The Way You Do the Things You Do; In the Name; Midnight Special; Born on the Bayou; I'm So Lonesome I Could Cry; Brown Sugar; Joy to the World

| December | *LP: Sunfighter* (Jefferson Starship) | Grunt LP-1002 |

NEW SONG: Bludgeon of a Bluecoat

**1972**

| c. January | *LP: Original Soundtrack: Dollars* | Reprise LP-2051 |

NEW SONGS: Money Is; Do It—to It

| c. January | *LP: Historical Figures & Ancient Heads* | United Artists LP-5557 |

NEW SONG: Rockin' with the King

| February | Rockin' with the King ◈/I Don't Care What You Tell Me | United Artists LP-50892 |
| September | *LP: The Second Coming* | Reprise LP-2017 |

NEW SONGS: Mockinbird Sally; The Saints; Sanctified Satisfied Toetapper; Nuki Suki; Thomasine; Rockin' Rockin' Boogie; It Ain't What You Do; Second Line; Prophet of Peace

| ? | *LP: Friends from the Beginning— Little Richard & Jimi Hendrix* | ALA LP-1972 |

NEW SONGS: Belle Stars; Funky Dish Rag; Why Don't You Love Me

| ? | Goodnight Irene/Why Don't You Love Me | ALA 1175 |

**1973**

| early | *LP: Right Now!* | United LP-7791 |

NEW SONGS: In the Name; Mississippi; Chains of Love; Don't You Know; Dock of the Bay; Chain Chain Chain; Hot Nuts; Geraldine Jones

| April | **FILM: Let the Good Times Roll (Columbia Pictures)** |

SONGS: Lucille; Good Golly Miss Molly; Rip It Up

| c. May | *LP: Original Soundtrack: Let the Good Times Roll* | Bell LP-9002 |

NEW SONGS: Lucille; Good Golly Miss Molly; Rip It Up

| c. May | Good Golly Miss Molly/no flip | Bell 1780 |

254

| | | |
|---|---|---|
| c. June | In the Middle of the Night/Where Will I Find a Place to Sleep This Evening | Greene Mountain 413 |
| ? | In the Name/Don't You Know | Kent 4568 |
| ? | LP: Rip It Up | Joy (UK) LP-260 |

NEW SONG: Jenny Jenny

| | | |
|---|---|---|
| ? | LP: Talking 'Bout Soul | Dynasty LP-7304 |

NEW SONGS: You Better Stop; Something Moves In My Heart

**1974**

| | | |
|---|---|---|
| ? | LP: Slippin' and Slidin' | Joy (UK) LP-270 |

NEW SONG: Every Time I Think about You

**1975**

| | | |
|---|---|---|
| c. December | Call My Name ◇106◇/Steal Miss Liza | Manticore 7007 |
| ? | Try to Help Your Brother/Funk Proof | Mainstream 5572 |
| ? | LP: Head On (B.T. Overdrive) | Mercury LP-1-1067 |

NEW SONGS: Take It Like a Man; Stay Alive

**1976**

| | | |
|---|---|---|
| ? | LP: Little Richard Live | K-Tel LP-462 |

NEW SONGS: rerecordings of 20 Specialty hits

**1979**

| | | |
|---|---|---|
| ? | LP: God's Beautiful City | World LP-1001 |

NEW SONGS: There is Someone Worse Off Than I; If You Got the Lord on Your Side; It Is No Secret; I Surrender All; What Am I Supposed to Do without Jesus; Come By Here, My Lord; God's Beautiful City; Little Richard's Testimony; Little Richard's Testimony (Part 2)

**1983**

| | | |
|---|---|---|
| c. September | Chicken Little Baby/Oh Why | Specialty 734 |

# WHAT'S MISSING?

*We have purposely omitted extensive documentation of a few Little Richard record releases, for reasons that will be obvious:* In 1964, Vee Jay issued a series of back-to-back hits on 45 rpm, coupling the rerecordings of old Specialty hits made for them in 1964. These 45s were not new releases per se, but were issued specifically for oldies stores.

In 1965, Modern did much the same thing as Vee Jay had a year earlier, coupling *another* set of rerecordings of old Specialty hits on a series of oldies 45s.

The Redita and Demand bootleg albums have not been included in the chronology (although they are in the session listings) as they were not legitimate releases.

Live recordings that were not intended for release (but available, more or less, on bootleg LPs and private collector's tapes) have not been included in either section.

# ACKNOWLEDGMENTS

This book was written because of my love for Little Richard and the inspiration he and his music have given me all my life. A devout follower and aficionado of the man for many years, I noted that there were hundreds of books about artists that Little Richard influenced—people like Elvis, Buddy Holly, the Beatles, the Stones, Jerry Lee Lewis, David Bowie, and many others, while there was nothing in print about Richard himself and his amazing contribution to twentieth-century music. I determined to put this injustice right and set about collecting material for a book that would give proper credit to the man. From being a spare-time project this snowballed to take over my life, and I was amazed at the worldwide interest in Richard when I let it be known that I was researching this work. All this was done without Richard's knowledge, and it was not until my research led me to Los Angeles that I actually met him (though I had interviewed him twice before, during his English tours of the 1960s). He felt that out of the dozens of people who had approached him over the years I was the one to write his life story. So we here have a Rock 'n' Roll legend telling his own story. It is the essence of America over the past half-century.

My thanks go to Little Richard for giving me the honor of being his official biographer and for holding back nothing in his answers to my close questioning. To Bumps Blackwell for bringing about my meeting with Richard, revealing his store of memories to me, and for his philosophy and advice in treading the contractual jungle of the U.S. literary world.

Little Richard and I would like to make a special tribute to Barry

257

Hampshire, who first encouraged me to write about rock music, and whose editorial skills helped me to put this book together.

To my wife, Ann, for her forbearance in my obsession, allowing her best room to be covered with clippings, records, magazines, photographs, and books, and for keeping the business going while I was in the United States.

Eternal gratitude to Esther Mitgang my editor, Ed Victor, and the staff at Harmony Books. To Lolly James "Lorelei," Lady Katharine Hampshire, Bill Millar, Adam Komorowski, Derek Glenister, Ray Topping, Cliff White, John Broven, Derek and Veronica Day, Rod Pearson, Tez Courtney, Stuart and Janet Colman, Tim Jibson, Marcel Guillou, John Graham, Phil Silverman, Joe Musella, Jonas Bernholm, Peter Goldsmith, Christopher Ebner, Norbert Hess, Robert Loers, Rein Jens, Bjorn Roswald, Michael Thonney, Jacques Barasamian, Professor B. Lee Cooper, Geoff Nunn, Alison Skilbeck, Anthony L. Wilkinson, Trevor Langton, Jamie "Dr. Elvis" Pearson and Julie, Patrick Humphries, Roger St. Pierre, Max "Waxie Maxie" Needham, Fred "Drastic" Drabble, Chris "Granpa" Found and the Twirls, Peter Ward, Stephen Shrimpton, Brenda Jenkins, Annie Bloom, Rod Pearson, Clive Anderson, Alan Stinton, Mike Vernon, Wayne Russell, Richard Wooton, Mark and Shelora Earl, Jean Hobson, and Pat O'Hara.

To all the people in the U.S. who helped me so readily. J. W. Alexander, H. B. Barnum, Johnny Otis, Johnny Guitar Watson, Joe Lutcher, Chuck Connors, Dewey Terry, Maybelle Jackson, Bo Diddley, Keith Winslow, Henry Nash, Sonny Knight, Eddie Fletcher, Bill House, Jose Wilson, Calvin Carter, Hal Blaine, John Marascalco, Lee Angel, Roy Star, John Daniel, Nona Raye, and Little Richard's family, Leva Mae Penniman, Peggie, Charles, Marquette, Walter, Robert, Silvia, Elaine, Peyton, Gail, Peaches, Deanie, Willard and Ernestine Campbell.

To all the artists who both recently and over the past years have given me their time in interviews and given credit to Little Richard—Buddy Holly, Jimi Hendrix, Chuck Berry, Jerry Lee Lewis, David Essex, Paul McCartney, Tony Crane, Carl Perkins, Wayne Fontana, Mick Jagger, Dewey Terry, Phil Everly, Wolfman Jack, Mickey Most, Billy Preston, David "Screaming Lord" Sutch, and Professor "Long Hair."

To the authors and writers of the books, magazines, and newspapers from which I have culled information over the years—Arnold Shaw's *Honkers and Shouters*, John Broven's *Walking to New Orleans*, Charlie Gillett's *The Sound of the City*, Phil Hardy and Dave Raine's *The Encyclopedia of Rock*, Lilian Roxon's *Rock Encyclopedia*, Jim Millar's *The Rolling Stone Illustrated History of Rock'n' Roll*, J. L. Rancural (France), Hans Ekestang (Sweden), Barry Ledingham (ATV) for photographs, Nik Cohn's *Pop from the Beginning*, David Ehrenstein and Bill Reed's *Rock on Film*, and Maureen Cleaves (*Observer*).

ACKNOWLEDGMENTS

My heartfelt gratitude to Bob Hyde who compiled the Sessiono-graphy, and Discography/Filmography—a task that had never before been attempted. For additional record information Tina McCarthy Vinces of CBS, Cathy McPeek of Warner Brothers, Sandy of Sonet, and "Little Walter" of Boston.

# INDEX

Page numbers in *italics* refer to passages in which indexed persons address the reader directly.

261

# PHOTO CREDITS